To: Laura
Thanks for ___ in my legs! May God bless you & your family. Hope you enjoy this book.

Cops...
Don't Just Eat Donuts!
Real Stories by Real Cops

By Gerald "Jerry" Borchers

Retired Detective

Kansas City Missouri Police Department

Gerald A. Borchers
9/25/2020

Copyright © 2012 Gerald Borchers
All rights reserved, including the right to reproduce this book or any portions thereof, in any form whatsoever, without the written permission of the author.

For information about special discounts for bulk purchases or to schedule a signing event with the author, please e-mail him at realcopstories@sbcglobal.net

ISBN-10: 1478321040
ISBN-13: 978-1478321040

This book is dedicated to my lovely wife, Carol, and our three daughters, Brenda, Bonnie, and Beverly. And to all the law enforcement personnel who contributed their stories to this book.

Table of Contents

Preface i

Acknowledgments iii

Introduction vii

Chapter 1: The Beginning 1

Chapter 2: Early Life 5

Chapter 3: Moving to California 9

Chapter 4: Joining the Air Force 13

Chapter 5: Back In Civilian Life 21

Chapter 6: Los Angeles Police Department 25

Chapter 7: Kansas City Missouri Police Department 37

Chapter 8: U.S. Federal Courthouse, KC, MO 81

Chapter 9: Edward J. Donahue 85

Chapter 10: Harold Vestal 91

Chapter 11: Benjamin E. (Ben) Way 97

Chapter 12: Dennis M. Gargotto 101

Chapter 13: Clyde W. (Randy) Pace, III 107

Chapter 14: Richard N. McKiddy 123

Chapter 15: Charles E. Weir 133

Chapter 16: Columbus L. (Leon) Cook 139

Chapter 17: Bob McConnell 143

Chapter 18: Jon D. Perry 147

Chapter 19: Ben C. Eyre 159

Chapter 20: Keith L. (Rocky) Gregory 165

Chapter 21: James G. Post 171

Chapter 22: John R. Stewart 177

Chapter 23: Jack Livella 187

Chapter 24: Kevin D. Eckhoff 193

Chapter 25: Joseph R. McCune 203

Chapter 26: Balfour J. Rast 205

Chapter 27: Glenn E. Cherry 215

Chapter 28: Earle C. Hammond 221

Chapter 29: Dwight L. Rhodes 229

Chapter 30: David Parker 239

Chapter 31: Richard Schwieterman 255

Chapter 32: Kathy M. Hentges 261

Chapter 33: Stephen W. Wright 273

Chapter 34: R. Wayne Staley 279

Chapter 35: David M. (Mike) Leavene 289

Chapter 36: David Eads 305

Chapter 37: John C. Cayton 317

Chapter 38: Rick Friesen 321

Chapter 39: J. Michael Brady 331

Chapter 40: Donald A. (Donnie) Bowerman 335

Chapter 41: Police Career's Impact on Family 341

Chapter 42: The Real Prowler Call 351

Preface

The first part of this book is an encapsulated story of my life, from childhood to adult, focusing on the events that led to my career in law enforcement. That, in turn, leads to some of the more memorable events that occurred during my employment on the Los Angeles, CA, Police Department (LAPD), the Kansas City, MO, Police Department (KCPD), as well as a few stories from the many years I spent in the military, both the active U.S. Air Force (pre-LAPD) and the U.S. Army Reserves, where I served in the 493rd Military Police/Criminal Investigations Detachment during the same period of time I was employed by KCPD.

The second part of the book is a compilation of stories written by other law enforcement officers with whom I worked, both during my career and after my retirement. They were kind enough to share their stories with me for this book. I hasten to add that these are their stories, written by them, either about themselves or some event in which they were engaged as a law enforcement official. I tried not to edit their stories in any way, except for maybe an errant comma, here or there. If I could trust the people with my life, who was I to think I had the right to "edit" their stories to fit some "approved" publishing format or the strict parameters of proper English?   Thanks, guys. I hasten to add that some of these stories do contain adult language. But, hey, law enforcement officers do not typically work in a Sunday school environment. If they all did, what would be the need for police, right?

My wife and three daughters also provided their own accounts of life as either the spouse or child of a career policeman. I cannot count the times they reminded me of how vitally important it was to separate my life at home from my job on the streets. Nor can I thank them enough for helping me stay sane in a seemingly insane world.

Acknowledgments

No acknowledgments from me could begin without first recognizing my family. I extend my deepest appreciation to my three daughters, Brenda, Bonnie, and Beverly, for encouraging me to write stories about my law enforcement career. To my dear wife, Carol, you know "beyond a reasonable doubt that you were, are, and shall forever remain the true love of my life. I am so grateful for the support you provided during these my literary efforts, meager as they are, and for keeping me mindful of the important events in our lives.

I also want to thank my uncle, Robert Jones, for helping me in the early stages of editing the manuscript, together with other members of my extended family for their constant support and encouragement. Special thanks go to the following officers for digging deep into their memories, emotions, and photo albums to contribute so many varied, but true cop stories: Ed Donahue, Harold Vestal, Ben Way, Dennis Gargotto, Clyde "Randy" Pace, Dick McKiddy, Charlie Weir, Jon Perry, Ben Eyre, Keith Gregory, Leon Cook, Jim Post, John Stewart, Jack Livella, Kevin Eckhoff, Joe McCune, Balfour "Bal" Rast, Glenn Cherry, Earle Hammond, Dwight Rhodes, David Parker, Richard Schwieterman, Kathleen Hentges, Steve Wright, Wayne Staley, Michael Leavene, David Eads, John Cayton, Rick Friesen, Donnie Bowerman, and J. Michael Brady.

I send my gratitude to Linda Pinkerton, sister of Karen Keeton, who, with a yet un-mended heart, shared the story of her sister's murder and the overwhelmingly emotional effect it had on the entire family. Thanks to KCPD detectives Roger Gibson and Jim Martin for sharing the story of their investigation of the Karen Keeton case and for their support of the family during the parole review hearings of her murderer, Stephen Gardner.

I especially want to thank Dena, with FirstEditing.com, whose many pertinent questions were especially valuable to me in the writing of this book.

Thanks to Denny Griffin, editor and author of many books including *Battle for Las Vegas, Cullotta, Killer in Pair-a-Dice, Policing Las Vegas, Vegas Vixen, The Morgue, Blood Money, One-Armed Bandit, Red Gold*, and *Pension* for his advice on authoring books.

I am especially grateful to Stan Cramer, a popular CBS (KCTV) television consumer-investigative news journalist, for reading my manuscript and offering helpful suggestions and encouragement. Thank you, Stan, for your diligent and pro-active involvement in the Gypsy investigation with KCPD detectives Dave Parker and Bill Cosgrove. Your 1984 national award-winning television series, entitled *Breaking the Spell*, encouraged Missouri state prosecutors to file charges in the case.

A special thanks to Alan Goforth, publisher and author of *Nitty Gritty Dirt Man, Tales from the Missouri Tigers, He Stood Tall*, and *Historic Photos of Missouri* for his generous assistance to this fledgling author!

For his valuable help with organizing, inserting and touching up the many photographs, I extend my sincerest appreciation to my good friend, Noel Shepard.

Thanks also to Chris Paxton, paxtoncreativeresources.com, for his assistance in formatting the contents and designing the front cover of this book.

Very special gratitude is reserved for Sonja Bartimus, author and friend. Author of my wife's grandmother's story, *The Delightful Miss Carrie*, and her own new novel, *The Silver Camel: a Texas Tale*, Sonja gave me that one external, encouraging "push" to write my own story.

Last, but certainly not least, I reserve my final round of applause for Donnie Bowerman, a longtime friend and co-worker in law enforcement and the U.S. military, together with several years we spent working off-duty at the Kansas City Royals' Kaufman Stadium. Early in 2012, after many years apart and then "re-discovering" each other on Facebook, Donnie volunteered his personal time and applied his considerable literary talents to just about every aspect of this book. Carol and I were thrilled at the suggestions, corrections, and additions he made to the book, and we will always be very appreciative for the gentle, yet aggressive manner in which he took my manuscript and gave it a thorough "top to bottom housecleaning." Thank you, Donnie, for your friendship and for the generous assistance you provided to help me get my book from rough manuscript to bookstore shelf.

Introduction

Most of us at some point have been urged to "follow our dreams," and, perhaps, we've been able to do so. But how many people can say, as I can, that they have also followed their nightmares?

Throughout my life, beginning when I was fourteen years old, growing up in Kansas City, Missouri, I would occasionally awaken in the night in a cold sweat, resulting from recurring images of being killed in the line of duty. I was terrified of becoming a cop because of those horrible visions, but, because our destinies don't always go according to plan, I became a cop, anyway.

This is my story, along with the stories of many other brave men and women I've had the pleasure of working with during my long journey from the Los Angeles Police Department to a U.S. Army CID Unit, followed by the Kansas City Missouri Police Department, and, finally, into retirement.

In this book, I have tried to offer a different perspective for those who think police officers, affectionately referred to throughout this book as cops, only eat doughnuts and "pull people over" for no good reason. This book is for those, like my wife and family, who worry about the cops they know; a tip-of-the-hat to their own unique bravery while they wait for their loved ones to come home at the end of their shift. For those of us policemen and policewomen who have made on-the-job mistakes, hopefully, some story in this book will serve up a few eye rolls or a good laugh.

The following stories aren't necessarily what the reader will generally find on TV. These are real cops, sharing their real observations and feelings. These are real cops who have spent countless hours poring over stacks of latent fingerprint cards, cataloguing evidence, or drinking lots of coffee during long, dark stakeouts. These are cops who sometimes went a little against the system, as in the case of Detectives Dave Parker and Bill Cosgrove who, when the state prosecutor's office wouldn't file charges to help break up a notorious Gypsy crime ring, went to a local television journalist to get the case the attention it deserved. These are cops with families, cops who have seen their fellow officers die in the line of duty, cops who have been caught in shoot-outs, robberies, and house fires.

The following stories run the entire gamut; from funny to horrible, from pathetic to heartwarming, from wild and exciting to downright unbelievable. Although none of these police officers wear capes, they're probably the closest thing this country has to everyday heroes. These are ordinary people who watch and wait for evil to manifest itself so they can track it down and snuff it out. And, yes, they will sometimes keep an eye open for regular folks who exceed the posted speed limits. These are real-world stories of good guys vs. bad guys, of life and death, and all the strange, funny, and ridiculous mistakes and mishaps that can happen to a police officer when he or she is "on (or off) duty."

Chapter 1

The Beginning

It had been an uneventful first two hours of patrol in the midtown police district in Kansas City. The weather was nasty--humid conditions, raining on and off. I was working a one-man car. I looked at my watch and couldn't believe I had not yet received a call-for-service.

While in the area of 23rd and Indiana, I finally received a call over the radio at 1 a.m. The police dispatcher instructed me to respond to 19th and College, on a prowler call. Because I was only a few blocks away, I thought I'd be able to catch the bad guy in the act.

It had started to sprinkle again, with flashes of lightning in the sky. It only took about a minute to arrive at the scene. There I met with a middle-aged woman who was standing in front of her home, awaiting my arrival. She told me that she was in her living room, standing near a window, when she heard a noise outside that window, and immediately called the police. The prowler appeared to be a rather large male staring in at her. She stated that after she called the police, she ran outside and observed a person running from her residence. He was headed north on College toward 18th Street.

I went over to her living room window, which was on the east side of the house. It was there that she had seen the prowler looking in the window. I saw shoe impressions in the mud below the window. The woman thought the prowler had gone across 18th Street, and then on into the Benson Lumber Co., on the north side of 18th Street and College.

It had begun pouring rain again, so I went back to my police car and donned my raincoat. I drove one block and parked my car facing north on College at 18th Street. I left the headlights on, so the whole front of Benson Lumber was illuminated.

I ran across the street and observed some muddy shoe prints on the sidewalk. The gate to the six-foot, chain-link fence that enclosed the lumber yard was locked. Because I also saw some mud on the fence, I guessed that the prowler had likely gone over the top and gained entry into the lumber yard. I placed my flashlight in my back pocket and began to climb over the fence. Just as I dropped down from the top of the fence, a dark figure rushed toward me from the side of the building.

I hadn't seen any sign of him earlier. He caught me off balance and began stabbing me with an extremely long knife. I fell to the ground with knife wounds in my chest and stomach. I tried to get up, but I couldn't move. I wondered if this was because the knife had completely gone through my chest and into my spinal column. I tried to remove my gun from the holster, but I was unable to move my arms or my hands. I was bleeding profusely from my chest and stomach.

I looked into the suspect's face, but everything was beginning to blur. I felt sharp pains in my chest, but then my body became numb all over. My life started slipping away. I thought to myself, how could this be happening? This was just a simple prowler call. This can't be happening to me. The rain hit me in the face as I lay dying on the ground of the Benson Lumber Company.

Suddenly, I awoke. I sat up in bed and noticed that my window was open. Wind-driven rain was coming in the window. The air was heavy with thunder and lightning. Sweat poured down my forehead. I was only fourteen-years-old and not a policeman, I had never even thought of becoming a policeman. But I could not go back to sleep; it was about 1:30 a.m. At this time, I lived on 19th Terrace between Indiana and College, which was about one block from the origin of the prowler call from my dream.

Why would I have such a dream? I tried to think back and reasoned that I, as well as several kids in the neighborhood, had a habit of climbing over the Benson Lumber fence to take a shortcut to the Grove swimming pool at Truman Road and Benton Blvd. There were also railroad tracks located on the north side of the lumber yard where we often stopped and played on the tracks, sometimes watching the trains pass by. I'll never forget the horror when one of the older neighborhood kids lost a leg trying to run beside a train to hop aboard for a ride.

The lumber yard had a guard on duty and railroad dicks would walk around the area. They would check the tracks for foul play, as well as for the possibility of catching transients hopping a train. Sometimes the railroad dicks would spot us kids and we would run from them. I also reasoned that I should not worry about the dream, because I was too young to be a police officer. Little did I know how much of an impact this dream would have on my life in the years that lay ahead!

Doreen (Brady) Borchers with her children, L-R: Jerry Borchers, age 9; Darlene Borchers, age 12; Fred Borchers, age 10. Above photo was taken near 427 Prospect in Kansas City in 1947. (Family Photo)

Chapter 2

Early Life

I was born in Kansas City, Missouri in the summer of 1938, the youngest of three siblings. My sister, Darlene, was three years older than I, and my brother, Freddie, was a year older. At this time, my family was changing. My father, Fred, and my Uncle Wilbur had both been drafted into the service during World War II. My Dad went into the Navy and my uncle into the Army. My parents had gotten divorced sometime before I turned 3 years old, but I never learned the reasons. I know that my mother wanted to make a better life for herself, and moving to California seemed to be the right decision for her at that time. She also wanted to be close to her sisters who had also moved to California and had obtained good-paying jobs.

My grandma, Maude Jesse, was married to my grandpa, Fred Henry. She was half-Sioux Indian, and grandpa's parents were from Germany. They were trying to raise all of us on my grandpa's small pension. Because this was particularly difficult on my grandparents during the war years, financially speaking, they made the decision to allow their good friends, Slim and Elizabeth Fowler to take care of one of us children. I was chosen, probably because I was the youngest.

The Fowlers resided near 19th and Agnes in Kansas City, just a couple of blocks from where I had previously lived. They raised me until the war ended in 1945. I remember the very first time I was taken by Mrs. Fowler to Yeager Grade School. Though only five-years-old, I, however, did not want to go to school. For motivation, Mrs. Fowler took a small branch off a tree and whipped my backside all the way to school, about three blocks away. That first day, I left the school just minutes after she dropped me off and I went back home, where Mrs. Fowler was waiting, and, again, she whipped me all the way back to school.

After that, I realized that, although I didn't like school, I disliked whippings even more. I did not give Mrs. Fowler any more trouble about attending school after that first episode. I continued to live with her and her husband for a couple more years until the war was over and my father returned home.

When my Dad came home from the Navy, he took a job at the historic Muelbach Hotel, located at 12th and Baltimore. The building, constructed in 1915, was twelve stories high, pretty tall by my standards. Dad worked as a bell captain and often told me stories about the New York Yankees staying at the hotel whenever the team was in town for games. My Dad became good friends with baseball's legendary Mickey Mantle and often told me that Mantle would have his legs wrapped in tape to help him run better during games.

My Dad remarried in 1949. Then, he, too, moved away. He started another family, eventually having two girls, Karen and Linda. My grandparents and my Uncle Wilbur, who was a bellboy at the Pickwick Hotel, continued to raise us three children after I had returned from the Fowlers. I had become very attached to the Fowlers and continued to visit with them throughout the days of my youth.

Jerry Borchers and Carol Walters at Reseda High School Prom Dance. (Courtesy of Whites Studios, Northridge, CA)

Chapter 3

Moving to California

In July 1953 (I was fifteen and my brother was sixteen), my mother, Doreen, arranged for us to come to California to live with her. Mother had recently remarried a man named Jewell Roark.

They lived in Van Nuys, which is in the San Fernando Valley, in Los Angeles County. Mother sent for all three of us children, but Darlene was old enough to already be engaged, and was married a short time later.

My Aunt Betty came back to Kansas City to escort my brother and me on the bus trip to California, which took us about three days. Jewel and my mother met us at the bus station in Los Angeles. We drove to their home on Hazeltine Avenue in Van Nuys. It was a small apartment with only one bedroom, one bathroom, a living room, and a kitchen. There was not enough room for two growing boys, but somehow we were able to manage.

I was starting the ninth grade at Robert Fulton Junior High. Fred was enrolled in Van Nuys High School. About six months later, Fred got homesick for his grandma, who had taken sick in Kansas City, and he eventually returned home.

When I was sixteen, Jewell and my mother bought a home on Saticoy Street in Canoga Park, which is at the extreme west end of the San Fernando Valley. This meant I would be going to Canoga Park High School.

While living in Canoga Park, I had the job of babysitting some small children a block from where we lived. The person for whom I was babysitting worked at one of the Hollywood studios as a cameraman. One day, when I went to his house to watch his children, he introduced me to two young actors by the names of Robert Wagner and Jeffrey Hunter. I shook hands with both. I was told that these young men would someday be great actors. This did not mean much to me at the time, but they did, in fact, become quite famous stars on the silver screen.

When a new high school opened in Reseda in 1956, I was transferred there to finish my last two years of high school. My parents also moved again, this time to the 7300 block of Yolanda Avenue in Reseda. This would prove to be the best move we ever made because we lived directly across the street from a family named Walters. They had a pretty young daughter named Carol. She was almost fifteen-years-old at the time, while I just turned eighteen.

I always tell everyone that she had a fishing rod and reel and cast her line across the street to hook me, then reeled me in for the big catch. Truth be told, I am certain it was the other way around.

By now I had acquired an old '49 Dodge Business Coupe and had been driving it to school. One morning I waited until Carol left her residence to walk to school. I let her get about a block down the street before I fired up my ride and drove alongside her. I opened the passenger door and asked if she wanted a ride. She told me no, but after several more tries in as many days, she finally agreed. That was how our courtship started. While at school, I would walk her to classes and sometimes carry her books. Back in the 1950s, you couldn't even hold hands in school without having them smacked by a teacher, which was usually followed by a stern warning from the vice principal. Oh, how times have changed!

During my junior year at Reseda High, I took a part-time job doing janitorial work at different banks. I had the keys to three different banks and cleaned them after all of the employees left home for the night. I thought this was really big stuff, having keys to banks and being my own boss. One night, I had just finished at the California Bank in Van Nuys. My car was not working, so I was waiting for a ride from my parents. I was leaning against the front of the California Bank, and a two-man police car drove up and questioned me about what I was doing. I told them that I had just cleaned the bank. I understand now why I should have used a different choice of words because that statement surely raised some eyebrows. The police got out of their car and frisked me. I took out a handful of keys and opened the front bank doors, much to their surprise. About this time, my parents drove up to give me a ride home. They explained that I did, in fact, have a job cleaning banks.

Carol and I continued to date for the next year and a half, and when I was a senior, I asked her to go to the prom. She accepted my offer with a resounding "yes." I will never forget how long it took me to make sure my Hollywood flattop was correctly combed. When I went across the street to get Carol, I was so nervous that I could not figure out how to pin the corsage on her beautiful dress. Carol's mother did the honor, and I was glad for her expertise. Every now and then, I run across that photo of us at the prom and can remember that evening as if it were yesterday.

Then, one night, during my senior year at Reseda High School, my old nightmare returned. I dreamt again that I was working as a police officer in the KCPD. The dream featured the same scenario with the same prowler call at the same location. As in the earlier dream, it was raining hard. As before, I dreamed that I climbed over the fence and that I was again stabbed to death and left lying on the ground of the lumber yard. This really shook me up, having such a vividly recurring dream some four years apart. Though I was only eighteen, I still had never given any thought to becoming a police officer.

About this same time, my brother was in the U.S. Navy. While on leave one weekend, he visited us and spent a couple of nights. He had a classy Navy uniform that he wore home. I asked him if I could wear it. He got me dressed and I went across the street in the uniform. I asked Carol if she wanted to go for a walk over to Reseda Boulevard to buy an ice cream cone at the Foster Freeze. As we walked back to our homes, I began talking seriously to Carol. We looked into each other's eyes, and it dawned on me that I was in love with her.

As the time for my high school graduation approached, my sister, Darlene, decided to attend. As I recall, Carol and I had been driven to Union Train Station in Los Angeles by my parents. We were meeting my sister and her two young daughters, Sherry and Carla.

Before Darlene and her daughters arrived, Carol and I were sitting on a bench in a garden area decorated with Spanish tile, talking about marriage and a white house with a white fence. We also talked about the first names of our future children, deciding that all of their names would start with the letter "B," so we could call them our little BBs. Carol reminded me that I had not really officially asked her to marry her. So, I got on my knees, took her hands in mine, and proposed. Our romantic moment apparently did not go unnoticed for the proposal was overheard by a number of people in the area. They clapped their hands and shouted their congratulations to us.

This photo was taken in San Antonio, TX, 1957. Airman Basic Gerald R. Borchers is in his Air Force uniform.

Chapter 4

Joining the Air Force

After graduating from high school in June 1957, I joined the U.S. Air Force and left on August 4th for boot camp in San Antonio, Texas. I had heard rumors about boot camp, and I was really not looking forward to arriving there and having my beautiful Hollywood flattop shaved off! Yet, the dreaded haircut was something that every recruit would have to endure, just like me, so the anxiety soon wore off. While in Basic Training, I made two great new friends. They had also boarded the train in Los Angeles to make the long ride to San Antonio. Boot Camp was a rude awakening for all of us. As we disembarked, our drill instructors were waiting for us, and all Hell broke loose!

Basic training was very hard, but I found that it was best not to draw attention to myself. Unfortunately, I made the mistake of being noticed right away. This was because of my ability to march well. I was made the 1st element leader, and all four columns of soldiers pivoted on my moves. After a week of the drill instructor yelling out my name, I began to wish that I had never been picked as the 1st element leader.

One day after our group marched back to the barracks, the drill instructor said he was going to do a laundry bag inspection. He bellowed to "get your butts inside and be ready for inspection." This really worried me, because we were only allowed to keep one dirty pair of underwear in the laundry bag, and I knew I had three. I ran into the barracks and took out two of the dirty pairs and placed them in my duffle bag beneath other clothing and boots.

I was the first person inspected because I was the 1st element leader and I was also bunked at the first bed. As I stood there at attention, the drill instructor said he was going to conduct a duffle bag inspection rather than a laundry bag inspection. The DI took my duffle bag from the foot of my bed and dumped all of the contents onto it. He discovered the two dirty pairs of underwear. He then got into my face and asked me if I was the 1st element leader, and I stated, "Yes Sir!"

The DI then grabbed my 1st element leader band from my arm and jerked it off. He then shouted "You were the 1st element leader." He told me to get my ass all the way down the barracks to the last bed and that I would never be an element leader again. I hurriedly went to the last bed and started thinking to myself that this was my dream come true. I would no longer have the pressure of screwing everyone up in marching drills. From then on, I was placed in the middle of the pack and was not noticed any more, especially when I started off on the wrong foot or goofed up the cadence.

While in Boot Camp, I took a battery of different tests to determine my job skill levels. I never liked mechanics, so I deliberately gave wrong answers to the questions on that subject. I didn't realize that the total scores would have a bearing on the jobs that would be offered. When I got the results, it was obvious that my total scores were not good, but I had done extremely well in the administrative area. I was offered jobs in administration: supply or postal services, cook or air policeman. Due to the two nightmares I'd had about being killed as a police officer, I chose to become a postal specialist, because I also did not like K.P. (Kitchen Patrol). I had already been assigned to work in the kitchen for a couple of days during training. I hated washing pots and pans or scrubbing the kitchen floor.

It was a happy day when I graduated from Boot Camp. I learned I was to be stationed at Norton Air Force Base in San Bernardino, CA, as a postal specialist. This made me happy because I would be close to Reseda and within reasonable proximity of Carol.

However, after only nine months, I was reassigned to Athens, Greece, for a scheduled two-and-a-half year tour. I was twenty-years-old at that time and really wanted to get married before I left. But Carol's parents wanted her to graduate from high school. They also preferred she turn eighteen before marrying me.

I was unhappy with their decision, but, in later years, I realized this was the proper thing to do at the time. Anyway, Carol and I were officially engaged. I gave her an engagement ring, as well as a wedding ring to keep until she graduated. I knew she was the right woman for me.

The U.S. Air Force Base in Athens was located within the commercial Athena International Airport. One of my duties was to pick up mail by truck from military and commercial cargo planes and from the ships in port and take it to the Air Mail Terminal (AMT). The mail was sorted by unit and division and then dispatched to the numerous APOs we serviced. I soon developed some very large calluses on my knuckles from handling all those mailbags.

Athens Air Force Base did not have living quarters for the soldiers, so while stationed there I lived at various locations off-base. Eventually, I moved to a white, two-story home on Perikleous Street in Old Phaleron, about ten miles from Athens and five miles from the base. A German shepherd dog named Ruff came with the house. Sophia, the landlady and her family, lived upstairs. I shared the downstairs with two other airmen. We each paid only $20 monthly rent, and this included laundry which the landlady did in her bathtub with a washboard.

Good old Ruff helped me out one time in particular. One day Sophia came down from her apartment and brought a large plate of spaghetti. The spaghetti was prepared differently than I was used to back home in the States, and I did not care much for the taste. Smelling the spaghetti, Ruff perked up his ears and started wagging his tail back and forth. After Sophia left, I placed the plate on the floor, and Ruff licked every last morsel from the plate.

When Sophia returned a few minutes later, she saw that all the food was gone and asked me if I liked it. I told her it was delicious so I wouldn't disappoint her. She said, "Poor boy, you are so hungry." She returned a couple minutes later with another full plate of spaghetti. I told her thanks. After she left, I looked at Ruff and asked if he was up to eating some more. He began to wag his tail, but a little slower than earlier. He was able to eat only about half of the spaghetti. After his last couple bites, his tail no longer was moving back and forth, and his ears were not as perky. It was apparent that Ruff had done his best. He gave it the old college try. I let the dog outside, because I was now worried what he might do to the room after devouring all that pasta and sauce!

Carol's graduation day finally came in June, 1959 and she bought her a ticket to fly over to Athens, Greece from the money we had both saved. I didn't have enough rank for the military to pay her way. Shortly after she arrived, we were married in the base theater, which also served as the base chapel on Sundays. The ceremony was held Saturday on a popcorn-covered floor after the kiddy cartoons and before the afternoon matinee. We had been apart for thirteen months. I was really nervous.

Around December 1960, Carol became pregnant with our first child. In June 1961, my tour was nearly up and Carol had to return to the states three months early because the military airlines didn't allow pregnant women to fly after their sixth month. She decided to go back to California to help out her mother until I could return. Her mother was now widowed.

I had made Airman First, but I still did not have enough time in the service to be eligible for the government to pay for Carol's trip home. Because she was six months pregnant, she did, however, qualify for a standby ride without having to pay for the airline ticket.

The first available standby flight was on a C-47 cargo plane on its way to Germany with a stop in Paris. Carol would then catch another standby flight to New York. Four airman, two sailors, and Carol were the only passengers. We said our tearful good-byes and I watched her plane take off.

Sometime, long after the fact, Carol told me of her adventure. After boarding, she saw there were only six passenger seats. The rest of the plane was an open cargo area with two hammocks attached to a side wall. After taking their seats, Carol learned the two sailors were coming off leave and were headed back to Paris for a connection to meet their ship. The Navy men were apparently very tired, and, after take-off, they lay down in the hammocks and were soon sound asleep.

After the plane had been in flight for some time, it was redirected on a different mission to pick up a high-ranking officer at Wheelus AFB just outside Tripoli, Libya. All of the passengers were informed of the change in flight plan except for the two sailors who were still fast asleep in the hammocks. Surely, they all thought, the steep, banking turn of the plane would wake the sailors, but they slept on. The passengers decided to let them be surprised. Just before landing, the sailors woke up and took their seats. It was pitch dark when the plane approached the Libyan airbase and, as the sailors looked out the window, they saw palm trees silhouetted in the bright airport lights. They immediately knew they were not in Paris. The other passengers took it in stride, except for the sailors, who were upset that they might miss their ship that was schedule to leave from the Port of France.

While Carol was stranded in Tripoli, waiting for a stand-by flight to the States, she met a female military medical nurse. The nurse spent time with Carol and took her off-base to show her the town. She said they had lots of fun together, touring the landmarks in the city, and browsing through the shops in the noisy, narrow streets. The nurse cautioned Carol about not staring at the Muslim women who wore long black dresses and veils over their faces. After only a three-day layover, Carol was on the first available flight to the States, eventually to California, but first by way of South Carolina!

Three months later our first child was born, whom we named Brenda. We kept our promise by sticking with first names beginning with the letter "B." Brenda was born at Williams AFB, located in Chandler, Ariz., my newest assignment.

Shortly after arriving at Williams AFB, my four-year enlistment was up. In August 1961, I was re-enlisted by Sergeant William Caskey, the same recruiter who convinced me to enlist in Los Angeles four years prior. This occasion made the Air Force Times, and our photograph was taken together. I was stationed at Williams AFB until the middle of June 1963.

It was on my 25th birthday in July, 1963, that I had to leave my pregnant wife and little Brenda to go to my new assignment at Don Maung AFB, in Thailand, fifteen miles from downtown Bangkok. Wives could join their husbands in Bangkok, but not at Don Maung AFB. What a difference fifteen miles makes! The farewell was heart-wrenching. To boot, the one-year assignment lasted 366 days because it was a Leap Year!

My assignment at Don Maung AFB was to again work at the AMT, basically performing the same duties I had in Athens. I had to drive to the commercial airport to meet planes, receive the mail, and return to the AMT, where the mail was sorted and directed to other APOs.

One particular night during the monsoon season, it was pouring rain. I was scheduled to meet a Pan American flight when it arrived. I backed up my truck to the doors of the plane to receive the mail.

Before giving me the manifest to check off the bags of mail, the crew on the plane started hurriedly throwing bag after bag of mail into the back of my covered truck, obviously trying to keep the mail from getting soaking wet. But I was also not expecting nearly that much mail.

When I finally was able to get the manifest and start checking off the mail bags, I became aware that some of the mailbags had an "X" by the number on the manifest. This meant the bag contained a large amount of money, in the form of cash. A member of the flight crew informed that this particular flight had been shot at when the plane was trying to land in South Vietnam. Because of that, the plane had been diverted to Bangkok. I could account for only some of the registered mail and assumed that the rest was already on my truck. Because of the heavy rainfall, I was unable to inventory the mail received there on the flight line. I signed the manifest, indicating that I had received all the mail. This turned out to be a serious mistake on my part. The pilot refused to hold up the plane and was in a hurry to take off, so I took the mail to the AMT. My fellow airmen and I took all the mail off of the truck and went through all the bags.

According to the manifest, we soon discovered that two bags of registered mail were missing, which I now desperately hoped that they were still on the plane that had already left. Still, I had to call my supervisor and get him out of bed. He reported to the AMT where he chewed me out, which was then followed by yet another phone call to the proper authorities to report the missing money bags.

Sometime around noon the next day, I was contacted in my living quarters by the FBI. I was interrogated for several hours and accused of being the kingpin that arranged for the plane to overfly Vietnam. They also accused me of arranging for some Thailand personnel to take the two money bags and that I had planned to split the money with them. I was informed that I would probably be busted in rank. They told me that I would be followed wherever I went and that every move I made would be watched. I tried to explain that I was only an airman with three stripes and could not have planned such an elaborate scheme. This went on for two days until I was contacted by my supervisor and told that the two missing mail bags had been found underneath some cargo equipment in New York City. I never received any apologies from anyone at anytime about the accusations made against me, but I did retain my rank of Airman First.

In October 1963, Carol delivered our second child, whom we named Bonnie. I was sent photos of Bonnie and was one proud father, all over again. When my tour was about up, I got a big surprise. T. J. Funderburk, with whom I had been stationed with in Athens, and who was also the Best Man at our wedding, was to be my replacement.

A few short months before I left Thailand, President John Kennedy was assassinated. I distinctly remember that it was a Saturday morning, the 23rd of November, and I had been taking a shower. I heard an airman yell out that the President had been shot and was dead. Back in Texas, it was a Friday afternoon, the day before, when Kennedy was killed --Thailand is twelve hours ahead of Texas time.

My one-year isolated assignment was over in Thailand. I left on my 26th birthday in 1964. That was the happiest day that I can remember because I knew I would soon be seeing Carol and our two beautiful daughters. Due to traveling east through the International Date Line, my birthday lasted two days!

I was one happy trooper when my plane landed in Los Angeles. My wife met me at the airport and we had a couple of days together at an old hotel on the beach…but we didn't notice it was old.

Before being reassigned, I had put in for two Air Force bases in California to be close to Carol's family. But I was awarded my third choice, McConnell AFB in Wichita, Kansas. I guessed it would be an OK assignment because it was only about a three-hour drive to my childhood hometown. I packed up Carol and the two girls, and the four of us moved to the Land of Oz!

Once at McConnell Air Force Base, I resumed my duties as a Postal Specialist with the rank of Airman 1st Class (E-4), with five years in grade. During my assignment, I was invited to attend the NCO Preparatory School on the base. This was a two-week assignment and around thirty airmen and a few staff sergeants were in the class. This was similar to Boot Camp, involving lots of academics, marching, and inspections.

At our graduation, we attended an appreciation banquet, and I was presented the Commandant's Award for having the most academic and training points. I knew I was pretty close to winning, but was not sure until my name was called. This award was for outstanding performance in military training, exceptional attitude, and meritorious personal achievement. Everyone yelled, "Speech!" I had to get up in front of high-ranking officers and gave a little speech. I was surprised and nervous, but got through it just fine. The award was presented to me on November 20th, 1964. I felt certain that I would have a chance to make Staff Sergeant (E-5), but it didn't happen.

While I was still stationed at McConnell and for the third time in my life, I had the same nightmare about being a Kansas City policeman. There were a few additional details, but it still ended the same way. I felt very strongly, by this time, that I was somehow being warned about something, though I had no idea what. Furthermore, I had no desire to be a police officer, nor did I have any plans to return to Kansas City to live. The time had come, however, to tell Carol about the dreams.

In mid-May 1965, I was notified by the base sergeant major that my name and Air Force Specialty Code (AFSC) number had been selected out of the computer. The Department of the Air Force wanted me to go on a temporary duty assignment (TDY) for 120 days to Vietnam. I had been picked because of my postal experience and for previously operating the military post office in Thailand. My assignment was to set up a field post office for the Marines, many more of whom were now being shipped to Vietnam as the conflict there escalated.

I talked with Carol about this assignment and we discussed my getting out of the service. Her mother needed our help now since she had become severely crippled with rheumatoid arthritis. Also, Carol wasn't very fond at all of another isolated assignment, it having only been a few months since I returned from Thailand. I advised the sergeant major that I did not have 120 days left on my second enlistment. He told me that I could not turn down the assignment and that I should extend my enlistment and re-enlist once I was in Vietnam.

I told him that I was very disappointed about not being promoted to staff sergeant and that I had over five years in grade. He told me that I would be promoted in Vietnam, if I took the assignment. I still refused, and he became angry. He told me that I would be red-lined and that he would stop me from re-enlisting. I told him to put me "on the list" for not re-enlisting, and that was the end of it. Up to that point I'd given the Air Force eight years of dedicated service, but the summer of 1965, marked the end of my Air Force career.

Chapter 5

Back in Civilian Life

Getting out of the Air Force left me with an uneasy feeling. During my eight years of service, our family may have had to live on a meager budget, but I did not have to worry about finding work or having to make career decisions – the military is pretty good about doing all that for you!

The next couple years became a very rude awakening for our family while I tried adjusting to civilian life and tried finding the right job to support our growing family. We rented a nice home near Carol's mother. Carol was rehired at Metropolitan Savings & Loan in Reseda, where she had worked before we were married.

My first job was with General Motors in Van Nuys, working on the assembly line in the trim section. I had to stay ahead of the cars coming by my work section every minute or so and assemble trim to have it ready to place on the cars. At first, I had trouble keeping up with the line of cars, but it was not long before I mastered this job and had time to even rest a little between cars. I don't remember how much I was paid an hour, but with Carol working and my wages, we were able to get by financially.

Carol became pregnant with our third child about the same time I was hired at GM. In order to have insurance to cover the birth, I had to have worked there for at least nine months. The baby was due on June 16, but the company health insurance would not begin until July 1. We did a lot of praying that our child would not be born on schedule. Thankfully, Beverly was born nearly three weeks late. Insurance covered the birth, which was great news. This may have had something to do with giving Beverly her middle name, Joy.

While working at GM, there were often rumors of layoffs. I

started looking for a better job that had some type of retirement benefits. I immediately thought of the nightmares I'd had about being a police officer and subsequently learned that the Los Angeles Police Department (LAPD) was hiring. I thought, well, this is LA, not KC. So, I applied and completed the written and psychological tests. I was then scheduled for a physical agility test and passed everything except for the overhand pull-ups. I was told to come back in a month and retry. This really discouraged me, so I gave up on the whole idea.

I then applied for the Los Angeles County Fire Department, located in Thousand Oaks. I passed the test and was immediately hired. This was an "on-the-job" type of training. We lived at the academy training facility, had classroom and field training during the day, and at night would be on-call to respond to fire alarms.

I was a little uneasy about being a fireman because I was just not very mechanically inclined. On the first day, we trained with the equipment on the various types of fire trucks. Each applicant had to run out a hose line from the fire truck and give a signal when he or she wanted the water turned on. I did everything right that first time, except for failing to brace myself when I gave the signal to "charge the line."

My oversight quickly became a disaster. The hose flayed out of control like some giant snake, high-pressure water spraying everywhere, quickly knocking our training fire captain to the ground before several of us brought the hose under control. When the situation finally calmed down, the captain reminded all of us that accidents can happen during training and to shake the incident off. It still bothered me that I had caused the accident.

The first night at the station, I tried to sleep while listening to the calls coming in over the radio. I did not sleep well, still thinking about that "eventful" hose incident. We did not get any calls that night, and the next day ended with regular classroom training. Shortly thereafter, I met with the captain in his office and told him I wanted to resign. He tried to talk me out of it, saying he didn't want to lose me, but I already had made up my mind; I did not want to be a fireman. I have often wondered if I could have made a good fireman, but the answer to that is something I will never know.

I was feeling pretty dejected when I arrived home that evening, even more so when I told Carol that I had quit. Sensing how I felt, she wrapped her arms around me to comfort me. I broke down and cried, not knowing where I would look next for work.

About that time, I met a man named Robert Wisherd, who lived up the street from us. He owned a large dump truck and worked in Sun Valley hauling asphalt to construction sites. He took me with him several times, and I became interested in the job. He had a relative with a truck for sale, and I decided to buy it. The truck was a 1961 GMC that could haul up to nine tons of asphalt. I borrowed money from Carol's mother for a down payment to purchase the truck. I tried this job for about four months, but the truck had too many mechanical problems, and everything that could go wrong…did.

Have you ever seen a nine-ton asphalt brick? One day, after picking up a full load of asphalt, the truck broke down in the Hollywood hills. The clutch plate and fly wheel went out. That meant I couldn't get the load of hot asphalt dumped out. By the time the repairs were made, the asphalt had hardened in the truck bed. It took copious gallons of diesel fuel, poured around the edge of the asphalt, before the "brick" would slide out of the raised bed. Because I was not a mechanically-inclined person, I decided to let the truck go back to the original owner and, once again, found myself seeking suitable employment.

This became a real low point in my life. I started to take on a series of low-paying jobs, if only to keep the lights on and put food on the table. During this time, Carol was amazing. She stood by me and offered her encouragement each time I explained to her that I had quit yet another job. Faithfully, she gave me the support to continue looking for the kind of work I liked.

Before long, I landed a job as a janitor with the Los Angeles School District. Whatever preconceived notion one may have about this kind of work, it was not a bad job, even though it did not pay much toward supporting my family. One of my specific tasks at the school was cleaning the gymnasium floor every night. I noticed a wooden ladder that had been installed against one of the walls. I decided to start practicing overhand pull-ups during my spare time, eventually making great improvement. This, of course, led to the idea of returning to the police academy and retaking my physical agility test. When I finally did, I passed the pull-up test with flying colors and was immediately selected to start training at the police academy in August 1967. I was now a twenty-nine-year-old husband and father of three wonderful young girls. Who would have thought?

Police Officer Jerry Borchers talks with citizens about crime prevention at a community meeting held in a local school in Granada Hills, CA, 1969. (Courtesy of Los Angeles Police Department)

Chapter 6

Los Angeles Police Department

LAPD Academy

In the back of my mind, I thought about the bad dreams I'd earlier had in my life. I had to put that particular nightmare behind me to make it through the rough academy training that I had to endure. After all, there I was in sunny California, a couple thousand miles from the Benson Lumber yard in Kansas City.

I truly believe that this training was harder than USAF boot camp. We started with 159 recruits, and it was not long before some were released. After about a month of training, we were instructed to fill out five pink slips, naming recruits that we believed would not make good officers. We also filled out five white slips of paper listing those we thought would make good officers. It was extremely hard on me to have to list the recruits' names on the pink slips. Perhaps, intuitively, the officers I listed on the pink slips would eventually be let go.

In the last part of our training, we only had to fill out two pink slips and two white slips. I was constantly afraid of having my name listed by someone, so I was careful not to criticize anyone or even use any profanity.

We had to run five miles at the end of each day and top it off with a round of "King-of-the-Hill." This was done at a muddy hill behind Dodger Stadium. The purpose of the exercise was to climb up the hill while keeping other recruits from reaching the top, pulling or pushing them back down. The idea was to not be the last one to the top of the hill. I was never last and I never lost. If someone had ever decided to form a company specifically created around this game, I would have become president in no time!

One day, during training, I ate a barbeque sandwich and baked beans for lunch. During the five-mile run at the end of the day, I got physically sick and stopped running. Soon, I began throwing up lunch. I was lying on the ground and the instructor, who came up beside me, asked me if I really wanted to be a police officer. I told him, "Yes, sir." He told me to get my butt up and continue running. I got to my feet, though it took every ounce of strength I had to continue the run. Still, after a few minor incidents, I successfully made it through the ten weeks of training and was among the 131 recruits that graduated in my class.

The LAPD had seventeen different district stations at that time, with approximately 7,000 policemen on the force. My first assignment was to the Foothill Police Station, located in the northeast area of the San Fernando Valley. I was assigned to patrol and automatically placed on three months' probation. I really enjoyed police work, and I believed that I had finally made the right career choice. The mental and physical efforts it took to become a police officer had stirred my interest even more. Through it all, this was the job that I knew I could do well.

I'd Like to Meet Your Wife

While at the Foothill Division, I had been assigned to work the front desk of the police station one evening shift. Carol had made me a nice lunch to eat because I would not be able to go out and buy lunch while working the desk. About an hour after I started working the front desk, I was informed that an older officer had suffered a minor injury and would be coming in from patrol to work the desk. We changed places; I took his assignment on patrol, and he worked the desk. I gave him my lunch to eat, not knowing what my wife had prepared, because I could now buy my dinner at a restaurant. About four hours later, I got a call to come to the station for information. When I walked in, several officers were standing around laughing. They looked at me and pointed to the bulletin board. I saw a personal note from my wife, stating "Oh Honey, you were wonderful last night, I really enjoyed it." The note was signed with Carol's name. The officer I had given my lunch to told me that my wife made a wonderful lunch and that he enjoyed the note he'd found in the lunch even more. He said he would like to meet my wife. I got a good laugh, as well. I have often thought of that note. This makes me wish today that I could "perform" like I did when I was only twenty-nine years old. However, I did request that Carol not place any more personal notes in my lunch again!

Missing Children

I was still assigned to the Foothill Division when I received a call while working with another officer named Gene Terrell. We were assigned to a two-man car, and it was late February 1969. Gene and I received notice to meet a woman regarding a missing child. For the preceding two months, the Valley had been experiencing some of its worst rains in thirty years. We were informed that three young boys, ages four to five-years-old, had been missing for more than three hours. They were last seen in the foothills close to the county line in Pacoima.

As we began searching the area, we spotted one of the children. The youngster said the other two boys were stuck on a cliff about three-quarters of a mile up the canyon.

There was no possible way to drive into the area, and it was about to turn dark. We had to hike in, and we found one boy clinging to a bush about fifty feet from the top of a 150-foot cliff. The other boy was spotted crouched on a ledge just a few feet below the other child.

I hiked back to the police car and called for assistance. I gave the dispatcher the exact location and the situation that the boys were in. During that time, Gene had climbed up the muddy hill to the child in the most danger. He removed his shirt and wrapped it around the boy. He then moved him to a safer area. Gene climbed further up to the top of the hill to wait for assistance.

Help came in the form of fire trucks, an ambulance, a helicopter, detectives and supervisors. It was pretty dark by this time, but the lights from the helicopter kept the boys in view. We wrapped a rope around Gene and lowered him down to each one of the children. Each of the boys was eventually pulled up the muddy hill to safety. Both boys were taken to the hospital by helicopter and were found to have only minor scratches and bruises. Gene and I were exhausted, wet and cold, but still on duty after our ordeal. Gene went to the Pacoima Hospital where he was treated and returned to duty after changing uniforms.

The following month, Gene and I were honored at a Sun Valley Optimist Club banquet. The main speaker was Lt. Gov. Ed Reineke. Some of the VIP's attending were Capt. W.A. Stephenson, Foothill commander Lt. Hoy Key, Foothill community relations officer, Councilman Louis Nowell, Capt. Richard Green, commander of the North Hollywood Division, and approximately two hundred local residents.

Lt. Gov. Reineke said, "Policemen, in everyday life, do an outstanding job, but every so often they do something that is beyond the requirements of the job." To this day, I have the award I received that night on an office wall in my basement and a photo of the two boys we rescued. Every once in a while, I wonder if either of those two boys might have been inspired to enter the law enforcement profession by what Gene and I did for them on that night so many years ago.

In April 1969, I was assigned to the Devonshire Police Station in Granada Hills. I put in for this assignment because it was much closer to our home; we had recently moved from Northridge to Sylvan Street in Woodland Hills. I was at first assigned to what was called the Basic Car Program. Devonshire Station was divided into several areas, each with a two-man car. Every shift, the two-man car stayed in a specific district. This allowed that two-man car to remain more in touch with the citizens and the crimes committed in the community they were patrolling.

Each month, different crime prevention issues were addressed during community meetings held in public schools. The three two-man cars that handled each of the three shifts met with community leaders to discuss the different crime problems that the community faced. The first part of the meeting was held in the auditorium, showing slides of the topics to be discussed. We then answered questions as a group. During the second portion of the meeting, the three two-man teams broke up by team and met in three separate rooms where the question and answer period could be, and usually proved to be, much less formal, though they were also far more productive for both the citizens and for those of us on the teams.

I remember one meeting, in particular, when I introduced myself as a policeman who loved Mexican food. I did not think much about it at the time. A few days later, my partner and I were on patrol and a car came up directly behind us. The driver began honking the car horn at us, waving at us to stop our vehicle.

I stopped the patrol car and two older ladies jumped out and ran up to us. I couldn't imagine what their problem was. They each called out our names and asked if we were headed to a particular Mexican restaurant. We told them that we had just come from there and thanked them for their concern. This simple contact confirmed to me that the program was working: the community was not avoiding the police, but was, instead, quite friendly toward us. Those of us on the police department hoped that, in this cooperative atmosphere, the local citizens would, in turn, be far more likely to report criminal activity when and where they observed it. Even today, just as then, there is not a police officer in this book who would not agree that a law enforcement agency's very first line of defense against crime is an alert and cooperative public.

Drunken Nude Lady

One night I had just gotten off duty from the night watch at Devonshire Station. I was about a mile from the station heading home, when I saw a middle-aged woman, completely nude, standing in the middle of the street, waving me down. I stopped my little red Volkswagen to keep from hitting her. She staggered over to my passenger door, opened it up, and got into my car. She reeked of alcohol.

I was in full police uniform, and she asked me to take her home. While debating what to do next, she then reached over and grabbed my groin, and I made up my mind; it was jail time!

I made a U-turn and headed back to the station. The woman told me that she did not live that way and wanted to know why I was going the wrong way. Before she knew it, I had pulled into the police station parking lot. I yelled to another policeman to grab a blanket out of his car and bring it to me. He retrieved one from the trunk of his patrol car and gave it to me as I got the woman out of my car and then wrapped the blanket around her.

Officers on the next shift were getting into their cars to leave the station. A number of them gathered around my car and laughed at me for not taking the woman home. Needless to say, I played this encounter safe and booked her for being drunk in public. Two things were prevented by doing what I did: first, I avoided the potential for false charges of inappropriate "contact," and, second, I did not have to worry about facing "the music" at home!

What's My Location?

One night, while working the dog watch (11 p.m. to 7 a.m.) in a one-man car, I found myself in an isolated area of the northwest end of the Valley. At all times, good police officer's should always know his or her location so as to be able to then inform the dispatcher when receiving a call or making a car or pedestrian stop for any reason.

This time, however, I really had not paid much attention to my location. I had driven up behind a parked car. There were four young men in the car, and as I walked up to it, I could distinctly smell the aroma of marijuana.

I pulled my revolver from my holster and ordered all of the individuals out of the car. I told the subjects to place their hands on the trunk. I asked for and was given each man's driver's license. Then I asked one of them to run down the road until he found some street signs to see what the location was. He returned a few minutes later and gave me the street names.

I then called the police dispatcher and asked for back-up. I explained that I had four subjects in custody. The individual who had gotten the location suddenly turned and looked at me. He said that he was stupid to return and that he should have kept on running. I held up his driver's license and explained that I would have gotten an arrest warrant for him and said that he had made the right decision. All four were booked for possession of marijuana after a couple baggies of the stuff were recovered from their pockets and car.

After various assignments in patrol, I was transferred to the Accident Investigation Unit where my primary duties were to investigate serious injury and/or fatal car accidents or accidents involving city property. My duties also included writing traffic tickets in high-frequency accident locations. My supervisors informed me that there were no such things as ticket quotas, but that I could write as many as I wanted.

Meeting Roy Rogers

One day I had handled a couple minor accidents and had some paperwork to catch up on. Typically, I would go to the station to finish my paperwork, but I stopped at a fast-food restaurant and got a malt and double cheeseburger.

I was close to Roy Rogers' ranch located near Topanga Canyon, so I decided to drive onto his property to let my food digest and to finish up some of my paperwork. I parked my vehicle on the hill at the intersection of Trigger Lane and Trigger Place. As I was finishing up a report, I apparently fell asleep with the report in my lap and my head resting against the driver's door window.

My sleep was disturbed by a car noise, and I looked out the window. I saw Roy Rogers himself in a pickup truck parked beside my car. He asked me if I was OK. I told him that I must have fallen asleep doing my reports. He laughed a little and told me that he was glad to have police officers looking over his property. He told me that officers were welcome at any time. As usual, I was embarrassed, but we had a nice conversation. When he drove, off I could not get over meeting the "King of the Cowboys." I eventually got an autographed photo of him on his horse, Trigger, which also hangs on the office wall of my basement.

Borrowed Pen

Two specific traffic tickets are still fresh in my mind today. I had just cleared from the station and was driving on Balboa Boulevard, north of Devonshire. I observed a car going approximately 20 miles over the speed limit.

Eventually I was able to get the driver to pull the car over to the side of the road. I walked up to the car and began conversing with the white male driver about his violation. I asked for and received his driver's license and took out my ticket book, but immediately realized that I did not have a pen to write the ticket. He told me he was an engineer, and I noticed that the front pocket of his shirt held several pens. I asked the gentleman if I could borrow one. He hesitated at first, but gave up one of his pens.

I gave him a 10-mile-an-hour over the speed limit break, which he accepted willingly. He then told me that he couldn't believe that his own pen had been used to write his ticket. I gave the pen back and told the man to have a nice day. When the driver left, I turned my patrol car around and headed back to the station to stock up on an ample supply of writing utensils!

Donald Duck

On another occasion, I had stopped yet another car and was in the process of writing the driver a traffic citation. I had the ticket completely written, except for the operator's signature. Suddenly, I heard an "Officer Needs Help" call come out near my location, and I asked the driver to hurry up and sign the ticket. As I hurriedly tore out his copy, I paid no attention to the name he signed, and closed my ticket book. The driver went on his way, and I went on the call to assist the officer in trouble.

After assisting the officer who had been in need of help, I drove directly to the Devonshire Police Station to drop off the traffic tickets I had written with the desk sergeant, then to be placed in the processing files. Thirty minutes later, I got a call from the desk sergeant to report back to the station. When I did, he told me that I should look at one of the tickets I had given him earlier. I verified that it was one I had written. When I checked the signature line, I saw the name "F--- YOU, DONALD DUCK." The desk sergeant advised me that it would be in my best interest to cancel the ticket, even though I could also request a warrant against the person. I totally agreed with the desk sergeant, knowing that I would very likely be the object of considerable scorn and laughter in a subsequent court procedure. I filled out a full report on why the ticket was cancelled, and "Donald Duck" never had his day in court.

Sylmar Earthquake

It was February 9, 1971, at approximately 5:50 a.m. when I decided to get up a little early for work. I already had put on my uniform and was ready to go out the door. I decided to rest another five minutes, so I lay back down on my bed next to Carol, who was still asleep.

At the time, we had a house guest, Carl Galbraith, a wonderful family friend from Ensenada, Mexico, who visited our family occasionally. He was a small wiry man who strongly resembled Don Knotts. He wore thick glasses and had worked as a dog catcher for the city of Los Angeles before retiring to a life of fishing. At this time, he was in his mid-70s. He had spent the night with us and was sleeping in Beverly's bedroom in the back of the house. It should be noted that there was a water heater on the other side of the wall from his bed.

At 6 a.m., Carol and I were shaken out of bed. I could hear a terrible roaring noise, one that I had never heard before. The house was rocking like a ship. Our bed was shaking up and down and moving from side to side. I immediately went to check on the girls in the bedroom next to ours, stumbling from wall to wall through the hallway. One of our daughters had been thrown out of the bunk bed and was crying. It was hard to get into their bedroom because their bed was wedged against the door.

I then went to the back bedroom to check on Carl. I called through the door to ask if he was okay, and he yelled out "Hell, that hot water heater sure is acting up." He did not realize there had been an earthquake. Finally, we all gathered in the living area and found that, fortunately, no one was hurt.

I did a quick inspection of the house. The only damage I found were marks on the ceiling where the chandelier hit as it swung from one side to the other. Some china had been thrown out of the cabinet and had broken. We were very fortunate. The single-story, wood-framed house had survived well. Later that day, we learned many other buildings had not.

I knew I would be needed at work, so I soon left. I arrived at the Devonshire Police Station in Granada Hills a little later than usual. A sergeant who had been working all night had been sitting on a toilet when the earthquake struck. His uniform was soaking wet, and he told us that he had held on to the base of the toilet to ride out the earthquake, which explained the condition of his uniform.

Our station was not badly damaged, but some of the walls were cracked and a section of ceiling tiles had fallen in.

I called Carol later and informed her I would be working 12-hour shifts. The earthquake had been measured at 6.6 and was centered in the Sylmar area across the Valley from our home. The Olive View Veterans' Administrative Hospital was badly damaged, and a number of people were trapped. Some died.

In the next few days, I was given a number of different jobs. One assignment was at the top of the Van Norman Dam, which had been badly damaged, leaving many to fear that it might break. People who lived below the dam had to be evacuated until the water could be released to relieve the pressure on the dam. This eventually took three days to accomplish. Another assignment was to protect the evacuees' homes and a number of small businesses from looters. This worried Carol because it meant I would be working below the dam. Thankfully, the dam did not fail.

Kansas City Beckons

Sometime in June 1971, I received a letter from my uncle, Pat Brady, who worked at the Harrigan Motors dealership in Kansas City. Pat informed me the Kansas City Missouri Police Department (KCPD) was in the process of hiring 300 new officers, all financed through a city earnings' tax that had been approved to fund the recruitment program.

I wrote back and forth to Pat and decided that I would fly back to Kansas City to see if I could get hired. My brother and sister both lived in Kansas City, and each of them had encouraged me to move back home. All of us dreamed of buying some farmland and living the good life. I had been separated from my siblings for many years and looked forward to being together again. I had mixed feelings about this move, however, because of the three nightmares I'd had. I certainly didn't want anything like that to actually occur. But since Carol's mother had passed away earlier in 1970, my family and I decided to explore the possibility of moving back to Kansas City.

I flew back to Kansas City to apply for and take the KCPD entrance examination. I was immediately accepted and asked to join the department. I returned to California and was quickly able to sell our home to a neighbor. I also informed the KCPD that I had accepted their job offer and that I would be there for the opening day of the new academy class, which was scheduled to begin in September.

I made arrangements to resign from LAPD, but still was uneasy about making the move. I had made many excellent friends on the LAPD, such as Sergeant John Bruns. He was a detective sergeant who worked with me at the Devonshire station. I told him that I would be leaving the department and would be living in Pleasant Hill, MO. I was completely surprised when he told me that he had been born there. He also said he would be retiring in three years and would then move back to Pleasant Hill to live on the same property where he was born.

I told him to look me up when he got back to God's Country. He did, in fact, look me up while I was working in the Juvenile Unit and even "rode along" with me a couple of times. I still go to Pleasant Hill Lake to visit him. He's torn down the old house that he was born in and built a beautiful home on the same property. John is in his 80s and getting along just fine.

Police Officer Jerry Borchers. Academy photo, 1971
(Courtesy of the KCPD)

Chapter 7

Kansas City MO Police Department

KCPD Academy

On September 7, 1971, I officially entered the Kansas City Police Academy which, at that time, was located at the northernmost end of Noland Road in Independence. The training was second nature to me, and I breezed through the training. At 33 years of age, I was the third oldest of the new recruits. Some of our instructors included Victor Kauzlarich, Fred Smith, James Lindell, and Mickey Bartow.

During one early morning formation, I was concerned about my daughter, Bonnie, who had come down with double pneumonia and had been admitted to the hospital. I told this to one of the recruits, James Fitzgerald, who probably told Sergeant Mickey Bartow during the inspection. He came up to me and asked me a few questions about Bonnie. After I verified that she was in the hospital, he told me to take off and be with my daughter. I had some reservations about leaving formation, but Sergeant Bartow told me a second time to leave. I thanked him and left. I could not get over the kindness of the KCPD training instructors. I will especially remember Mickey's kind deed. Several years later I saw him again and he had made the rank of Captain. I thanked him for his kindness on that day and, to my surprise, he remembered the incident.

One thing I quickly learned was not to compare LAPD to KCPD on many levels, particularly patrol tactics. The instructors became upset with me when I brought up that it was done differently on the LAPD. They also thought my remarks were distracting to the class. I was called into the office and warned to not compare the departments while in training. I agreed, and everything was great from that time on. We finally graduated in mid-November 1971, with thirty-nine recruits completing the training. During the graduation ceremony, Police Chief Clarence Kelley congratulated everyone and also honored the families of the recruits. One of his remarks stayed with me throughout my entire career. He said, "It's okay to make a mistake of the mind, but not to make a mistake of the heart." The Chief left KCPD in 1973, after he had been appointed by President Richard Nixon to become the second permanent director of the FBI, following the death of the legendary John Edgar Hoover.

Years later, I met "Chief" Kelley when I was working off-duty at the K.C. Royals Baseball Stadium. He had since retired from the FBI as its director. He saw me, walked up to me, and, to my great surprise, called me by my first name. He asked me if I was putting people in jail. I got a puzzled look on my face, and said, "No." I thought he was referring to arrests at the ballpark. He then said, "No, no, I mean are you putting the bad guys in jail out there on the streets?" I answered, "Oh, yes, sir, I still am." He reached over and pinched my face with his big hand, shaking my cheek, and said, "That's the way to go!"

My first assignment with KCPD was with the dog watch shift at the East Patrol Station at 27th & Van Brunt. My break-in officer was Bob Greenwood. I don't think all of the personnel I worked with accepted me at first because I was an outsider from the LAPD. I had to gain everyone's confidence, even though I felt that I was already a seasoned officer.

One of the first calls that I was told to handle was a family disturbance. Officer Greenwood told me that I would handle the call by myself and that he would only be observing. As we approached the front door, we could hear arguing coming from inside. I knocked on the door and then a woman's voice yell out, "Who's there?" I replied "The police." The woman again asked, "Whooo?" I again said, "The police." She again said "Whooo?" I again said, "The police."

At this time Greenwood said, "Let me show you how to handle this call." He took out his leather slapper and banged on the door, and bellowed, "This is the PO-leece." The woman than stated, "Oh, the PO-leece," after which the door quickly opened. I handled the dispute and we left everyone in a calm state. I learned that I needed to learn a different way of speaking, depending on the neighborhood in which I was working.

I was still on probation and had not yet fully proven myself to Greenwood. Bob always told me that I was a hell of a secretary but he had some reservations about me being a good police officer. One night while I was driving, we got into a car chase that ended at a cul-de-sac. The person driving attempted to drive his car over an officer who had stepped out of his vehicle. The officer was able to dodge out of the vehicle's path. I jumped out of our car, pulled out my nightstick and ran over to the suspect's vehicle. I told the suspect to get out. He would not get out or roll down his window. I took my nightstick and broke out his driver's side window to get him out. I dragged him out of the car and put him on the ground. I handcuffed the suspect and took him into custody. It turned out later that the suspect had just stolen the vehicle, so we booked him with auto theft.

When we got off duty at the end of our shift, Greenwood invited me to have a drink with him. Funny thing was that shortly after that I was off probation! I was assigned to a one-man car and was accepted as one of the guys. My area of assignment was in a pretty safe area near what is now called Kauffman Stadium, the home of the Royals' baseball team. Things were somewhat slow…in that area with just the usual minor calls.

I believe it was March of 1972, when I had the same dream again about that prowler call at 19th and College that led to me being stabbed to death in the lot of the Benson Lumber Co. This time Carol woke me up. I told her that I had had the same nightmare. I still was not working in that area, but I was now a Kansas City police officer. This dream was getting closer to coming true.

Almost Fatal Traffic Stop

Early one morning, about 5 a.m., I was patrolling near 43rd and Van Brunt. I decided to get a cup of coffee at a convenience store. I brought the coffee back to my patrol car and headed down the road. An older model car traveling southbound on Van Brunt went by me while I was waiting at an intersection. The car was driven by a white male. I noticed that the car didn't have taillights or any illumination lights above the license plate. I got behind the car and activated my red lights. The car pulled over at Clary and Van Brunt. I got out and conducted a one-man car check like I was trained. I ran the license plates, and there were no warrants. I did not call for an assisting car. I planned to just give the driver a verbal warning.

I walked to within a couple of feet behind the driver's door and asked for his driver's license, and he said he had left it home. I told him that I was not going to give him a ticket but I needed to go back to my car to write down certain information on my activity sheet. He seemed nervous, and I finally decided to call for back-up. I also decided I was going to arrest him for not having a driver's license, even though it was a non-moving violation.

I went back to my car, called for back-up, and waited just a minute or so until it arrived. I also called for a tow truck. When my assisting car arrived, the other officer went up to the passenger side of the vehicle while I returned to the driver's door. I had the subject get out of his car and had him place his hands on the trunk while I searched him for weapons. I told him I was arresting him and cuffed his hands behind his back.

During this time, the other officer yelled out to me that he had found a loaded .38 revolver under the driver's seat. I had recovered weapons in other cars in the past, so this did not particularly bother me at that time. As I was driving the suspect to the station to be booked, he looked over at me. He told me he had his gun in his hand and his finger was on the trigger when I first walked up to his car. But he told me that when he realized that I was not going to give him a ticket, he decided not to shoot me. After I got him to the station, I found that he had an extensive record. He had just been released from prison for serving time on an armed robbery. I quickly began to realize that he probably would have shot me if he thought I was going to arrest him.

This still didn't bother me too much until I was driving home to my family a couple hours later. I began to wonder how my family would have dealt with my being shot. I also thought of those nightmares I'd had over the years. I started shaking so badly that I had to stop my car and pause for a few minutes. I began to think of all the other times that someone else, somewhere, might have also been about to shoot me without my knowing it. I went home and told Carol. In hindsight, I probably should not have told her about this incident.

Rape in Progress

On yet another dog watch shift, I was assigned to work with Officer Gary Smith. It was around 6 a.m. and we were dispatched to a house on Benton Boulevard near 33rd Street. The complaint concerned a possible rape in progress.

When we arrived, a young teenage girl answered the door. She informed us that she had called the police and that her uncle was upstairs raping her older sister. With our guns drawn, we ran upstairs, where we observed a black man in his late 30s having sex with a young woman. She was crying out, and we told the man to get up and that he was under arrest. The young woman ran out of the room as we attempted to handcuff the man. He was about 5'8," weighed around 200 pounds, and was bald-headed. He appeared to be a weightlifter. His pupils were pinpointed, and he backed away from us. He said, "You are not taking me to jail." I had placed my revolver back into my holster. Gary, my partner, had his gun pointing toward the man. As I started to handcuff the man, he went for my partner's revolver. I removed my baton and swung it down on top of his head. Blood started spurting out, and he backed away from my partner, saying "I'm hurt, I'm hurt."

He finally fell and got wedged between the edge of the bed and the wall. We still had not handcuffed him. Gary and I took out our mace and squirted him. The mace got on the wall and each of us more than the man, but we finally got him turned over on his stomach. It took both sets of our handcuffs to finish cuffing him. By this time we had used our walkie-talkies to call for back up. Our supervisor and several other officers arrived at the house to help. It was winter and had begun snowing quite heavily. We dragged the man down the stairs, through the snow, and placed him in the police paddy wagon. I told the wagon driver to take him to the hospital because of the injury to his head.

I worried about this arrest because of the injury that I caused to his head. I was not surprised; however, to later learn that he was an escapee from a mental institution in California. His relatives wrote us a letter of commendation for putting the man away and stopping the rape of the young woman.

Give Me a Light

Early one morning when it was barely light, my partner and I were on patrol on Stadium Drive. We spotted an older man staggering on the sidewalk with a cigarette in his mouth. We got out of our car and asked the man where he was headed. It was obvious that he was intoxicated and had no idea where he was going.

He looked at both of us and started mumbling that he needed a light for his cigarette. My partner turned his flashlight on and held it up to the cigarette and the man puffed away, thinking that his cigarette had been lit. He hesitated, looked at me, and, in a drunken, mumbling voice, asked me for another light. I obliged and turned on my flashlight and held it up to his cigarette. He puffed away again and thanked us for the light.

I looked at my partner and said, "I think that he passed the drunken test." We could have taken him to the station and booked him for being drunk in public, but after checking his identity through the dispatcher, we found he did not have any warrants. The dispatcher notified us that he lived a block away, so we took him home to sleep it off.

You Killed My Dog

Officer Raul Guerrero and I were working during the last hour of our shift. We had a warrant sheet and noticed that one particular individual had numerous misdemeanor warrants. This would be an easy way to end our shift, so we knocked on his door. He answered the door and identified himself with the same name that was on the warrant.

We told him to go get dressed. We were going to arrest him for his outstanding warrants. He started to turn around and then yelled his dog's name. A very large and very mean-looking German shepherd appeared from the kitchen. The man commanded the dog to attack, and it started running toward us with its mouth open and teeth showing. I froze, waiting for the dog to lunge. My partner, being an excellent shot, removed his revolver from its holster and fired one shot, striking the dog in the mouth. The gunshot killed the dog instantly. The man started yelling, "You killed my dog!" We advised the man that he was right, and we were also placing him under arrest for telling his dog to attack us, and that was in addition to being arrested for the outstanding warrants.

My partner had to complete a lengthy arrest report and a Discharge of Firearm report, explaining why he had shot the dog. Our original idea to get off work on time did not go quite like we had planned!

Outhouse Surprise

One of the most memorable calls I ever experienced involved a heavyset woman who had been screaming outside a park area. Upon arrival, the woman was contacted. She was hysterical, jumping up and down yelling "He's in there!" She kept on yelling and pointing at an outside bathroom in the park. I walked over to the outhouse restroom and opened the door. I did not see anyone inside the restroom.

I told her that the person had already gone. Still pointing to the toilet, she yelled again, "Heee-Heee-He's in there!" I went back inside and again looked around. Then I looked down inside the toilet. I couldn't believe what I saw. There was a man standing, knee-high, in "stuff," looking up through the toilet with a big smile on his face. I went outside and opened the back trap door and told him to come out. I told him he was under arrest. He told me that he was not doing anything wrong. He was only watching women as they went to the bathroom. He admitted that he got excited with the last woman and could not resist reaching up and tickling her bottom.

I called the Fire Department to respond and hose him off. Another officer soon arrived with the paddy wagon, angry with me for dispatching him to the call. But I thought it was one of the funniest calls that I'd ever handled.

Joining the Army Reserves

While I was still in East Patrol, I started thinking about the eight years that I had spent in the Air Force and how I hadn't gotten credit for that time. I attempted to get in the Air Force Reserves, but was only offered Airman Second because I had been out of the service for such a long time. I also was told that any job I received would be in the administrative field and that I could not get into the air police.

About that time, I met with Sergeant Edward Wolters, one of the police sergeants I occasionally worked for at EPD. He advised me that he was a warrant officer with the Army Reserves. He suggested that I apply with the 493rd Military Police Detachment (CID) and that I might eventually make warrant officer.

I took his good advice and applied, passing high on the general aptitude test. I could not believe it. I was accepted and brought into the Army Reserves as a Sergeant (E-5). That was one rank higher than what I had obtained in the eight years with the active Air Force. I met wonderful friends, worked hard, completed 86 hours of college classes and rose up through the ranks to Sergeant First Class (E-7) in a few years. I put in for warrant officer about the same time I made the rank of SFC.

In 1980, I was awarded Warrant Officer One (WO1). Lt. Col Fred McDaniel of the 159th M.P. Battalion gave me the oath of office. McDaniel was also a KCPD captain, at the time. I had previously worked for him as an evidence technician.

I was assigned to be the training officer in charge of developing crime scene scenarios for the CID agents on weekend drills. Sometimes the agents signed up with the KCPD Ride-Along program to ride with me on duty to receive additional training points. This gave the agents an opportunity to observe and train at real crime scenes.

During one of our two-week ADTs at Fort Riley, Kansas, I was assigned to work with CID Special Agent Wayne Staley. Wayne taught me the Army method for investigating crimes. We worked together well and solved a couple cases during that two-week period. The best result of this training assignment was that Wayne and I became great friends. He went on to have interesting assignments, both in the military and later when he came to work at the Kansas City Regional Crime Laboratory. He shares some of his stories later in this book.

I spent a total of twenty-four years in the Army CID Reserves and retired in 1996, as a Chief Warrant Officer Four (CWO4).

Crime Scene Investigation Unit (CSIU)

During late 1974, I decided to make a change in my police career. I put in for an opening in the Crime Scene Investigation Unit as an evidence technician. At the time I applied, there were several openings available, and I was selected along with John Young, William

Cosgrove, Frank Brumfield, Fred Spilker, Ed Stawicki, Charles Pottinger, Tom Allen, John Sprayberry and Stephen Wright to fill the various vacancies.

When our CSI training class graduated, we were not yet detectives. We worked out of several of the police stations where other evidence technicians had been assigned. I was first assigned to East Patrol. For my new training, I was teamed with Chester Lucas who took me by the hand and taught me the finer points of processing crime scenes.

It was not long before he and I received my first call to investigate a homicide. A man had been killed in a heavily-frequented, adult book store. One should be able to imagine how many cards of latent fingerprints we lifted, considering all the people that had been in and out of the store. As I recall, we lifted more than 40 cards of latent fingerprints, which, for the CSI wannabes out there, is a lot of cards!

Following the actual processing of the physical crime scene location, we left to go to the county morgue where we performed the most important phase of our job, the examination of the victim's body. Police around the world have learned over the centuries, as law enforcement has evolved and forensic science has perfected a host of new investigative techniques, that the human body, particularly in a homicide case, is the source of some of the most crucial evidence in the case. I will never forget when it came time to get elimination fingerprints from the victim. Chester made me take the victim's prints several times before he was satisfied with the results. I ended up getting a nice letter from the Fingerprint I.D. Unit that mentioned I had submitted the best elimination prints that they had seen in some time. Because of our work, the fingerprint I.D. technicians were able to identify the victim's prints on half of the cards. I owed it all to Chester Lucas. Together, we would partner up on several other homicides during the time we spent together in CSI.

Radio Shack Double Homicide

One homicide call I remember quite vividly occurred at the Radio Shack on Grand Boulevard. The two male victims were 18 and 20 years of age. After being robbed, they were shot in the head and killed by a person who was later identified as having killed several other persons in the robberies he had perpetrated. The suspect had a habit of kicking victims in the head to get them to lie on the floor of the businesses he robbed. He would then shoot them, execution-style, while they were in that defenseless position.

When he was arrested after the Radio Shack murders, other CSI personnel found trace evidence, human hair, to be exact, on his shoes. With this information, Chester and I were dispatched to a funeral home in Kansas City, Kansas, to collect hair standards from one of the victims who had been killed at Radio Shack. We also were instructed to view the victim's forehead to see if he had any bruises, possibly having come from being kicked in the head by the suspect.

As we entered the funeral home, I saw a banner on the victim's casket that read "So long, Freddie." We had the relatives ushered out of the room so we could examine the victim's body in private. We obtained hair standards from his head and also observed a slight bruise on the side of his left temple. We wiped off the makeup from the bruised area of his left temple and took several photographs to later show as evidence. This was not like processing a dead body at a morgue. This examination was the first that I had conducted in a funeral home, and it was a little unsettling to me.

Pillowcase Rapist

My partner, Tom Allen, and I worked together for a couple years handling numerous major crimes, including the Pillowcase Rapist, whose modus operandi (M.O.) was to take a pillowcase and put it over the victim's head before the rape. We had worked several of these specific rape cases.

One night I was working by myself and got a call regarding another one of these rapes, which had occurred in the same general vicinity as many of the others. I took my time and did the best job that I could, lifting latent fingerprints and performing the other typical crime scene processing duties. This was one bad guy I desperately wanted to help take off the streets of Kansas City!

As I was leaving the scene, I decided to take fingerprint lifts from the smooth front door, up high above the doorknob. I started developing a whole complete palm print. I took a lot of time in making sure that I lifted the large latent print successfully. I was proud of myself and, when I was done, I took the prints I'd collected personally and directly to the Fingerprint Identification Unit. I advised Richard Schwieterman of the Fingerprint I.D. Unit that I was sure that I had the suspect's prints. I knew I need not ask him to give it a high priority; Richard already understood how important my latent prints were to the case.

I told him that I was going home and to call me if the suspect was identified, even if he had to wake me up. He told me he would get right on it. It was about four hours later that I received a telephone call from Richard. He had good news and bad news. I told him to give me the good news first, and he told me that he had identified the suspect's palm print. I asked him who it was and he then told me the bad news; it was my own. This was not the first time that my prints were identified at crime scenes, nor would it be the last. I realized that I had opened the door high above the door knob when I first entered the victim's apartment. Regardless of this particular setback, the Pillowcase Rapist was arrested during the commission of another rape.

Fingerprint Lifted From Homicide Vehicle

One afternoon I was assigned to respond to our police garage on Prospect Avenue to process a vehicle that had been involved in a homicide. I took several photographs and searched the vehicle, but did not find any weapons. I vacuumed the inside and processed the interior and exterior for latent fingerprints.

I remember that I had lifted some latent prints from the back of the rearview mirror, an area that a suspect will sometimes touch as they get ready to drive. Most people, including criminals, fail to recall touching that portion of the mirror. The cards of latent prints were submitted to the Fingerprint I.D. Unit for examination. A few days later, I was informed that a suspect had been arrested for the homicide. The arrest was the result of the fingerprints I had lifted from the back of the rearview mirror.

For several hours, the suspect adamantly denied that he was involved. He also had an alibi as to his whereabouts during the homicide. The detectives questioned the suspect as to where he had been working. Six years before, he had worked at the General Motors plant where one of his jobs was to install rearview mirrors. It was then learned that the suspect had actually installed this specific rearview mirror six years earlier when he worked at the plant.

I was notified by the Homicide Detectives when and why he was released. I was also surprised that the person released had actually installed the rearview mirror six years prior to the homicide. Capt. Fred McDaniel, who was my CSIU Captain, kids me today about how thorough I was on processing this vehicle. He stated to me "If I ever committed a crime I would not want you processing the crime scene." I took that as a compliment.

Take the Body Back to the Crime Scene

Occasionally, when any of the five patrol districts were short on personnel, an evidence tech, like me, would be pulled on that job and sent to fill in wherever needed. As it turned out, I was working the Central Patrol desk one night while my CSI partner, Tom Allen, was assigned to the evidence van. At that time, CSI officers were not yet considered detectives. The practice of pulling someone off an investigation and placing that officer on patrol was discontinued when CSI personnel were finally classified as detectives. The practice was reversed, however, if there was a major crime. The Patrol Bureau would pull a person that was on patrol and have him or her work with his partner on the major crime scene investigation.

At any rate, Tom had been working a suicide on this particular night. A young man had jumped from a bridge overpass on Grand Avenue. A police car had been sent to pick me up at the station. When I got to the scene, Tom was taking photos of the body and the overall crime scene. I assisted him by gathering all the measurements relating the location of the body so a detailed crime scene diagram could be drawn later. Detective Fred Jordan, of the Homicide Unit, was in charge of the investigation. We had the body transported to the old General Hospital morgue for examination.

At the morgue, Tom continued to take photos of the body after I had undressed the victim. Our various investigative tasks at the morgue were many and, at times, very extensive. One aspect consisted of the recovery of all clothing and personal property so that it could be packaged and sent to the crime lab for further analysis or to the Property Room for safekeeping, depending on which it was. In a dead body case, we might take several rolls of film. Regarding that, I noticed that Tom had not changed the film in the camera, so I asked him what number the film indicator was on. He told me number 42. I knew that the rolls of film we used in the CSI Unit only held 36 photos. I suggested that he check the film. To Tom's surprise and dismay, the camera was empty!

I looked at Tom, he looked at me, and then we both looked at Detective Jordan. We told him that we had to take the body back to where he jumped off the bridge. We had all the measurements regarding the body's location at the scene. We told Fred that we could make sure the body would be in the exact position and we would retake our photos to prove the victim had jumped off the bridge... and no one would be the wiser!

Detective Jordan got red-faced and told us that he was in charge of the investigation and that he would not allow us to take the body back for photos we should have taken in the first place. We had just been kidding with him—we knew that we could not do that, but we also knew we were in trouble by not having those photos.

The CSI Unit commander was Captain Fred McDaniel. We had to tell him what had happened, and he got furious, telling us that he felt like transferring both of us back to patrol. "Freddy Mac," as he was affectionately called by all of us who knew him at KCPD and in the local USAR's 159th Military Police Battalion, was definitely the type of boss you wanted on your good side, bad side, not a good idea at all! And we were on his bad side that night, for sure!

Meanwhile, the parents of the suicide victim had arrived in Kansas City, from out of state. They wanted to see the photos of their son lying under the bridge where he had been found dead. They simply could not believe that their son would jump from a bridge and commit suicide, a very typical and understandable human response. Capt. McDaniel, in a way that few people had the capacity to do, was able to compassionately explain to the parents what had happened and assure them that there was no doubt as to the nature of their son's death.

Captain McDaniel took care of us, but then he also changed the unit policy concerning who was responsible for changing the film in the cameras carried onboard each of the evidence vans. And, sometime later, Tom and I both made detective and were no longer pulled off of the evidence van to fill in for patrol vacancies.

Captain McDaniel is known to most law enforcement officers as

"Freddie Mac." He administered my oath of office when I made warrant officer while in the 493rd M.P. Detachment (CID). He served with the 159th Military Police Battalion as the battalion commander and the Provost Marshal at the Richards-Gebaur Air Force Base in Belton, MO, where the battalion was located. Fred retired from the Army Reserves as a lieutenant colonel. He also retired from KCPD in 1986, and became the chief of police of the Riverside Police Department in MO. As of the final edit of this book, Fred is currently serving as a minister and chaplain with a number of public safety agencies in MO.

Juvenile Unit

In 1977, I transferred to the Juvenile Unit. It was located on the sixth floor of police headquarters at 1125 Locust in downtown Kansas City. I was placed on the day watch and worked with detectives Thomas Marquis, Robert Landzettal, John Kirby, Robert Keys, Herb Roberts, Edward Sanford, and Harold Vestal. Captain Richard McKiddy was our commander.

Our principal duty was to handle any person under the age of seventeen who had committed or was charged with committing any sort of crime. We also handled missing persons' reports and child abuse and/or neglect investigations. As juveniles were brought into our booking facility, we would see what type of record they had and make a determination as to what we would do with them. Most of the juveniles would be warned and released back to their parents, obviously depending on the severity of the charges. Sometimes the juveniles had extensive records. These kids were taken directly to the Jackson County Juvenile Detention Facility, where the juveniles were housed until their court hearings.

While processing their charges, I would talk to the youths, saying things to them that I hoped would help them get back on the right track. One day, I talked with a 16-year-old, a young black male, and told him that I was concerned about the way his life was going. I wanted to show him how he could straighten himself out. I took out a piece of blank paper and drew a line up the middle of the paper and a line across the top, making a "T." I placed the words "Wrong Side of Law" on the left of the center line along with the word "Friends." I placed the words "Right Side of Law" on the right of the line and also placed the word "Friends."

I drew several small circles indicating small holes and a few larger circles on the left indicating larger holes. I told him that going through life was sometimes tough and that a person needed to stay on the right side of the line and avoid falling into the holes on the left side. I also told him that he was going to experience peer pressure from friends on the left side that would cause him to fall into these little holes. Eventually, if he did not make the right decisions, he would land in one of the larger holes. I told him that if he fell into one of the larger holes, he may not be able to get out and might go to prison for a long time.

I further told him that he needed to choose the friends on the right and stay on the right side of the law. I told him that if he stayed on the right side he would get through life just fine and become successful. His eyes opened wide and he asked if he could keep the diagram. He folded up the piece of paper, and I did not see him again for a long time.

Five years later, a man looked me up at police headquarters when I was assigned to the Forgery Unit. I did not remember his face, but he reminded me of the diagram I had drawn for him about staying on the right side of the law. He then removed a worn, folded piece of paper that had my diagram on it. He told me that he had kept this piece of paper on his person for the last five years. He told me that my talk with him gave him the courage to avoid the friends on the left side of the law. He then told me he was about to graduate from college and become an engineer. Apparently, the talk I had given him had turned his life around and he shook my hand. I remember we both started crying.

I received many awards during my career for a variety of acts related to job performance or some significant arrest. This particular award came with no public accolades of any kind, no newspaper photos, and no handshakes with the chief of police or the president of the Board of Police Commissioners, but this one was, without any doubt whatsoever, the best one I ever received.

This is a photo of Karen Keeton that was taken a couple years before she was raped and killed by George (Tiny) Mercer in 1978

This is a photo of Karen Keeton's sister,
Linda Pinkerton taken in 1976.

Karen Keeton Case

On September 1, 1978, I was working the Juvenile Unit. I was acting sergeant that day. It was about 4 p.m. and I was getting ready to call it a day. I received a telephone call on a missing person from the mother of Karen Keeton. I was informed that she had last been seen at the Blue 7 Lounge in Grandview, where she was a waitress, on the night of August 30th.

Karen was a beautiful 22-year-old woman. She was last seen leaving the lounge with a man named Stephen Gardner, a frequent patron of the lounge. Karen's landlady had been over to her apartment and found her dog, without food or water, which was not like Karen. I immediately started collecting information for the report. Normally, we waited seventy-two hours after the individual had gone missing before taking the report, but I had a serious gut feeling that this case needed to be handled immediately. I stayed over on the next shift, where I developed valuable information about Gardner being involved with a George "Tiny" Mercer, who lived in Belton and was a member of a motorcycle gang.

A couple of days into this investigation, we learned more about Mercer. He was being investigated for the rape of a 17-year-old. I was asked to continue on the case, but I had to go on my two weeks Army Reserve training at Fort Riley. Detective Edward Sanford continued my work on the investigation for a couple days and then he had to leave for his annual two weeks of Air Force training. It was then decided by the command staff to turn the case over to a special squad of detectives, formed to handle this particular case. I would become involved again with the case when Stephen Gardner was brought to trial.

I was working off-duty at the Westport Bank on Broadway and Westport Road when I received a call from my supervisor that the Gardner trial had started at the Boone County Court House in Columbia, MO, and that I had to be in court immediately. I was needed to testify about the missing person report and the portion of the investigation that I had conducted. I was told that in five minutes a Highway Patrol officer would be at the bank to pick me up and take me to Columbia to testify.

I agreed and notified the bank personnel I had to leave. It was only four minutes later a highway patrolman arrived in his state patrol car. I practically jumped into it and away we went like a bat out of hell. Normally, it would take a solid two hours to get to Columbia from Kansas City on a good day with little traffic, but I believe we made it in half that time. The cruiser arrived at the courthouse. The trooper and I practically ran into the courtroom. I learned the case was close to being dismissed if I had not arrived there to testify. I was called immediately to the stand to testify to the missing person report I had taken.

Karen Keeton – Murder Investigation
By Detectives James Martin and Roger Gibson

In August 1978, Karen A. Keeton, an attractive 22-year-old Lake Lotawana resident, was working as a waitress at the Blue 7 Lounge in Kansas City. She disappeared August 31, 1978, after it had been reported that she was last seen with Stephen M. Gardner. A subsequent investigation revealed that Ms. Keeton had been murdered in Belton, MO, and her body dumped alongside a country road in Johnson County, KS.

Upon completion of a missing persons report by the Kansas City Police Department and several days of preliminary investigation, two members of the Crimes Against Property Division, Detectives Roger Gibson and Roscoe Reed, and two members of the Juvenile Unit, Detectives Thomas Marquis and Jim Martin, were placed on special assignment to conduct an investigation into the disappearance of Karen Keeton. Captain Elmer Meyer and Captain Richard McKiddy commanded the Property Division and Juvenile Division, respectively.

The investigation revealed that Karen Keeton had last been seen in the company of Stephen Gardner and was reported to have left the Blue 7 Lounge with him on the evening of her disappearance. Her vehicle was found parked in the lot of the lounge the next morning. Stephen Gardner, when interviewed, stated that he and Ms. Keeton had just ridden around for awhile and he then dropped her off in the parking lot of the lounge and he last saw her getting into her car.

Investigation revealed that the facts were that Stephen Gardner asked Ms. Keeton out for the evening of August 31, 1978. He then drove her to an address in Belton, MO, where they met with

George "Tiny" Mercer and two other male individuals. They sat around the kitchen table and had drinks. Then, suddenly, George Mercer tapped Karen Keeton on the head with a sawed-off shotgun and started forcing her up the stairway to a bedroom. Karen was crying and shouted to Gardner, "Steve, help me, help me!" Gardner laughed and stated, "Happy Birthday, Tiny."

Karen Keeton was forced up the stairs into a bedroom and was forced to have sexual contact with at least three of the four male subjects at the residence. The investigation revealed that while Mercer was raping Ms. Keeton, Gardner was going through her purse. Gardner then raped Ms. Keeton. Afterwards, in a conversation between Mercer and Gardner, Mercer asked Gardner what they should do with 'her' and Gardner reportedly stated, "Kill the bitch." As these criminal acts were occurring, George Mercer's very young daughter was asleep in a bedroom on the first level of the residence.

Near the end of the evening, Stephen Gardner asked Mercer if he needed help getting rid of the body, and Mercer replied, "No." Gardner then stated that he was going to leave because he needed to establish an alibi.

Gardner and one of the other males left the residence and George Mercer strangled Karen Keeton to death. He and an accomplice then rolled her body up in the bedding, placed her in the back of a pickup truck, and transported her body to a rural road in Johnson County, KS, where they placed the body in some woods.

As the investigation continued, the accomplice that owned the truck was questioned and his truck was processed. He became frightened and left the city and state. He later contacted an attorney and, with the aid of the attorney, contacted the KCPD with the location of the body.

As the investigation into the disappearance of Karen Keeton was being conducted, George Mercer was in custody in the Cass County Jail on an unrelated rape case. Stephen Gardner was arrested in Lenexa, KS. George Mercer was charged and tried for the capital murder of Karen Keeton in Greene County, MO. He received the death penalty and was executed by the State of Missouri. His was the last execution to take place in the converted gas chamber in the Missouri Penitentiary in Jefferson City in 1989.

Stephen Gardner was tried for capital murder in the death of Karen Keeton in Columbia, MO. He was convicted and sentenced to fifty years, without the possibility of parole. Due to an error in the instruction given to the jury by the judge, a new trial was ordered. Then, through plea bargaining, Gardner received a life sentence, which he is currently serving in the Missouri Penitentiary in Moberly. The two accomplices gave state's evidence and were not prosecuted.

Karen Keeton's mother, along with other family members, has attended every parole hearing that has occurred, since Gardner became eligible for parole, in order to request that Gardner's parole be denied. To date, the family has been successful. Two of the detectives assigned to the case, now retired, have attended these hearings and testified for denial on behalf of the family.

Karen Keeton's Disappearance and Tragic Ending
By Linda Pinkerton (Karen's Sister)

Shortly before Labor Day in 1978, my sister, Karen Keeton, called my mother and said she was coming for a visit. My mother called me and my siblings, Debbie and David, to see if we could meet for lunch, and we did. My daughter, Leah, had dance class on Saturday, so we met at a Mexican restaurant afterward. Karen told us that a guy she knows, Stephen Gardner, had sent her a dozen roses. She made it clear to him that she had a boyfriend. Little did we know fate brought us together that day and, soon after, fate would take her away from us forever!

My mom called me over Labor Day weekend to see if I had heard from Karen because she had been unable to contact her. It was a holiday weekend so we assumed she went to the lake. However, there was one fact that had us baffled. Her beloved Maltese, Bon Ti, was still at her apartment and, when we called, her landlady said no one had been asked to take care of him. Karen would never leave her dog unattended. We tried calling nonstop all weekend but there was never an answer and our concern grew with each attempt.

Mom called the police and filed a missing person's report even though they normally do not create one until a certain amount of time has passed. Detective Jerry Borchers recognized there were some facts that stood out as abnormal and took the report.

In the meantime we went to Karen's and picked up Bon Ti, her beloved dog. We also had to pick up her car from the Blue 7 Lounge parking lot. One thing that was discovered at that time is that her car would not start because the wires had been tampered with, so Karen would never have been able to drive her car. We knew that was not a good sign. Karen did not leave that parking lot of her own free will.

The police were very active in the whole ordeal. They interviewed over 100 people during the long and gut-wrenching month that Karen was missing. I remember calling the detectives day and night to see if anything new had transpired, and they always had time to talk to me and reassure me that they were actively and aggressively working the case.

The day Mom and I went to post reward money for information regarding Karen's disappearance, we returned home and were informed that Karen's body had been found. This was approximately 30 days after her disappearance. They had to verify via dental records but were pretty certain it was her.

We thought the waiting was horrible but this result was sickening. My beautiful, gentle sister who would never hurt anything and had never caused anyone trouble had been murdered. Now we knew where she was and had to plan a funeral for her decomposed body. I still clearly remember going into a fabric shop and selecting material to cover her battered body in the casket. It took everything we had to complete these tasks as the hurt and pain was unbearable. One memory that still stands out in my mind is when my seven-year-old daughter, Leah, asked, "Why would anyone want to kill my Aunt Kaki," (Karen's nickname.) I thought, good question, I didn't understand it myself.

We thought we would bury Karen with dignity and move forward with the recovering from our grief. Instead, we faced the nightmare of two separate trials where we listened, blow by blow, to the details of Karen's death. It made me want to scream. The end result was George Mercer received a capital murder death sentence and Stephen Gardner received a capital murder sentence for a life term. Gardner's sentence was later reduced due to a legal technicality, even though he was the man who set Karen up as a birthday gift for Mercer. The police were actively involved and supportive of my family during the entire difficult process.

The legal technicality resulted in my family's ongoing attendance at parole board hearings where we continue to be victimized by being forced to relive one of the worst times of our lives. Fortunately, we do not have to go it alone. James Martin and Roger Gibson, who were active during the case and are now retired from the police force, still travel many hours to attend the parole board hearings. They sit in support of our family and give factual information to the parole board regarding the case in an effort to keep a guilty man in jail. We cannot adequately express our gratitude to these dedicated detectives, as well as everyone else involved in the case, who kept us in mind, informed, and became our heroes in more ways than they will ever know. To this day, after all of these years in jail, Gardner still has not expressed any remorse for Karen's death.

Losing a family member to murder is something you think could not possibly happen to your family, but I am constantly surprised by the number of people I know who have been affected by the murder of a friend or family member. Every time I learn of someone who is missing, I recall our pain and empathize with what the family is experiencing. Society needs to understand we need stricter laws for offenders. If Mercer had not been released on parole for a prior offense, Karen may well be alive today. We also need to provide more understanding and support to victim's survivors during the difficult times. Due process is a necessity, but the legal and public focus given to the murderers instead of the survivors needs to be more balanced. The pain of my sister's murder never goes away... even writing these words brings tears to my eyes as memories from long ago linger in my mind and heart.

I am thankful Mercer was sent to his death, though this does not relieve the pain and loss, and I hope that Gardner also receives his just reward.

Transferred to Forgery Unit

In January 1980, I found out that the Juvenile Unit would no longer be investigating juvenile crimes and that several of the detectives would be transferred to other investigative units.

I was getting on the elevator at GHQ one day with Captain Lester Hash, who was commander of the Bomb and Arson Unit. I had worked with his unit on several large arson cases, helping out by photographing some of their major fire scenes, which had taken place when I was in the Crime Scene Unit. Captain Hash asked me if I was happy with my job in the Juvenile Unit. I told him that I was not happy playing the role of a detention officer. I further responded that I felt I was unable to use my experience that I had gained investigating crimes. One day later, Captain Hash called me at home to tell me that he did not have an opening in his unit, but that he could get me transferred to the Forgery Unit. Once there, I would be working for Sergeant John LePage. He told me that it was already arranged and that I would be transferred in two days.

I worked in the Forgery Unit for Sergeant LePage for the next five years. My average monthly caseload was thirty open cases, and I would close about twenty cases every month. The Forgery Unit was on the third floor of police headquarters, right next to the Fraud Unit, where Sergeant Ron Closterman was in charge. Both units worked side by side on many cases and, of course, always shared pertinent information on those cases that had overlapping suspects, victims, or any other important factors. It was typical to have at least a couple "in-custody cases" waiting for us each morning (people who had been arrested the night before).

Robert Green Forgeries

On a number of occasions during the five years of working forgery cases, I came in contact with a black male named Robert Green. He had his own techniques of using stolen business checks and creating fraudulent identifications for individuals to cash them. He mainly got street people and prostitutes to cash the checks using the false IDs. I had put him in jail a couple of times, but each time he got out, he would continue his check-cashing schemes.

Sergeant LePage typically gave me all the forgery reports in which he believed Green was involved. I worked these cases together to be sent to the state prosecutor's office to have warrants filed for Green. Each time Green was arrested, he went to jail for around a year and things got fairly quiet for a while in the world of forgeries in Kansas

City. After a couple years, our unit started getting a lot of counterfeit checks. We noticed that the checks being cashed had similarities to the operation that Green had used before he had last gone to jail. I checked with the Bureau of Prisons and learned that Green had once again been released.

One Saturday morning, I was on call and was advised that a prostitute had been arrested cashing one of these counterfeit checks. Her false identification was similar to what Green had been fraudulently producing. After a couple hours of questioning the woman, I received a confession and she identified Green in a photo lineup. She told me that she had been cashing checks for Green for a couple of weeks and that he gave her $50 for each check she cashed. She gave me the address and room number of the hotel where he was staying.

My partner, Dennis Trabue, and I went to Green's hotel room and found him there along with several other individuals. They all were getting ready to leave and cash more forged checks. All of the persons were taken into custody, and all of the checks and forged instruments were recovered from the hotel room. While we were getting ready to leave the room, three more individuals knocked on the door. We let them in, and they were also arrested. Their faces each matched one of the fraudulent identification cards that Green had made.

Detective Trabue and I worked a long twelve hours to finish this investigation. We cleared approximately forty forgeries and made nine apprehensions that day. We also recovered a large amount of cash.

Needless to say, Mr. Green went back to jail for a long time. I interrogated him, but he would not admit anything. He told me that he respected me and that he was good at his game, while I was a proficient detective. He always seemed to have a smile on his face when I arrested him and was, generally speaking, a nice, gentle fellow. I knew that he had a problem with drugs and needed to obtain money to support his habit.

Detective Trabue and I received a Certificate of Commendation from Chief of Police Norman Caron. As a result of the investigation, nine persons were charged with forgery, a crime that victimized banks and businesses. The businesses, alone, suffered financial losses in excess of $65,000.

Burglary Unit

I was assigned to the South Patrol Burglary Unit from 1984 to 1989. I worked for Sergeant Tom Theison for most of those five years. I also worked with detectives Bill Irvin, Dennis Gargotto, Carl White, Andrew Daniels, and V.L. Davis while assigned to that unit. I found that burglaries were probably the hardest to solve of any of the crimes that I worked. Our unit also investigated auto thefts. That crime seemed to be fairly easy to solve, usually because the suspects were riding in the stolen vehicles at the time they were arrested. We also were able to rapidly solve a high number of car thefts by lifting the suspects' latent fingerprints from the vehicles when they were recovered.

We also got a lot of gas drive-offs. These, too, were fairly easy to solve because the license plates were usually available to identify the owner of the vehicle. Convenience stores were normally not interested in prosecuting the suspects in these crimes; they only wanted to be reimbursed for the gas.

Return to CSI

Gary Howell, director of the Kansas City Regional Crime Laboratory, approached me in late 1991. I knew him fairly well from my earlier assignment to the CSI Unit. Gary also served in the same Army CID unit with me. He told me that there was an opening on the dog watch in the Crime Scene Unit and that he would like me to transfer back to that unit. I agreed and found myself transferred almost immediately.

It had been fourteen years since I had last worked in that unit, so I needed to receive refresher training regarding the latest techniques in CSI work, and I needed to become familiar with the new type of cameras and other new equipment that were being used. I was back on dog watch again and worked with Detective Gary Parker, along with civilian crime scene investigators Ian Ledoux, Diane Lutman and, Charlie Closson. Our supervisor was Sergeant Edmund Stawicki who had been in my crime scene training class in 1975. After Sergeant Stawicki left for another assignment in the department, Sergeant Roger O'Connell became our shift supervisor. During this period of time, non-sworn, civilian crime scene technicians were slowly replacing all sworn crime scene detectives. I really liked my job in CSI, and I would have preferred to remain in this assignment until I retired, but the days were numbered for those of us who were detectives.

Processing Victims at the Morgue

I found that the job in CSIU was basically the same as before, but we now had much better equipment, and there were a number significantly improved techniques we employed in collecting and preserving evidence. We still handled the investigations of homicides, rape, robberies, and other major crimes; those that the FBI identifies as Part 1 Crimes in their Uniformed Crime Report, which it publishes annually in October. The processing of dead human beings, whether their deaths were caused by justifiable, unjustifiable, accidental, or unknown means, was an almost daily responsibility. Of all the various duties and job requirements of a CSI member, whether civilian tech or detective, this particular duty was one that always seemed to "separate the men from the boys." In decades past, very, very few police officers who made the "Detectives' List" would eagerly accept, much less volunteer for an assignment in the CSIU because of this one specific job requirement. I would not be surprised if that particular statistic hasn't changed a bit in the years since I retired. Those of us who chose to work in CSIU did so because we found the pursuit of the unknown to be rewarding and challenging. In the daily "routines" of police work, no matter where across the globe, crimes involving dead bodies will always be the ultimate investigative challenge, and being able to successfully put the perpetrator in prison for murder is one of the greater rewards CSI personnel face.

Investigating dead bodies requires taking copious photos of the victims, first at the crime scene itself, in the exact condition and location in which the victims are found. We always pay particular attention to recognizable trace evidence on the bodies, on their clothing, and any observed lying in the vicinity of the victim, that will need to be collected later. Once collected and placed in various types of bags, bottles, or cans, depending on the nature of the evidence collected, these would then be sealed with evidence tape, upon which the CSI member inscribes his or her initials, the date collected, together with a description of the contents of the bag. Personal property, like jewelry and money, was always collected separately. All of paper money had to be listed, complete with the serial numbers of each bill. In many cases, items like these were not evidence per se, and could be released to next of kin without much delay and paperwork.

At the initial crime scene or later at the county morgue, the victim's body would be thoroughly checked for trace evidence. For example, obtaining scrapings of the contents from under the fingernails was of particular importance. If the victim had defended against a physical attack, such fingernail scrapings could contain physiological evidence of the suspect, that all-important and irrefutable DNA, or, as we highly-trained crime scene personnel always refer to it, Deoxyribonucleic Acid (and if you believe that, I will mail you the title to some ocean-front property in Idaho!). At the morgue, the victim was stripped and all clothing recovered was "bagged and tagged." Once this was accomplished, more photographs were taken, paying specific attention to obvious wounds or signs of injury. Exact measurements were taken of these marks on the body so a "Wound Diagram" could be produced detailing the type and location of every such visible wound or injury to the body. Elimination fingerprints were also taken, for two reasons: to confirm the identity of the deceased and to "eliminate" the victim's fingerprints from others obtained at the crime scene. If the victim was a female, careful attention was given to the vaginal area, especially if sexual assault was suspected.

Deceased crime victims generally arrived at the morgue shrouded one of two ways: covered with the ubiquitous white cloth sheet, usually indicating that the body was reasonably "fresh," or in the equally common, but much more infamous black vinyl, zippered bag. It was the later that was most likely the reason that law enforcement personnel would not "jump" at the chance to become a CSI detective. I'm sure my readers can conclude for themselves the condition of the body that had to be transported in such a container!

After the body of the victim was completely processed for evidence, all the "bagged and tagged" evidence and personal property was taken to the CSI unit to be properly labeled and included on, what usually became, several evidence and property inventory reports. Personal property would be sent to the police property room and evidence would be delivered to the Regional Crime Lab for scientific examination.

The use of the term "normally" does not apply to just about anything in police work. However, normally, it would take two CSI people three hours or so to process an original crime scene, then a couple more hours of investigative work at the morgue. All that would be followed by three to four hours back at the unit to complete all the reports and diagrams associated with the crime scene detectives' portion of the entire investigation. Maybe then you could go home because your shift was over or you could go out for something to eat!

Deadly Helicopter Crash

Ask any American older than sixty where they were and what they were doing the day President Kennedy was shot and every one of them will be able to recite exactly who, what, where and when. Ask me what I did the night of December 1, 1992, and I will be prepared to relate to you one of the most tragic events that occurred during my KCPD career. I had prepared to go work at the CSI Unit, and had left my house at around 10:15 p.m. I had the car radio on and heard the news that a KCPD helicopter, with two officers aboard, had crashed in a wooded area near 23rd and Topping. Sergeant Jack Shepley was the pilot and Officer Stephen Faulkner was the observer. The helicopter had left the pad and been in the air just 20 minutes; it had been called to assist police officers on the ground in a foot chase. On their way to the call, Officer Faulkner radioed to the dispatcher that they were going down near 23rd and Topping. That was the last radio transmission that was heard from the officers. Though a Kansas City firehouse was located fairly close to the crash site, and several emergency vehicles were dispatched to the location, the helicopter was completely engulfed in flames, and the two officers had been killed. This crash occurred at 8:51 p.m., and the CSIs from the evening shift had been on the scene for almost two hours by the time I arrived at the unit.

With only one pressing matter on his mind, Sergeant Edmund Stawicki began Roll Call by informing us of the death of the two officers. He asked if any of us knew either of them. Most in the room raised their hand. I didn't really know them personally, so I didn't raise my hand. A lot like "drawing the short straw," Sergeant Stawicki assigned another CSIU member and me to go to the morgue to process the two officers' bodies. It was my understanding that the rest of the CSIU dog-watch personnel would go to the crash site to relieve the evening CSI crews. I don't recall which CSI individual went with me to the morgue, but I was dreading every moment the closer we got to Truman West Hospital where the county morgue was and is still located. After arriving at the morgue and getting set up to perform our part of the investigation, the body of Sergeant Shepley was brought in first, followed by that of Officer Faulkner. To this day, I do not know how I got through that night, but I did what I was trained to do and I did it to the very best of my ability. I will not relate to you or tell you the condition that the two officer's bodies were in. All I can say is that I will never forget the dreadful sight I had to view. Still, all I could think about was those officers' wives and children who were left behind. That tragic event deeply affected me and the entire department, each one of us vividly reminded that any shift we start could also be the one we do not finish.

Burglary and Homicide

A little after midnight one night, my partner, Ian Ledoux, and I received a call on a burglary and shooting that had occurred near 24th and Holmes. We arrived in our evidence van and were met by several uniformed officers, along with two homicide detectives. The detective in charge stated that some time in the early evening the occupants of the residence had left their home, returning around 11:30 p.m.

When the occupants first arrived, the wife got out of the car and walked onto the front porch to unlock the front door. As she did this, her husband got out of the car after parking it in the driveway. The wife told the detectives that when she entered their house she heard a loud noise outside that sounded like a gunshot. The woman went back outside and found her husband, who had been shot in the chest while attempting to unlock the double gate to their fence. He was lying on the driveway, barely conscious. An ambulance had been ordered before we arrived and the victim already had been transported to Truman West Hospital.

I was told that the suspect, who may have done the shooting, had entered the residence by forcing open the rear door. He had probably left the house the same way when he heard the victim's wife enter the front door. Our first observations were that of blood spattered in the driveway in front of the victim's car, just outside the gate.

This residence was an older two-story, wood-frame house. It had a backyard that was completely fenced in by a cement block wall. The end of the driveway had a chain-link fence that was still closed. A padlock on the chain link fence was unlocked but not removed, which seemed to indicate that the victim had unlocked it, but had not yet removed the padlock before he was shot. The interior of the home had been ransacked. The woman was unable to determine if anything had been removed from the residence. The rear door appeared to have been the point of entry, as well as exit.

Ian and I started taking photographs of the house and yard. We noticed a folded, black plastic garbage bag lying on the ground inside the yard near the south end of the cement block wall. It was an autumn night with leaves lying on the ground throughout the yard, but no leaves were on the bag. Things like that just naturally shout, "Hey, look, I'm evidence." Well, not exactly, but to a trained CSI guy like myself, it did not fail to catch my attention. The suspect may have brought the bag with him to carry out any property that he intended to steal. We photographed the bag and took measurements of its location in the yard, so we could include its position on our subsequent crime scene diagram. We collected the black plastic garbage bag as evidence, and would later forward it to the regional crime lab to be examined for any latent fingerprints.

While Ian and I were finishing our investigation, another CSI unit went to Truman West Hospital to check on the victim's condition and learned that he had died of a small-caliber gunshot wound to the chest. We were informed that the bullet had pierced the victim's heart and that he had bled to death. We also were told that the victim was in his 30s, and that he was actually studying to be a neurosurgeon there at Truman West Hospital where he died.

A few days later, I was contacted by the Fingerprint Identification Unit and informed that fingerprints, belonging to a suspect who had since been identified, were on the black plastic garbage bag that we had recovered from the victim's yard. The suspect was a seventeen-year-old black male who lived just a couple doors south of the victim's residence. He had been fingerprinted just a year earlier by order of the Jackson County Juvenile Court. A few weeks later, I received a nice letter, signed by many of the staff of Truman West Hospital, thanking Ian and me for helping to find the suspect who had killed one of their promising surgical interns.

Forgery and Fraud Unit

With only three more years left of service to obtain my twenty-five years for retirement, I was offered the opportunity to transfer back to the Forgery and Fraud Unit (FFU), which I accepted in 1993. Nearly all sworn law enforcement personnel were now gone from the CSIU, except a couple of us. Quite a number of civilians had been trained as CSI technicians and were doing a wonderful job. So, I "saw the handwriting on the wall," and returned to another of my old department stomping grounds. The Forgery and Fraud Unit worked very closely with the FBI, Secret Service, and U.S.P.S. postal inspectors because a number of the crimes we investigated crossed state lines, and some of the thefts occurred through the U.S. mail, and still others involved stolen credit cards.

Controlled Mail Drop

Steve Cline, a U.S.P.S. postal inspector assigned to the Kansas City office, occasionally contacted me and would ask if personnel in our office could help him catch a thief by making a controlled mail or merchandise drop at a particular address where certain merchandise was scheduled to be delivered. During one such case, a woman was using the address of a vacant house located next door to her own home. The rightful owner of a credit card had discovered that her card had been used to buy merchandise she did not order. She contacted the police and filed a Fraudulent Use of a Credit Device report. Eventually, this case made its way to Steve Cline.

During this particular case, the suspect ordered numerous size 18 dresses. The owner of the credit card was only a size 10. With this information, we used our powers of deductive reasoning to conclude that the suspect was probably a large woman. Inspector Cline and I decided that we would perform a controlled delivery of suspected, fraudulently obtained merchandise to the vacant residence I just mentioned. We borrowed a UPS delivery truck, uniforms, and made the delivery to the address. Steve rang the doorbell several times, but no one answered. As we continued to stand on the front porch, a large woman appeared on the porch of the house next door. We did not want to leave the packages on the porch because we needed to get the suspect to sign for the items, using the victim's name.

We started to leave with the merchandise and she ran over to us. She said that the package was meant for her. She identified herself as having the same name as the victim. She told us the package had been mailed to the wrong address and it was intended to be mailed to her. We told her that she had to sign for the merchandise, and she signed the lawful credit card holder's name. That pretty much made our case, and the woman was immediately arrested. She was not a happy camper when we told her we were taking her to jail. We did, however, get a confession, where she admitted to ordering the dresses through the mail with the stolen credit card that she had removed from the victim's purse. Inspector Cline and I worked twenty or more cases together during the time that I was assigned to the FFU, and it was always a real pleasure "doing business with him."

Stolen Identities and Western Union Checks

While working in the FFU, I became involved in a number of cases in which stolen credit card information was used to order Western Union checks, which were subsequently delivered to a number of individuals who were in on the fraud. Most of these checks were wired from Western Union offices to, of all places, grocery stores. In order to cash the checks, the suspects would use fake identification cards made out in the names that were printed on the Western Union checks. The case involved more than a hundred Western Union checks that had been cashed in several states. The majority of the checks had been cashed in the Kansas City area. Probably based upon that one factor alone, the local FBI office brought the case to the FFU, hoping they could get us to handle it. They claimed they did not have the man-hours or the manpower to solve the case...uh-huh, yep, sure!

It took me a while to get a grip on how the scheme worked, not because I am a slow learner, but because I am very methodical! The key was to find out how all the information from the credit cards was being compromised. This meant calling approximately twenty-five different individuals whose credit card names and numbers had been used in the frauds. I finally learned that each of these people had rented a car at Kansas City International Airport (KCI) over a period of six months. I made arrangements to go to the car rental agency in question, before which I ran criminal records' checks on all the employees at the agency and could not find any with noteworthy criminal history. My next step was to determine how the suspects obtained the credit card holders' information. I discovered that the car rental application came in triplicate form and that one of the copies was given to the person renting the car. A second copy was filed for the rental agency records. I asked about the third copy and was told that it was simply thrown in the trash. I obtained the pertinent rental records, informing the rental company personnel that these documents were evidence in the crimes that I was investigating. My investigation quickly pointed to someone who had been picking up the trash. I contacted the trash company and obtained the name of the individual who was responsible for picking up the trash at the car rental agency. A quick records' check revealed that the individual had an extensive arrest record. I will call this person the Suspect Number Two.

I obtained his address and found that he was living in the Northeast Patrol area along with a person that I will call the Suspect Number One. Suspect number one had one of those "long as your arm" arrest records that involved several states. I learned that suspect number one had been living in California and Colorado, using the same credit card scheme to cash Western Union checks. These checks were also part of my ever-expanding case file.

My FFU co-workers and I started visiting all the grocery stores where people had been cashing the checks. We found a few of the suspects were prostitutes and drug addicts who had used their real names to cash the checks. Most of the checks, however, were cashed by persons using fake identification in the names of the persons to whom the checks were made out. We were in luck at some of the stores because they had cameras that took pictures of people transacting check cashing-related business. These photos were referred to as regiscope photos that allowed us to determine the actual names of some of the persons that cashed the checks. Most of the checks ranged in amounts from $400 to $600.

With this information, I assembled a photo lineup of six different people of similar description that included the mug-photos of suspect number one and suspect number two. Most of the people I'd arrested for cashing the checks identified suspect number one, and some identified suspect number two as arranging for them to cash checks. In a couple of the regiscope photos, both suspects number one and number two were observed standing in the background, a short distance from the person cashing the checks. Warrants were subsequently issued for the two primary suspects, both of whom were later arrested on multiple felony charges. When the two primary suspects were arrested, they confessed to the offenses. Suspect number one admitted being the kingpin. Suspect number two admitted to removing the application forms from the trash of the car rental agency at KCI. Both admitted to making phone calls to Western Union offices to have checks mailed to different grocery stores using the credit card holders' personal information.

I hasten to add that one day during the investigation I drove by the residence where both suspects had been staying and noticed a trash bag by the street in front of their house. I picked up the bag and went through it. Believe it or not, I actually found some of the car rental applications with the credit card holders' names and credit card information, complete with their phone numbers and addresses. The forms also showed the date that the credit card holders had rented the cars and the information relative to the cars that they had rented. Talk about "icing on the cake?" Needless to say, the application forms were collected as evidence.

I worked on this case for several weeks while still working others assigned to me. When I completed my investigation, the entire file was given back to the FBI, which then took full (and public) credit for solving the cases. Now, if that don't beat all?

Retirement from KCPD

In May 1996, Police Chief Floyd Bartch presented 25-year anniversary rings to our Class of 1971, in a ceremony at KCPD Headquarters. After the ceremony, all the officers receiving their 25-year rings assembled outside in front of headquarters for a group photograph. We were positioned on the front stairs, standing in the same position that we'd been in when our original academy class photo was taken. Only a few of the original thirty-nine recruits were present to receive their retirement rings on that day. I do not know exactly how many of the original officers made it all the way to retirement.

When I officially retired on December 17, 1996, Postal Inspector Steve Cline attended my retirement party and presented me with a letter of appreciation for my valuable contributions to the United States Postal Inspection Service. It's now 2012, and I am still waiting for a similar letter from the Federal Bureau of Investigation...uh-huh!

This photo was taken in 1975 of the CSI Class.
Front row, L-R: John Young, (3) Bill Cosgrove, (4) Frank Brumfield, (5) Fred Spilker. Middle row, L-R: Edmund Stawicki, (3) Charles Pottinger, (4) Thomas Allen. Back row, L-R: (2) Stephen Wright, (3), Jerry Borchers, (5) William Sprayberry. (Courtesy of the KCPD)

Jerry Borchers pictured with his wife and daughters in 1976. L–R: Brenda, Carol, Jerry, Bonnie and Beverly. Taken late Christmas Eve before Santa was to arrive. (Borchers family photograph)

CSI Jerry Borchers getting off duty after restocking evidence van, 1976 (Courtesy of the KCPD)

Above: Lieutenant Colonel, Fred McDaniel promoting Jerry Borchers to Warrant Officer One (WO1), 613 Hardesty Avenue, Kansas City, MO, 1980. Below: Jerry's wife, Carol, pinning on his new rank. (Courtesy of 493rd MP Detachment (CID), Reserve Unit)

493rd MP Detachment (CID) reserve unit on a week-end exercise at Richards Gebaur AFB, Belton, MO, 1981
Front row L-R: Billy Smithart, Richard McKiddy. Back row L-R: Michael Riorden, Jerry Borchers, Major Fred Potter, Stephen Clark, Robert Chapman, Cecil O'Rear, and William Price. (Courtesy of Don Meador, 493rd MP Detachment (CID) Reserve Unit)

Chief Norman Caron, center, presented Certificates of Commendation to Detectives Dennis Trabue (L) and Jerry Borchers (R) for the arrest of Robert Green whose commission of numerous forgeries resulted in monetary losses of over $60,000 to area businesses. The award was presented in 1981. (Courtesy of the KCPD)

Chief Floyd Bartch, on the left, presented Det. Jerry Borchers his 25-year anniversary ring for the academy class of 1971. Jerry is accompanied by his wife, Carol. Photo taken in 1996
(Courtesy of the KCPD)

Court Security Officers that were present at the opening of the new Charles Evans Whitaker Federal Court House on October 23, 1998, located at 400 E. 9th Street, Kansas City, MO. Front row L-R: Louis Zacharias, Harold Vestal, Lynn Kinder, V.L. Davis, Owen Williams, Lester Hash. Back Row, L-R: John Oyler, Ronald Breedlove, Dale Trigg, Clarence Gibson, Walter Massey, Wilfred Crespo, Edward Glynn, Karen Pruitt, Fred Honeywell, Harry Thomure, Jerry Borchers, Ronald Hogue, Jerry Curtis, Ray Freeman, Warren Eckstein, George Hiller (not in photo) (Courtesy of John Falk. Original photo resides in the Federal Court Library Archives.)

Chapter 8

U.S. Federal Courthouse, Kansas City, MO

After retiring in 1996, from the Army Reserves on December 16th and from KCPD one day later on December 17th, I filled my free time with fishing and bowling and helping family members with anything and everything. After two years of this, I decided I missed the work and the camaraderie of fellow officers. While conducting personal business one day at the KCPD benefits building, I found out the U.S. Marshall Service was hiring additional staff for the new federal courthouse, which was scheduled to open soon. I was hired by AKAL Security, Inc., a private contractor, to provide security for the building and the courtrooms contained therein. I began working in the old United States Court House and Post Office, also known as the Federal Courts Building, located at 811 Grand in Kansas City. The old court house opened in 1939, with a construction cost of $3,300,000, the funds being appropriated by Congress.

    Three months after I was hired, the Charles Evans Whitaker Federal Courthouse was completed at 400 E. 9th Street in Kansas City, and we quickly made the transition to the new building. It is a beautiful white, crescent-shaped, 12-story building. I was informed that this new structure cost in excess of $110,000,000, if you're keeping track of the cost of construction these days! The new courthouse was named to honor a Missouri federal judge who was appointed to the United States Supreme Court by President Dwight Eisenhower, serving as an Associate Justice from 1957 to 1962. The original federal courthouse I mentioned has since been remodeled into attractive loft-style apartments.

As court security officers (CSOs), we had the following duties: assure the security of sixteen courtrooms; ensure the interior and exterior premises were secure; and screen all persons, vehicles, and objects entering and exiting the building. We also operated the cameras in the command center which monitored special areas of the premises, including the areas in which prisoners were held before and after court appearances. In addition, at least one of us was assigned to a courtroom during court hearings to keep order and to assist with the traffic flow of persons viewing the hearings. The security of the judges was of upmost importance while they presided over the cases. My duty, when working the command center, was to ensure that the rotation of all CSOs from one post to the next occurred smoothly and that all posts were covered.

Once a month, about 120 people and their families would arrive for naturalization ceremonies and would become new citizens. It was an exciting day for the new citizens; however, we dreaded this day because every person had to be screened (as tightly as airport security).

After the swearing-in, many of the newly naturalized Americans wanted their pictures taken with the judges and there was much congratulating going on. The judges usually shared their own family immigration stories, which delighted the new citizens. All in all, we tried to make them feel welcome while providing the necessary security. One day, I was privileged to witness the swearing-in of a special friend—Gabriele, a beautiful German woman I had introduced to my good friend, Wayne Staley, whom he later married.

In all the years I worked at the federal courthouse, I saw several court case hearings involving murder cases. One stands out that I will never forget. It was the trial involving the incredibly heinous murder of Bobbie Jo Stinnett. In December 2004, the young woman was found dead at her home in Skidmore, MO. Her unborn baby had literally been cut out of her womb and the baby was missing. The investigation revealed that the defendant, Lisa Montgomery, had cut the baby from Stinnett's womb while the young mother was still alive. The defendant kidnapped the baby after she strangled the victim to death. The next day after the victim was found dead;

Lisa Montgomery had shown the baby to friends and neighbors and claimed the baby was hers. Montgomery was quickly arrested, and the baby was released to and is still living with the victim's family today. The jury trial started in the early part of October 2007, and ended with a guilty verdict about 3 weeks later. The jury reached their verdict after only 4 hours of deliberation. On April 4, 2008, Montgomery was sentenced to death by District Federal Judge Gary Fenner, who had presided over the case. Over the forty-two years I spent in law enforcement and courthouse security, I had been an actual witness in, or a witness spectator, if you will, to hundreds of court cases over the span of my entire career. This one, however, was, regrettably, one of the most notorious and sickening trials I will ever remember.

My job in courthouse security was a wonderful and rewarding experience, and I continued to work at the new facility for a total of thirteen years. But I retired yet again, on March 3, 2011, after deciding it was finally time to quit working and write a book about some of the eventful adventures I had in law enforcement.

This photo is of Police Officer, Edward Donahue taken around 1965, while he was in the KCPD Academy. (Courtesy of the KCPD)

Chapter 9

Edward J. Donahue

Retired Detective, KCPD, 1965-1969 and 1972-1996

I was born in 1937 in Kansas City. My father, Clarence Donahue, was on KCPD from about 1931 to 1940. I was the youngest of three children, and I went to Milton Moore Elementary School, Central Junior High, and then Central High School. When I was 17, I joined the Navy, spent about three-and-a-half years there and was honorably discharged.

I got a job at Bendix Corporation and worked there until 1965, when I went full-time with the KCPD. I was in the 100th academy class. I worked in patrol, and later I was assigned to the Tactical Support Unit. I left the department in 1969 to go back to work at Bendix, because it was a better-paying job. I continued to work there until I realized I missed police work.

I met with Chief Clarence Kelley in 1972, and was approved to be rehired. I had to go through the academy again due to the length of time I had been gone from the department. What I really liked about the police department was that I was able to work several areas of law enforcement. I worked in Patrol, three times in the Tactical Unit, Staff Management, Internal Affairs, the Burglary Unit, the Arson Unit, and I finished up the last several years in the academy, directing and planning training and scheduling in-service training.

Shooting at Brass Rail Tavern

On February 1, 1968, my partner, Hugh L. Butler, and I were working together in a two-man car. This was the first night that we had ridden together. Butler had transferred into the Tactical Unit about a month earlier, and my regular partner was off that night. We had been working on surveillance from 7 p.m. to approximately midnight, and then Sergeant Bumpus assigned us to work a high-crime area.

We were wearing civilian clothes at the time, on patrol around 35th and Troost Ave. We had stopped to assist a uniformed officer in that location and were flagged down by an unknown person who said there was a disturbance in the Brass Rail Tavern at 3502 Troost. We were advised that a white male, later identified as Terry McCullough, was armed with a gun inside the tavern. He was reported to have shot two people, plus a cigarette machine and the jukebox.

I was the first officer to go inside the tavern and Butler entered behind me. We identified ourselves as police officers as we entered. The lighting was poor inside, and I observed a white male suspect holding a woman as a shield, standing behind her with a gun in his hand. He started firing shots at me, and I fired a shot at him. The next thing I knew, my revolver fell from my hand to the floor. I felt a sharp burning sensation in my right hand and wrist. I didn't know at that time that I had been shot.

During the same time that shots were being fired, my attention was directed toward a young boy who was screaming and running into the line of fire. My back was turned as I tried to protect the boy and get him in a safe area. When I turned back, I observed the white male suspect on the floor with his gun near him. I went over and kicked his gun away from him.

Officer Butler apparently had gone back outside after also being shot by the suspect and was found lying near our police car in front of the tavern. It was revealed later that Butler had been shot in the back a couple times by a uniformed police officer, who had mistaken him as the suspect. Officer Butler was taken to Menorah Hospital where he was pronounced dead just a half hour after the shooting. I had sustained a gunshot wound to the right wrist area when the suspect had fired at me.

Two other patrons in the tavern had been shot by the suspect and also were taken to the hospital. McCullough had been shot in the chest and left leg and also received treatment. He survived to stand trial. Investigation revealed that one of the .25-caliber bullets that McCullough was firing struck Butler in the arm and lodged in his back but was not the bullet that took his life. Butler had three gunshot wounds to the back, and his death was regarded as accidental. The shooting was described as a "tragedy," but no charges would be filed against the officer.

McCullough was found guilty by a Jackson County jury of assault in the shooting of me. The jury assessed a penalty of two years imprisonment. He also was charged with two other counts of assault and a charge of carrying a concealed weapon. This trial was held in September 1968, and I always wished I could have done more at the time.

Later I purchased a bench in Hugh L. Butler's name to be placed on the Trail of Heroes, located on the campus of the Kansas City Regional Police Academy and Shoal Creek Patrol Division. The one-and-a-half-mile trail honors fallen department members. I had seen the trail at the November 2007 academy dedication and thought it was a nice idea and a good way to honor my former partner. The commander of the Patrol Bureau, Building Operations, and the Kansas City Police Historical Society attended the dedication.

This photo is of police officer, Hugh L. Butler taken of his early days on the KCPD. He was killed in a shooting at the Brass Rail Tavern at 3502 Troost in 1968. (Courtesy of the KCPD)

Edward J. Donahue

This is a photo of police officer, Ed Donahue honoring his fallen officer that was killed during a disturbance and shooting at the Brass Rail Tavern located at 3502 Troost in 1968. Donahue is donating a bench to Butler on the Trail Of Heroes.

This photo is of police officer, Harold Vestal taken in 1965. He had just graduated from the academy. (Courtesy of the KCPD)

Chapter 10

Harold Vestal

Retired Detective, KCPD, 1960-1986

The date was November 3, 1937. I was told the weather was very cold the day I was born. My mother, Uva Vestal, was lying on an old wrought-iron bed in the front bedroom of our old farmhouse, which was located on the outskirts of Huntsville, MO. I was named Harold Earl Vestal and was the last of seven children.

My childhood was uneventful. I went to West Park Elementary School, (aka Nanny Goat School, where we had goats that grazed on the grass on the playground), and then attended Moberly Junior High. I quit school after completing the 10th grade. My close buddy, Ivan Manning, and I enlisted in the U.S. Army.

I completed four years of military service and was discharged in 1960. The job situation was really bad, and after pounding the streets looking for a job, I saw two job listings in the Kansas City Star. One was for a mail carrier and the other was for the KCPD as a probationary police officer. Then the waiting period began, to hear who had hired me.

About a month later, I received a letter from the police. I was told to respond to the personnel unit for additional testing. After responding on the date specified, I talked to a shrink and then took a polygraph test and passed both. I was informed that I would be hired as a probationary police officer and would be notified as to when and where to report for duty.

The very next day I received a letter from the U.S. Postal Service telling me that I had been hired. I called the post office, spoke to a clerk, and informed him that I was taking a job with the police department. That's how my career as a police officer started.

Joining the KCPD

I received a letter telling me I would start my class work in the academy in the basement of the police communication center at 27th and Van Brunt. My class was the 78th recruit class, and we all completed the basic skills to become a probationary police officer. Our training required 760 hours, and we all made it through. I felt this training was not unlike my basic training in the U.S. Army. I thought it was much harder because it was more mental than physical, but to this day I have never regretted my chosen path. Looking back on how I became a police officer, I have come to realize it was either a fluke of luck or maybe it was karma.

First Assignment, District 1 - 1125 S. Locust

After my class graduated, we were assigned to various stations for duty. I was assigned to work out of District No. 1, located in the main police building at 1125 Locust St. Our office was on the first floor, and we had roll call in the squad room off the garage entrance. My first chief was Bernard C. Brannon, and my first desk sergeant was Frank Ratliff. I was assigned to Sergeant Russell Chittum's squad. If I knew how downright demanding Sergeant Chittum would be, I probably would have resigned!

To this day, I don't remember the name of my break-in officer, but on my first day he told me before I even got into the squad car to shut up and talk only when I was spoken to. He also told me that I was to write all reports, even the daily activity sheet. He told me to always remember the four "Ws"—Who, What, When and Where—when writing reports, but I guess he forgot to tell me the "How."

Getting back to Sergeant Chittum, he had an unusual way of reading and correcting any report that was given to him by any recruit. Instead of reading and underlining mistakes in red pencil, he tore the report in half and gave it back to you stating, "It's wrong, write it again." After rewriting the same report two or three times, he would then take your report and, without reading it, tell you it was just OK. The real lesson that was learned from this was to take really good notes and never give him your note pad. If you did, it was gone.

The first day on the street with my break-in officer, I, along with all the other recruits, realized that what we had been taught in the academy was good training, but that our real police education had just begun. Working the streets was real, not like the academy. What we saw, heard, and did sometimes was not what we were taught.

Nature Unknown Call

After my break-in period, I was assigned to the 130 sector. Around mid-morning of a beautiful day, another car and I were dispatched to the 2700 block of Woodland. It was to investigate a "Nature Unknown Call." I can't recall my assisting officer's name, but when we arrived we were met by an upset older lady. She said her husband told her he was going to the basement to clean his shotgun before he went hunting. A little while later, she told us, she heard a gunshot from the basement. She had called to her husband to tell him about the noise, but he did not respond. When asked why she did not actually go downstairs, she said she thought her husband had killed himself but didn't know why.

We proceeded to the basement and, as we got to the bottom of the steps, we saw the husband sitting in a straight-back chair. His right shoe and sock were removed from his foot. There was a shotgun lying at his feet. The room had a strong acrid smell. As we walked over to the gentleman, we saw a lot of blood, bone and brain matter on the floor and wall. I had spent three years in the U.S. Army and had been in Korea (not during war time) and seen a lot of devastation, but this was the first time I had seen a person with the top of his skull blown off.

We then went back upstairs and told the lady that her husband was dead. After my field sergeant arrived and learned of the situation and what had been said to the victim's wife, he took me aside and really reamed my butt out for telling the lady her husband was dead. He asked me if, at any time while I was in the police academy, I had been taught the duties of a county coroner. You can bet

I never told a family member that one of their loved ones was dead ever again, even if it was so.

The Detective Bureau

Of all the units I was ever assigned to, I think my most enjoyable and exciting time was spent while assigned to the Detective Bureau.

One day while I was on patrol, I received a radio call to report to Major Sidney Harlow's office. I went to the Detective Bureau and was met by Sergeant Jerry Happy, who was Major Harlow's operations officer. Sergeant Happy followed me into the major's office, where I was instructed to have a seat. I did not know what to expect, but I didn't think I had done anything that I was to be reprimanded for. I remember Major Harlow asking me if I could keep a secret. I said that I could and would.

He then informed me that from this minute on, until further notice, I would be assigned to work out of his office on a special undercover assignment. I was then told to go with Sergeant Happy and he would fill me in on what my assignment would be. Sergeant Happy told me that the police department and the Bureau of Alcohol, Tobacco and Firearms were going to conduct a large, reverse sting operation. I asked Sergeant Happy what my job would be. He said that I, along with Special Agent Jack Malooly, would be installing all of the audio and video equipment and man the operation whenever we bought stolen property. Thus, began one of the most enjoyable and difficult jobs I have had while being a police detective.

The reverse sting was set up in April 1977, and closed down nine long months later. The sting was set up in a building at 2717 Truman Road in a little storefront operating under the name of A. Picaro & Associates, which would take almost anything and pay fair prices. Tony Picaro and the rest of the fence's employees were either KCPD officers or ATF agents. A total of 753 people came in to check the place out, and 288 of them stayed to sell stolen merchandise, ranging from a small electric fan to semi-trailers and their contents. A total of $1.5 million worth of stolen merchandise was brought into the store, and only $133,000 in Law Enforcement Assistance Administration (LEAA) funds had been spent to buy the stolen property.

The three dozen officers and agents bought 146 guns, 139 stolen automobiles, two motorcycles, three tractor-trailer rigs and large quantities of explosives and drugs. Another 13 civilian employees worked behind the scenes processing the stacks of information. Dozens of arrests were made on this particular sting. The building later was put up for rent; however, whoever moves into the building in the future will have to live with the ghost of one of the area's most successful crime-fighting efforts.

My Personal Thoughts on the Police Department

In the 1960s, during personnel background checks, the KCPD would ask the families of new recruits what their feelings were about one of the family members becoming a police officer. If the response was negative, you probably would not have been hired. Because I wasn't married at the time of the check, my wife-to-be was not interviewed. If we had been married, I believe she would have given me thumbs up.

Of all the professions that I could have picked, I truly believe the one that was chosen for me was the best. The time on the job, surrounded by and working with my peers, was without a doubt the best. I have gotten to experience the highest of highs and the lowest of low feelings while on the job. I would like to state that police officers sometimes fail to give enough recognition to our spouses and families. Without their love and moral support, our jobs would be a lot tougher. I married my current wife, Doris, in 1961, and we have three children. The oldest is Randal Vestal, who is now 49, and also on the KCPD; Rachelle, who is 45; and Robert Vestal, who is 40. I concluded my career with the KCPD in July 1986, after serving 25 good years.

Above photo shows Sergeant Benjamin Way, with his signature cigar, hard at work at his desk, as the operations sergeant in the Traffic Division. This photo was taken in 1975 or 1976.
(Courtesy of the KCPD)

Chapter 11

Benjamin E. (Ben) Way

Retired Sergeant, KCPD, 1957-1985

I was born in Kansas City, MO in 1930, and started my police career in Douglas County in Lawrence, KS in 1954, as a deputy sheriff. At that time, I was only making $240 a month. I was promoted to Undersheriff in 1957, with a pay raise to $270 a month.

Some of my memorable investigations were working traffic accidents. One of the first accidents that I investigated was a head-on collision where a westbound car crossed the center line, sideswiped a truck, then hit an eastbound car head-on, killing that driver. The driver who crossed the center line had his arm torn off at the shoulder. I checked the driver, and I could not believe that he didn't even bleed. He was drunk, testing .25 blood alcohol. When I told the driver that he had killed a woman driver, he replied "F—k her." He was found guilty and was placed in prison.

Another fatal accident that really upset me was in Lawrence on Massachusetts Street. A school bus driver let a little girl off the bus and then ran over her, flattening her head. She had blonde hair fixed in a ponytail. My daughter was about the same age and also had a ponytail. This was very upsetting to me, knowing my daughter could have been killed in that manner.

During 1957, I noticed an ad in the Kansas City Star seeking police officers. I applied and joined the KCPD in 1957, making a starting salary of $330 per month. This was a nice pay increase for me.

Some of my assignments were Central Patrol, Detention, Police Dispatcher, Traffic Motorcycle Officer, Accident Investigator and Operations Sergeant of the Traffic Division. Of these assignments, I enjoyed Traffic Investigator the most. You see the best and worst of people's attitudes. You see death and near-death of both young and old. You learn how to notify parents and relatives of their loved ones being killed in accidents, and you learn to feel their sorrow. You review autopsies and start to become callous. In Traffic, I was involved in many assignments from writing tickets to escorting, and the security of presidential visits. I handled the visits of President Nixon, Ford, Carter, Reagan, and Bush Sr. on my watch.

During my time on the KCPD, I went to Southern Police Institute at Louisville, KY. I also attended the Hazmat Police Academy in Louisiana, the National Fire Academy at Kansas University, and the Accident Reconstruction School in Florida. I was certified as an expert in accident reconstruction and testified in many civil and criminal cases.

After I retired I went to work at the Kansas Law Enforcement Training Center, located south of Hutchison, Kansas, at the old Naval Air Training Station, as a Police Instructor. I was there for a total of ten years. I taught accident reconstruction investigation, radar, and assisted at the pistol range.

Coates House Fire

Fires could also be a horrifying thing. I never wanted to be a fireman. I guess I was more afraid of fire and smoke more than confronting an armed criminal suspect.

On January 28, 1978, early in the morning at around 4:00 a.m., I was working as a sergeant in the Accident Investigation Unit, out of the old 28th and Main Street Station. I was on patrol in a one-man car and I remember it was well below freezing. As I drove northbound on Broadway approaching the Coates House Hotel, between 12th and 11th Streets, I noticed fire billowing from the building, with heavy smoke coming from the six-story structure. I did not see any emergency equipment or fire apparatus at the building, so I got on the radio and contacted our dispatcher to tell him the Coates House Hotel was engulfed in flames. I got out of my police vehicle, but the fire and smoke was so bad that I could not enter the lobby of the hotel. Only a fireman with the proper equipment could have entered the building.

As I was standing on the sidewalk at the southwest corner of the building of the hotel, I could hear the sounds of people calling out for help. I looked up near the top floors and saw two people jump from the upper portion of the building and fall to the pavement only about five feet from where I was standing. I could not tell which floor they jumped from because of the heavy smoke. They appeared to be male victims dressed only in slacks and shirts. I checked their bodies and it was evident that they had been killed in the fall to the pavement. I got on the radio again, reported what I had seen and requested ambulances for the victims. I also requested fire trucks and more police to help out, along with traffic units to block off the streets. I was upset that there was nothing I could do to save the people in the fire.

Immediately after I called the dispatcher, fire trucks, ambulances and other policemen started arriving at the scene. I stayed at the scene helping out until the area was secured. I later learned that two more people had jumped from the windows to their death and that several others had perished in the flames.

I was later released from the scene to continue my accident investigation duties. I want to add that I have nothing but high praise for the firemen who responded and went inside to rescue occupants.

Later that morning, I remembered that my grandfather had lived in the Coates House Hotel in the early 1940s. My mother had taken me there for a visit. I understand that this was a nice place to live in during its earlier days; but, I was not impressed because the bathroom was down the hall and there was only one for each floor. My grandpa seemed to be happy there. At that time, there was no smoke alarms so there would not have been any warning if a fire broke out. I'm glad that my grandpa wasn't there to die in the fire.

This photo was taken of Police Officer, Dennis Gargotto while he was in the police academy in 1971

Chapter 12

Dennis M. Gargotto

**Retired Detective, KCPD, 1972-1996;
Reserve Detective, KCPD, 1996-2006**

I was born in Kansas City, Missouri in 1948. I went to Southeast High School and, after graduating, served two tours in Vietnam.

I always wanted to be a Kansas City Missouri Police Department officer. So, in 1972, I applied. The police academy was held at the Regional Center for Criminal Justice. The academy trained officers for the KCPD, as well as other surrounding agencies. After graduating from the academy, I was assigned to patrol, as was required for most new officers.

I attended evidence technician training for the department, which is now commonly referred to as Crime Scene Investigator (CSI). There were around ten KCPD officers that completed the CSI training.

For three years, I served in the evidence technician unit and was later made a detective. I remained there for most of my career, working in various assignments.

I was a member of the Major Case Squad, commonly referred to as the Metro Squad, and also served on the protection detail for the sitting Governor of Missouri, along with protecting his family.

Coates House Fire

While serving as an evidence technician, on the morning of January 28, 1978, we did not have a roll call which normally was standard procedure. Instead, we responded to the morgue at the Truman Medical Center (TMC) to process 13 victims that had been brought there from a fire at the Coates House in downtown Kansas City.

These victims had either jumped to their death from windows or had been recovered dead from the charred remains of the building. We were attempting to identify the victims by any means possible. It was extremely difficult to identify some of the victims due to the burned condition of their bodies. Some of the victims could only be identified through their fingerprints. And this was even difficult due to some of the victims' fingers being so badly burned and not available to print.

At the beginning of the investigation, I was instructed by my sergeant, John Sprayberry to call my good friend and partner, Andy Daniels, who was assigned to the unit, but was on a scheduled day off. I called Andy and told him that we were at Truman Medical Center (TMC) and that we had 13 dead bodies from the Coates House fire. He thought I was joking with him on his day off, so he hung up the phone. My sergeant, John Sprayberry had to confirm what I had told him was, in fact, true. Andy then responded from his house to the morgue, and he and I began processing the victims. This was unusual because we were not normally called from our home to a homicide scene.

This investigation lasted several days at the location of the fire scene. Most of the days were very cold with the temperatures being around five degrees. The cold was amplified by the winds that were almost constant in the downtown area, whipping between the tall buildings, and the thick ice, which developed from the water laid down by the firemen extinguishing the large blaze.

The cold was so extreme that we could only work fifteen minutes at a time while exposed to the elements. We used hand rakes to sift through the charred and burned debris in an attempt to locate other victims. We would alternate entering a Blue Bird bus which served as our command post parked at the scene. It provided some warmth while others continued the search. After fifteen minutes of rest, we would go back outside and this would continue for many hours each day.

For days, a bulldozer would gather buckets of debris and then spread the debris out on the ground to allow us to sift through it. Other victims were located in some human form, but some were not. There were bodies so badly charred that they were hard to see in the black debris surrounding the entire scene, or to even recognize as human remains. One such find was a mass of frozen flesh and bone which we transported to the morgue only to be informed later that they were the remains of a dog.

Among the obvious were two things that really impacted those present. We had been told that a man on the south side of the building had tossed what appeared to be an infant to the ground during the fire. After that, he reportedly went back inside the apartment building and was never seen again by those witnessing the fire. The child's body was later found intact, but was brown in color, probably from the intense heat of the fire. The body was also frozen from the extreme freezing temperatures.

The second was a man in the upper north side of the structure that had been apparently hanging out of the window when the floor behind him collapsed, leaving him suspended on the remaining windowsill. Ice from the fire hoses had formed on his upper torso which hung on the outside of the structure and also on his legs and feet, which remained hanging inside. The ice formed an eerie sight with long gray and black long icicles hanging off his body, which I assume kept his body balanced a day or two before he could be brought down.

After finishing this assignment, we were returned to our regular crime scene duties, waiting for another call to major crime scenes such as homicide, rape, and other crimes committed in our city.

During my time assigned to the Crime Scene Unit, I would say that this particular scene was one of the most horrific scenes that our unit had to deal with.

This is a photo showing the CSI personnel gathered to process the crime scene of the Coates House fire in 1978. Pictured Left to right with their faces showing, CSI SGT. Dan Barr, Capt. Fred McDaniel, CSI Bill Cosgrove, and CSI James Barbee. The other two CSI's are unknown with their backs to the camera.
(Courtesy of CSI Sergeant John Sprayberry)

Dennis M. Gargotto

This photo shows two unknown CSI personnel digging in burnt debris, where they discovered a burnt body at the Coates House fire in 1978. The arrow points to the remains of the dead body found in the debris.
(Courtesy of CSI Sergeant, John Sprayberry)

Chief Warrant Officer Four (CWO4) Clyde W. Pace pictured in full dress army uniform. He was warrant officer in charge of the 493rd MP Detachment (CID), reserve unit at Richards Gebaur AFB, Belton, MO. (Courtesy of Clyde Pace)

Chapter 13

Clyde W. (Randy) Pace, III

Police Officer, Accident Re-Constructionist, Department Safety Officer, KCPD, 1972-1988; U.S. Army CID Reserves, CWO4, Special Agent, 1972-1997

Bulldog vs. Indian Joe

William F. "Bulldog" Price was a great friend, mentor and all-around super guy. One of those guys that when you thought of him, you couldn't help but smile. He got his nickname because he spent nearly seventeen years, as a sergeant, in the Homicide Unit of the KCPD. He was tenacious as all hell, and if your name appeared in the "Suspect Block" of a homicide report, your butt was in big trouble.

Well, Bulldog wasn't that way only about homicides. Everything he did, he did with purpose, and he tried to do it well, just as the great majority of all of us tried to do. However, none of us in law enforcement are without incidents that leave us, if only to ourselves, shaking our heads in disbelief as to what's just occurred. In fact, one story about Bulldog working as a new patrolman out of the old Sheffield Station, that was located on Winner Road, bears repeating.

As the story goes, Bill (as they called him then) was dispatched to the old City Market area down by the Missouri River on a drunk involved in a disturbance. Little did our young officer know that he had been set up? The "drunk" was, in fact, very drunk and was an individual known by veteran officers and the public as "Indian Joe." He was a large man about 6'4" or 6' 5," depending upon who's telling the story, and weighing in around 270 pounds. With a snootfull, he became strong and mean as hell once he was placed inside a confined space, such as a police car. Stories are told of Indian Joe literally tearing apart the inside of a cop car once he realized he was "captive" and would be headed for jail.

Well, here was Bill, young, inexperienced, but as with most "newbie's," a little full of himself and cocky, just now dispatched on a disturbance call. He was ostensibly sent alone on the call as a part of his "break-in" as a new officer. As he pulled up to the address, he saw Indian Joe sitting on the sidewalk, obviously intoxicated, and a couple of drifters were leaning against a building, a respectful distance away. Out jumped our hero, who walked right up to Indian Joe and ordered him to stand up and lean against the police car so he could be searched for any weapons. This was done without incident. As he finished the pat down, he spun Indian Joe around, pulled the front passenger door open and began to stuff him into the front seat.

The word had spread quickly that the new officer was headed back to the station with an arrest but that he had not requested any help. Everyone had to see how that was possible. Indian Joe, being drunk and unsteady on his feet and, being as big as he was, did one thing: he grabbed the top of the car at the gutter area with his right hand to lower himself into the seat. Officer Bill didn't see this or it didn't register with his brain. Bill slammed the door hard. The four fingers of Indian Joe were caught in the top of the door jamb between the top of the door. Once this happened, Indian Joe let out a squall in pain. But Officer Bill didn't hear that because he was walking around to the driver's side of the police car. Once inside, a casual glance told him everything was OK with his inebriated passenger, and he cleared from the scene over the two-way, put the car in gear, and started back to the station with his arrest.

I'm told that it looked like all the monkeys in the zoo were staring at the parking lot when Officer Bill and Indian Joe arrived. The windows of Sheffield Station were full of faces peering out, watching.

Bill pulled up to the rear entrance, the closest one to the booking desk, got out of the car, and walked around to the passenger side. Upon reaching for the door handle, he got his first view of the fingers, now purple, sticking out of the top of the door frame. He did the only thing he could. He opened the door, and Indian Joe, who had not done anything during the ride from the City Market to the station, except make a few groaning sounds, pulled his hand inside, held it, and then looked at Officer Bill. That's right, all he did was stare at him, got out of the police car, and walked as meekly as he could, up the back stairs, and into booking.

From that day, whenever Indian Joe saw Officer Bill, he'd reach over, touch his own right hand, stare at Bill, and then do whatever Bill told him to do.

Bad Weather and Maneuvers

At 0200 hours, sometime during the winter of 1963, the siren in our barracks at Flak Caserne went off, waking the barracks for another "Alert," a monthly exercise that always happened at 0200 hours, for some diabolical reason. There were always two constants with an alert: the time and the weather, both always bad. We groaned when we got outside after hurriedly getting dressed. We found fresh snow over a layer of ice.

Now, personally, I like winter. It's great to step outside on a cold and windless night and see your breath in the crisp air with moonlight enhancing the vapor. But I didn't like it when we had to investigate accidents and injuries to German nationals and GIs because some knucklehead didn't bother to look outside before they hit the switch and put fully one-third of the division on alert. Oh, pardon me...that should have been "Knucklehead, Sir."

We were barely creeping along in our MP jeep when we got a call: "Respond to Schlock Idling on a vehicular accident involving an M-48 tank and a building." This was a little town, located almost due south from Augsburg, with a traditional castle, hills, old buildings, residences and narrow streets. It's actually west of Immerse, a really beautiful lake. All of this was made much worse now because of the snow on top of the ice. As luck would have it, the tank, driver and crew, although out of Gilligan Caserne, the home of the armor units of the 24th Division, were new to Germany. Somewhat fresh out of Fort Knox, KY, they had only seen wet roads. Hazards, such as buildings built to the edge of the streets, were "foreign" to them, and the driver had never been on snow, much less with ice underneath.

So, because of the alert, every tank was in battle-ready mode, not transport mode, with the gun turret was facing the front of the tank, not to the rear. Too bad, because as he made a sharp 90-degree turn in the narrow street at the top of the hill, the gun tube struck the corner of a building and sent the tank askew and down the hill. Fortunately, not much damage was done to the building.

However, by this time the hapless tank was now going sort of sideways down this rather steep hill, and it was totally out of control. Gaining speed, the driver had fully locked the tracks and now was terrified to realize that at the bottom of the hill was a "T" intersection. Beyond the little picket fence in the yard, now looming ever closer, was a house. What happens when you lock up the brakes on your own vehicle in the ice and snow? Yep, same thing happens with a tank. No steering. No stopping. No shit, except I think the driver actually did mess his pants.

Well, the tank took out the fence without even a shudder and careened across the yard, slowing down little, when it struck a small line of fruit trees before burying itself about halfway into the house. Now it was about 0430 hours, and Frau and Herr were still in bed at the back part of the house. They were uninjured as the tank came into their home, went through the living room, bathroom, and ended up nudging their bed.

The tank engine was still running when we got there, and they had a tank retriever supposedly on the way. We didn't want to work that wreck either. Uninjured as they were, you would have thought World War III had occurred. Herr Whomever was mad as hops and demanding much more than my German could comprehend. They both looked a bit silly in their traditional long-flowing night shirts and night caps. We took the report and I tried to assure them that their rich uncle (Sam) would take care of their trees, their fence, and their home.

We'll just wait for the next alert to see whether or not they change the route. If the route is not changed, will the couple have a new house that we can destroy?

Another German Winter Spectacle!

My son-in-law, Mark Brady, recently retired as an Army LTC, armor officer. He's now employed as a civilian at Fort Leavenworth, KS. He's had two tours in Iraq and a short tour in Afghanistan. He was fortunate; he didn't earn a Purple Heart.

As an enlisted MP over twenty-five years ago, he also was in Germany in the winter. He was called to a massive 100-plus-vehicle accident on the autobahn, somewhere around Stuttgart. The primary cause of this accident was people driving too fast under deplorable conditions. The secondary cause was that German nationals, even after more than sixty years of occupation, still don't understand that they shouldn't try to cut in and out of military convoys with their own vehicles.

Anyway, Mark was a Sergeant E-5 at this point and was the patrol supervisor. As he stood on glare ice, a brigadier general walked up behind him and placed his hand on Mark's shoulder to ask him a question. When he touched Mark's shoulder, it was just enough to cause Mark to slip and he began to fall. The only thing Mark could instinctively grab on his way down was the general. That brought them both to the ground in a heap.

Mark said it was at that moment he saw his military career flash before his eyes. However, the general was most apologetic and told Mark not to worry because it was the general's fault for placing his hand on Mark's shoulder. Then the general asked Mark: "Do you think you can get this all cleaned up in a half hour? I've got to get my convoy moving."

Mark told me it was at that moment he saw his military career flash before his eyes, again.

OCS, Not!

It was close to the end of my tour in Germany. The 24th Infantry Division, and its MP Company, was on maneuvers on the north side of Vohrenbach on Field Training Exercise "Frosty Lion" in the Black Forest. It was December 1964. About two feet of snow was on the ground, and I was now a "hard stripe" corporal, in charge of the general's security. I had been assigned this rank as a junior NCO because as a Specialist Four, I completed the 24th Infantry Division's NCO Academy in July 1964, as part of my quest to get into Officer's Candidate School (OCS). I completed the NCO Academy in the top five, so I was eligible to make Buck Sergeant, but my Military Police job specialist code (MOS) was frozen for further promotions. So, they converted me from Specialist Four (SP4) to Corporal. Let's see... that's more responsibility with the same pay.

A really great captain, David J. Puehl, who was our MP company commander and also the military legal attorney for the division, had taken me under his wing and was making sure all the "I's" were dotted and "T's" were crossed on my application. We were both waiting for word that I would be headed toward OCS in the next few weeks.

Early in the morning, the CQ runner (soldier on 24-hour duty after hours) for the orderly room came down to my tent, awakened me, and told me to report to Capt. Puehl because he had a set of orders for me. I got dressed, ran through fresh snow to the orderly room, entered, saluted and said, "Corporal Pace, reporting as ordered."

My salute was returned and Capt. Puehl said," Pace, I don't know what happened but here are your orders. You're being discharged and you leave out of Bremerhaven mid-January on the troop ship." The orders were signed by General Rose.

Well, I was pissed. I just gave him a "Thank you, sir," came to attention, saluted, did an about face and walked out of the orderly room. All that work and just a boot in the butt to send me home. After I got back to my squad tent, I put a "short-timers" calendar on my helmet band and started telling my squad that I was "a short timer" (meaning I was about to get out). I wrote a letter to my parents, giving them all the details with a copy of my orders. Now I was ready to go home.

About three days later, we still were in the Black Forest. Again, in the early morning, the CQ runner awakened me with a now familiar message. I reported to Capt. Puehl, and he said: "Congratulations Pace, you've been assigned to Class 65-5, OCS, Fort Benning, Ga. You leave out of Rein-Mien Air Base in Frankfort in five days."

I said, "Sir, if this Army can't figure out if they want me to go home or go to OCS within one week, I respectfully decline. I've already written my folks, told everyone here that I'm leaving the Army and it's going to stay that way." I saluted, did an about face, and walked out of the orderly room.

A few years later I thought about this rather startling and somewhat knee-jerk reaction to something I thought I really wanted. I began to realize that this was the start of the Vietnam War and they were training second lieutenants like crazy. Then it hit me -- I probably saved my own life with this decision. The average life of a second lieutenant in the heat of a fire fight in the boonies of Vietnam was about 10 seconds.

I had joined the 493rd MP Detachment (CID) Reserve Unit, based out of Kansas City and, around 1978, I had been promoted to Warrant Officer One (WO1). Our unit had been assigned to Fort Leavenworth to assist the active Army agents during our annual two-week assignment.

It was during this time that I ran across Colonel Puehl's signature block on a report from the USDB. He was the commandant of the USDB. I got down there pronto, went into the front entrance and asked for him. The E-7 looked me up and down, and then I showed him my CID credentials. He immediately changed his tune, and I gave him my name.

It wasn't a couple of minutes later that Colonel Dave Puehl came around the corner with a quizzical look on his face, and when he saw me, he broke out into the biggest grin I'd ever seen on him. He spent about 30 minutes with me, and we caught up on lots of things. That was the last time I ever saw him. I heard he was up for a brigadier general promotion and had been transferred from the USDB (where military prisoners are housed) and was now the provost marshal of TRADOC (U.S. Army Training and Doctrine Commander). Several years ago, I tried to find out more about him, but never could. What a great guy!

Two Blondes and a Traffic Stop

For one of my longtime attorney friends, John Chick, this is his favorite story. This was my first use of my limited, German language skills on a traffic stop. I learned a bit of German during my nearly two years as an MP in Germany from 1963 to 1964

After getting out of the Army and becoming a policeman in Kansas City, I was part of a Traffic Enforcement Squad in midtown. My supervisor was Sergeant Dave Courtney. Sometime in the early fall of 1977, he had us working something we called "line beats," trying to look for hazardous moving violations during rush-hour traffic.

I was in an unmarked car with a siren under the hood, red lights behind the grill, no markings, just a four-door sedan with a one-quarter, wave-length antenna. I was the first vehicle behind the stop line, sitting at Westport Road and Broadway, facing east, stopped at the red signal, waiting for southbound traffic on Broadway to stop for their red light.

Just after my light turned green, a white Mercedes-Benz 230SL convertible with two pretty blonde ladies in it went southbound on Broadway through the intersection at a high speed, obviously running their red signal.

I made a right turn, pulled in behind them, pulled the switch for the emergency lights behind the grill and hit the heavy-duty foot switch on the floorboard for the old wind-up federal siren under the hood. The blonde driving the vehicle pulled over quickly an as the old siren wound down, I pulled in carefully behind her vehicle.

If I had been more observant, I should have been more aware of what was coming. An oval "D" sticker (for Deutschland) was on the left rear trunk lid and a Johnson County, Kansas tag was screwed over an international license plate on the rear of the vehicle. Because the top was down on the convertible, it was easy to observe the driver and passenger.

I walked up to the driver and said, "Good afternoon, traffic violation, you've just run the traffic light southbound on Broadway at Westport, I need to see your driver's license."

This lovely young lady looked me right in the eye and said, "Ich spreche kein Englisch."

I said, "Das macht keinen Unterschied, Ich meckta bitte haben sie Führerschein." Loosely translated, that was. "That makes no difference; I'd like to have your driver's license, please." Then I said, "Englisch oder Deutsch, macht es keinen Unterschied."

At that point, the passenger let out a kind of rasping noise, covered her forehead with her hands, and buried her head against the dashboard. The driver turned crimson and said in broken English, "I vill speak to you in English," then searched through her purse and gave me her license.

After I walked back to my unmarked police car, I began to write the ticket for failing to stop for a red traffic signal and also was able to observe both ladies. The passenger still had her face buried in the dash, but you could tell she was trying her best to stifle laughter. The driver had her face buried against the steering wheel and was slowly shaking her head left and right.

I finished the ticket in a couple of minutes and walked back up to the driver's door. She slowly looked up at me. I told her that I'd written her a ticket for failing to stop at a red traffic signal, described how she could contact the court for payment, told her because she and her vehicle were "local," I wouldn't require her to post a cash bond even though she was "out of state" and concluded my traffic stop with: "By the way, you speak very good English, why did you tell me you couldn't speak English when I first spoke with you?"

Again, she turned a very nice shade of crimson and said, "It always before vorked"! Needless to say, she paid the fine ahead of the court date, and I never saw her again.

To Shoot or Not to Shoot

Sometime, in the summer of 1978, while working out of Metro Patrol Division, I responded to a disturbance call, "party armed," that was somewhere on 67th Street. The lady who called was standing outside the battered, two-story frame house, yelling at me that a man had a knife and tried to kill her. I confirmed she was uninjured, told her where she should stand to keep out of the way, and told her I needed to wait for my backup officer who was just a couple of blocks away.

The lady was screaming at me to do something, so I started for the front door. My backup officer had just driven up and was getting out of his car. I kicked the door open with my foot, yelling "Police" as I did so. What I heard from inside was: "I'm in here, M....r F....r!" My service revolver already was pulled and at the ready position, with my partner's footsteps quickly growing louder behind me. I stepped into the living room behind a large, rather tall-backed couch.

On the other side was the suspect, tossing a large knife back and forth between his hands, staring at me. I ordered him to drop the weapon. He didn't say anything but just kept tossing and staring. Again, I ordered him to drop the knife and pointed my revolver directly at him. He made a step or two toward me and I said: "Drop the knife or you're a dead man!"

At this point my backup officer yelled: "Shoot him, shoot him!" I gauged the distance between the suspect and myself and determined that at that exact moment I was not in imminent peril, so I didn't shoot. Again my backup officer yelled: "Shoot him, Shoot him!"

I began to squeeze the trigger, knowing that at this point if he lunged at me there was still the large couch between us, and I felt I could drop him in his tracks. My backup officer was now screaming at me to shoot him. Probably it was that screaming that caused the suspect to throw away the knife. Once that happened, we jumped on the suspect, subdued and cuffed him.

I was glad I hadn't pulled the trigger. My partner was beet red, still screaming at me for being a pussy and afraid to shoot someone threatening me with a knife. I've looked back on that situation and remain grateful that I gave the guy that extra moment to make a right decision. And I don't have to search my soul for unnecessarily killing someone.

That officer and I worked only one more incident together when he arrived on a car check of mine that he had been dispatched to as my backup. Things were smooth for me, but when he arrived he began to agitate my arrest and then tried to get him into a fight. I told him this was my arrest and to get the hell away from me and him. He got in his car and drove off.

When It Rains

One day in September 1977, the Kansas City Teacher's Union was voting to go on strike; heavy rain was predicted. I was scheduled to report to the Helicopter Unit at 0500 for a roll call and from there to be sent to a school for security. I was driving in torrential rain. I was at Raytown Road and turned southbound onto Eastern. It was raining so hard I couldn't tell any difference in the rain hitting the water on the road surface and the rain hitting the water on the creek that had come up and had flooded Eastern about 4 feet deep.

Not realizing the creek was totally out of its banks, I drove my Datsun station wagon right into the water. I felt that initial floating feeling that turned within a couple of minutes to that sinking feeling; I realized all too quickly that I was in trouble. I rolled down the window of my little car and (I still don't know how I did it) crawled out the window and onto the top of my car - in full police uniform -- without getting into the water.

After standing there for awhile, I sized up the situation and realized that my next step, if the car started to move from the rising waters that were now flowing faster, was to grab a telephone pole that I could barely reach and, for a very short time, hang onto, if the car was pulled away by the current.

It was still raining and there was no traffic, so I felt I needed to be pro-active in getting myself out of this unexpected jam. I had three viable options at this time: I could use my voice, my traffic whistle, and the last resort would be my department-issued .38 caliber revolver, with about 18 extra rounds. At that time, nobody had any "take-home" radio equipment. Unlike today, there were no cell phones. Knowing that I could always escalate my priorities, I started with just yelling, "HELP, HELP, and HELP." Then, waiting a few moments, I began blowing my Acme Thunderer-issued whistle with four long blasts. I did this for awhile until I became hoarse, deciding that wasn't working too well either.

By this time the water around my little Datsun had already entered the windows and was about 6 inches from coming over the top of the car. I was beginning to get a little nervous because nothing had headed my way. I was thinking about my next move, and then a spotlight hit me from the north side of the flooded creek. I was most glad to see a KCPD-marked car parked at the edge of the water.

A voice called out, "Are you all right?" "Yes," I answered, "Just get me out of here."

The voice again, "Who are you?"

Just get me out of here" I responded.

The voice, "WHO are you?"

By this time, I knew I was in for some real ribbing and I also now recognized the voice. It was a good friend, Officer Steve Weinberg, from the Accident Investigation Unit.

He had to know, or eventually would know, who I was anyway, which also meant that the whole damn department would know. So I yelled out, "Clyde Pace." Steve collapsed against the side of his police car, roaring with laughter. I yelled, "Stop laughing, and get me out of this water!" Through his laughter, he said the fire department was on the way.

And, by the way, did I know that the Plaza was under water? I yelled back I didn't know anything about the Plaza. This was the first morning of the start of the big Plaza flood that claimed seventeen lives across the city. Oh, yes, the teachers didn't vote and didn't go on strike because they couldn't get to their schools. School was cancelled for at least a week or more. Waiting for the fire department, I asked Steve how he knew I was there. He said the dispatcher sent him on a call at Raytown Road and Eastern because someone had reported someone yelling for help and blowing a whistle.

The fire department showed up with a big ladder truck. They extended the ladder horizontally over the water, and a firefighter hooked me up with a rope with which they pulled me off the top of my now totally submerged vehicle. My good friend, Officer Weinberg, laughed about that for years.

Later that day, as the water began to recede, a private tow truck arrived to hook up my little station wagon. The driver walked out in waist-deep water with a tow cable. When he got to the rear of my car, he broke out in a fit of laughter; he'd seen the sticker on the top of my rear window. It said, "I'd Rather be Sailing."

Halloween Traffic Stop

Late afternoon on Halloween in 1983, I was working out of the Traffic Division's Enforcement Unit, running radar on westbound 63rd Street, about three-quarters of a mile east of the Kansas City Zoo entrance. Pickings were pretty good, and I'd written several tickets for 10- to 15-plus mph over the posted limit of 45. I'd just gotten set up again for my last ticket. My shift was ending and I was ready to check traffic from the rear when the radar alert sounded and the unit locked on 81 mph. One quick look and it was a VW Bug, with one occupant. I knew I wouldn't have any problems getting him stopped.

But he didn't stop or even try to stop. Now pursuing him, I hit my siren again and was prepared to call dispatch and tell them I was in a car chase. But, after he figured out I was after him, he slammed on his brakes and the little bug skidded in gravel to a stop on the right shoulder of westbound 63rd Street, about 200 yards east of Hardesty.

As I was behind him, I thought I noticed a bit of erratic steering and wondered just what I had with this guy. I gave the dispatcher my location, the license and description of the vehicle, and then got out of my marked unit and started to walk up to the VW.

The driver's door sprang open, and out hopped (literally) a guy in a rabbit costume. This was a complete costume, with a head, nose and nice big ears. Oh, yes, he was wearing a bib around his neck that was embroidered with "Mommy Loves Me." I've seen plenty in my years of law enforcement, but this was a first. I was probably nearly laughing by this time. Not only was he in a rabbit costume but, as he tried to explain, the costume had no pockets. Therefore, he had no license. The car license information didn't come back to the name he gave me and all he could say was that he was on his way to a party and had borrowed the car from a friend.

A little closer interaction with the driver revealed that perhaps his party had started earlier. I detected alcohol on his breath. I did a field sobriety check with him, and he didn't do well with the one-foot balance and walking a straight line. Admittedly, he looked quite silly performing all these things while wearing the full costume.

I called for a city tow, cuffed him and called for a paddy wagon. I didn't put him in my car, because the weather was just fine. Besides, I rather enjoyed the other drivers going by, honking and laughing at this guy in a rabbit costume, standing by the road in handcuffs. During this time, an assisting traffic car showed up, and he turned out to be one of the guys working a little overtime with an emphasis on drunk drivers. He asked if he could have the paddy wagon take this driver to Metro Patrol Division and he would administer the Breathalyzer and handle the arrest from that point. I had no problem with that because it would free me up to head back to the Traffic Division and complete my tour of duty.

I often wondered how this guy was treated by the other prisoners in the Metro Patrol Division lockup before he posted bond. I can't imagine his treatment by the inmates at Police Headquarters if he couldn't post bond at the Metro Police Department and had to spend the night downtown.

Hop-fully (or hopefully), he learned his lesson and hasn't had any more hare-brained activities behind the wheel.

Nitro Hodel

Sergeant Dick Hodel was one of my instructors when I went through the police academy in November 1972. He was a nice fellow and didn't use his position to "harass" us as entrant officers, but was there to make sure we learned and got as much out of the program we could.

Soon after the academy started, we began to hear stories about him and learned of his nickname, "Nitro." The story goes something like this: as a District sergeant, he was assigned to East Patrol Division and was sent, along with other district cars, to a disturbance in a bar where one of the involved parties had threatened the customers and staff with a vial of straw-colored liquid that he claimed was nitro-glycerin. Frightened nearly beyond words, the call came in from someone behind the bar to send help immediately.

After the police arrived at the bar, the altercation situation was eventually resolved and arrests were made. The glass vial of straw-colored liquid, with its rubber stopper, was left lying on the bar counter, with everyone just looking at it.

Now Sergeant Hodel sprung into action. He knew that calling out the Bomb Squad was time-consuming and expensive; he took it upon himself to "test" the liquid first, to authenticate the liquid as nitro-glycerin before making that overtime call to the squad.

He cleared a wide area around the front of the bar and gingerly lifted the glass test tube of liquid. Ever so carefully, he began to twist and pull the rubber stopper out of the end of the vial. Finally, he got it loose and, ever so carefully he tilted the test tube just enough to touch his forefinger into the liquid. When he does this, he smells the liquid and tastes it on his tongue. He then placed the rubber stopper back on the vial carefully laid the test tube on the bar counter, and stepped away.

At this point, he said to the gathered officers: "Yep, its nitro, order the Bomb Squad." When the bomb guys arrived, they listened to Hodel's description of the incident and confirmed the location of the vial of liquid. Everyone had to leave the bar as the squad expertly moved in.

In just a few minutes the squad supervisor was contacted by radio from the guys inside and went in. Shortly after that, he came out saying the situation had been "neutralized." Everyone was elated. The bomb guys had done their job. How did they work so fast? They also removed the stopper from the vial and ran a small piece of litmus paper into the liquid to check it. The results revealed that it was urine.

This photo is of Police Officer, Richard McKiddy taken around 1961 after graduating from the academy. (Courtesy of the KCPD)

Chapter 14

Richard N. McKiddy

Retired Captain, KCPD, 1961-1991;
U.S. Army CID Reserves, Sergeant First Class, 1975-1991

I was still in the 493rd CID Unit when I retired from the KCPD on January 21, 1991. Eighteen days later, I reported to active duty in Desert Storm to my assignment with the CID Protective Services Unit (PSU). I served on a team for General Colin Powell, Chairman of the Joint Chiefs of Staff; Richard (Dick) Cheney, Defense Secretary; General Gordon Sullivan, Chief of Staff, U.S. Army; and many other high-ranking military officers and foreign defense ministers.

In April 1991, I was informed by a CID officer to start preparations for retirement from the U.S. Army. I was about to turn 60. I explained to the CID officer that I was scheduled to join three other CID agents on a mission to Tegucigalpa, Honduras. The CID officer said I should begin the retirement processing immediately. I told him we were to depart even more immediately by air to Honduras. I hinted that Gen. Powell might not be too happy to have on board a person with no knowledge or participation in the mission planning. The CID officer cleared me for the last PSU through April 1991. I was able to complete the mission without any problems. A few days later, I walked out of the Army in St. Louis as a civilian.

I was honored in May 1991, for my total of 28½ years service with the U.S. Army. I wore my dress blue uniform, and there were more than 100 people at my retirement party at John Knox Village in Lee's Summit, MO. My wife, Barbara, also was present.

Calling 422

I was lucky to have a job where every day was different. I can't truly say I remember every day, but my head is still full of memories. As with most jobs, there were good days and bad days.

On the first day of my new job with the KCPD, my field sergeant told me to sit at a shopping mall and if I got a call and didn't know where it was located, call him or one of the other cars and they would tell me how to get there. Well, it wasn't actually my first day on the job. I'd just graduated from the police academy and was assigned to a patrol district that covered about 60 square miles of relatively unpopulated real estate at that time. There were only six patrol cars to cover that area and, as luck would have it, they were all 10-7 (out of service) on other calls when I got the call.

"Calling 422," the dispatcher said. I picked up the mike and responded, "422's at Vivian and North Antioch." The dispatcher said, "422, at Baugham and Barry Road, a vehicular accident, car off a bridge into a creek." I started to look at my map, not having the faintest idea where Baugham Road was. It was a good 10 or 15 miles northwest of my location. I flipped on the reds and stepped on the button on the floor that activated the old-fashioned, top-mounted siren and started going northwest, all the time trying to call one of the other cars or the sergeant on my three-way. In those days, you had to flip a switch back and forth to talk to the dispatcher and the other cars in your sector.

As I was driving toward the call, the dispatcher called me periodically to update me on the status of my call. She said the car had gone off a small, one-lane wooden bridge. Luck must have been with me, because I had been unable to contact anyone in my sector when I flashed past a street sign that read Baugham Road.

About a mile up the road, I came to the bridge. As I approached it, I shut down the bubble gum machine and the noisemaker and slid to a stop. Exiting the car, I looked the bridge over and seeing no damage, I looked over the side and down to the small creek. There, in the creek, waist-high in water, sat an old junky Ford. On top of the Ford sat a skinny old man, taking a pull from a half-pint. I yelled down and asked, "You OK?"

He looked at me and pitched the empty bottle into the creek.

"Yep," he said, "but I reckon I might need a tow truck." The old geezer had just missed the turn onto the bridge and driven down a 3-foot embankment.

I called for a tow truck, and I also called for a paddy wagon to give Mr. Wet Britches a free ride down to the friendly Gray Bar Hotel. When the tow truck arrived, I gave the driver the old man's name, address and other information, and loaded the old man into the paddy wagon. As it turned out, it was good that I ordered a wagon for the transport. The officer driving it told me later that the old guy kept banging on the steel walls of the wagon and yelling, "Any chance we can stop for a quick drink?"

But, hey, that old guy was number one in my book. Arrest book, that is.

Off-Beat Work

It was a hot summer day in 1967. I was assigned to the evening shift at the old Northeast Street Station. I was on my way to work, slowly driving through the streets in the ghetto neighborhood near where the old station was located when I saw an elderly black man who seemed to be having a hard time walking. He was nattily dressed in a suit, white shirt, and tie. I pulled over to the curb, got out of my car and asked if I might help him. Upon closer inspection, it appeared that the suit was a circa-1943 model, with lapels wide enough to make seat covers from. I was in my police uniform, and he looked at me with a confused look on his wrinkled face. I was in my own car, a bright red sporty model, and perhaps that accounted for the look of confusion. I asked him where he lived and he just looked at me with big brown, confused eyes. Then I smelled the distinct aroma of alcohol on his breath. Aha, I thought, the old gent is trying to make it home.

I looked at my watch. It was early, so I had a few minutes to make roll call at the station. I thought I'd see if I could find out where he lived and get him there. I asked for some identification, and he brought out his billfold. There was a dollar in it and no ID papers. I explained to the old man that I just wanted to help him get home. He told me he lived in the apartment building down the block, nodding his head in the direction of a six-plex.

I got him in my car, drove him to the old apartment building and helped him inside. "Which floor?" I asked. He held up two gnarled fingers while he pawed about in his pants pockets, apparently looking for his keys. We creaked up the weak stairs to the second floor hallway where he stopped at a door. I asked him, "Is this where you live?" He looked at me with his watery bloodshot eyes and said "Yes."

I'd been in these apartments, which were built in the 1930s, and I knew they had a two-foot by two-foot "grocery delivery door" off the hallway where the kitchen pantries were located. Using my credit card, I slipped the lock and opened the small door. I told the old man to get down and slide through. He mumbled, but got down on all fours and managed to squeeze through the small opening. Feeling that the mission was accomplished, I strolled off down the hallway and was about to creak back down the stairs.

When my foot met the first step, a woman in a robe burst from the apartment screaming, "There's a man breaking into my apartment!" I gulped, then reacted quickly, "Don't worry lady, I'll get him," I said. While she stood in the hallway, I went in and retrieved her "burglar" and took him to my car and loaded him in. He was asleep before the wheels began turning.

I drove him to the station where I took him inside. I told a patrolman who worked for me, "Collect him after roll call and check with the Missing Persons Unit to see if anyone is missing a grandpa. If not, take him to General Hospital for safekeeping." I started to walk off to check the crime activity report. Then, I turned to Murphy, the young cop and said, "And do not ask him to show you where he lives, OK?"

Dog Watch in a Junkyard

Gibby rolled out of the Sheffield Station parking lot in his patrol car. It was the start of another long, dark night. The evening shift had just turned over the night to the dog-watch crews. Because it was shortly after midnight, he decided to rattle some doors, which was the colloquialism used to describe a patrol activity. While not many doors were actually rattled, the process called for a visual check of buildings within the officer's patrol area, called "districts," and, in some cases, "beats." In the Midwest, beats are thought of as walking patrol areas, which there were few of in the 1960s. Not all buildings received equal scrutiny. Most seasoned officers knew their districts and had a historical record filed away somewhere in their brains of the most vulnerable locations.

Most business burglaries occur during the night at times of opportunity, like around shift change time, when all the cars are at the stations, and on the darkest of nights. Moonlit nights, as most police officers know, are not preferred by burglars, but they do have some weird effects of their own. This is especially true on hot summer, moonlit nights which keep patrol cars busy running from one fight or disturbance to the next, or policing crazies wanting to jump from high buildings or bridges or run naked through the streets.

Gibby was thinking of all this as he rolled into dark alleys, throwing his spotlight on back doors and loading docks and parked cars. Occasionally, he would dismount and actually check a door to ensure it was locked. Then, having satisfied himself as much as possible that his district was OK, he turned his car toward the east side of the district.

His destination was a seedy neighborhood of small decrepit houses scattered among a slew of junkyards. He knew that there was only one reason to check this area and that was to see if there was any criminal activity at the junkyards. He also knew that junkyards are not pretty. These surely were not. These were sitting in a boggy area near a small river that ran through the industrial/residential area. Policemen generally make a practice of either sitting quietly in a dark area listening or watching, or sometimes cruising industrial areas with lights out, radio turned low and slipping the transmission in and out of low range, just enough to keep rolling as silently as possible. Most of the time the left hand is on the spotlight handle, and thumb on the toggle switch that activates the powerful light. It can get creepy in the dark, and you try to maximize your odds by being ready.

Gibby already had checked a couple of yards and was creeping slowly down a dark street, nearing the remotest of the area junkyards. He eased up to the corner and looked to his right, down the street toward the junkyard. He observed an old truck near the fence next to the street. He watched it as he turned the volume even lower on his police radio. Patrol cars didn't have air conditioning then, and, on hot nights, all the windows were lowered.

He flipped the toggle switch on the radio to "three way," allowing him to talk to other district officers in his sector. He could hear their frequent chatter, including a transmission from a neighboring car. Very little formality was used on the three-way band. In a low voice, he asked the neighboring car to roll his way. He said that he might have prowlers at the Manchester junkyard. Keep your lights off and sneak in, he advised.

Catching some movement, he saw a figure on the bed of the truck. Then, a second figure was seen heaving something over the fence, assisted by the man in the back of the truck. He watched and listened to the radio at the same time, thinking his backup should be close. The radio came to life again. His backup had just been dispatched on the main frequency to a possible vehicular accident involving an overturned car. He flipped to the three-way again and told the backup that he was all right alone.

He checked the vertically-mounted shotgun rack, making sure it was unlocked. Checking his radio, he flipped it to the main frequency and reported possible prowlers at the junkyard and gave the address. The dispatcher acknowledged the information and dispatched an assisting car from another sector several miles away.

One man came over the fence and the other man jumped down from the bed of the truck. Gibby slipped the gear selector into drive, pulled the headlights on, and hit the dimmer switch on the floor to bring up the bright lights. He flipped the switch on the spotlight and, in a swift wrist motion, directed the bright light into the eyes of the startled men. This was all happening as he gunned the cruiser down the street straight at the parked truck, screeching to an abrupt halt a few yards away. He grabbed the shotgun out of the rack, threw the driver's door open and, using it as cover, shouting commands to, "Come out from behind the truck."

When the backup arrived, the men were taken into custody, searched, handcuffed and placed into a paddy wagon which had instinctively responded to the scene. Investigating the truck, Gibby found one 30-gallon drum and two 55-gallon drums of what appeared to be scrapped copper. The 30-gallon drum was labeled "Clean Copper Wire." A photograph was taken showing the three drums in the truck. Samples were taken from each drum to be used as evidence in court.

The men pled guilty and never appeared in court. Gibby, like all policemen in patrol duties at the time, rotated shifts every month, from dog watch, day watch to the evening watch. When he was on days, he'd occasionally drop by the junkyard and chat with the owner, a man named Angelo, have a cup of coffee, and get circulation back in his butt. He and Angelo got to be pretty good friends and he enjoyed the break in the day's activities.

Time passed and one day Gibby needed a radiator for his 1956 Plymouth. Remembering a similar car he'd seen at the junkyard, he dropped by and Angelo sold him the radiator for $12.50. They had coffee and chatted for a few minutes. The conversation ranged all over the place, from police work to junkyard work to family and current events. Only once before, shortly after the burglary, had the arrest been discussed. As Gibby was loading the radiator into the trunk of his cruiser Angelo said, "Gibby, I need to be totally honest with you. You remember those three barrels of copper you guys recovered for me? Well before you guys showed up, I only had one; the other two barrels wasn't mine."

My Thoughts on Police Work

What other line of work has been followed as closely as police work? Look at television, and it won't be long before you are watching a cop show, or some news reporter, or news analyst, or news correspondent sounding off about some police-related event, be it a car chase, a murder investigation, a massive search for a missing person believed to have fallen victim to foul play or corruption or abuse of authority by a police official or officer. The obsession by the news media, and probably the general public, as well, with police-related events or police work, in general, seems apparent. At least it does to those of us who spent long careers in the profession. And we wonder why.

Police work is supposed by most outsiders to be an action-packed job, full of adventure and excitement, as well as back-to-back episodes of involvement in hair-rising entanglement with the "criminal element." Not to mention car chases, mob scenes during riots, and the joys of sticking it to errant motorists for minor traffic violations. If it were true, a 30-year career would tick away rather suddenly. No, it is said by insiders (that is, law enforcement officers), that police work is 90 percent boredom and 10 percent panic. From my experience, I'd consider that pretty much on track.

Oh, there are times when it's like draining a swamp full of alligators, calls coming back to back, whole precincts "blacked out" with all available cars dispatched. During times of mass demonstrations, such as in 1968, it was necessary to activate the National Guard and bring in state patrol troopers to augment law enforcement in most major cities in America. And things as simple as a Beatles concert can change the whole law enforcement apparatus's way of responding to it and regular law enforcement activities. And when our dear political folks decide to pay us a visit, the Secret Service may make a simple little request for 100 police officers to escort, provide route security (like a man on every bridge that the convoy passes under), as well as helicopter patrol preceding the convoy to its destinations. No problem, hocus pocus, pull 100 cops in on overtime. Now, of course, we have a new problem – national security issues. We are then required to have special training for reacting to terrorist threats or actual incidents of terrorist activity.

Doesn't sound too much like action-packed excitement and adventure when you put it in that context, does it? We know, of course, that most perceptions of police work by the general public probably were garnered over the years from watching Badge 714, Car 54, Where are You, Barney Miller, NYPD Blue, CSI, and on and on ad infinitum. Most of the shows, at least the recent ones, are so far from reality to be true. I did enjoy Barney Miller, and Car 54 was fun to watch.

But, hey, folks, NYPD Blue and the "serious" police shows were and still are gag-and-vomit bad! Lots of cops watch the shows, but sometimes as examples of how NOT to do their jobs. I can't even believe that chief executives of law enforcement departments would give the camera cowboys access to film the many screw-ups of weapons security and other dangerous activity carried out during the filming.

Photo was taken in 1991, at John Knox Village, Lee's Summit, MO celebrating Richard McKiddy's 28½ years in the Army. Also pictured is his wife, Barbara McKiddy. (Courtesy of 493rd MP Detachment (CID) Reserve Unit)

This photo is of Sergeant Charles Weir, taken in 1975. He is standing by Rockhurst College, taking a coffee break between classes. (Courtesy of the KCPD)

Chapter 15

Charles E. Weir

Retired Sergeant, KCPD, 1968-1996

Who Would Have Thought?

It was sometime in the early 1970s that President Richard Nixon was visiting Kansas City. Several police officers were sent to provide security for the President in the area where he was staying. Officer Jerry Pearce and I were assigned to a post guarding some obscure entrance at what I remember to be a building near Municipal Auditorium. This was a big deal, but our assignment placed us completely out of view of any pedestrian or traffic movements. It proved to be three or four hours of boredom. Absolutely no one came or went through the side entrance except for a routine check made by a roving Secret Service Agent.

Suddenly, a black government vehicle pulled up and several agents jumped out. Just as quickly, out of our entrance stepped Nixon and several more agents. The President inadvertently stepped on Jerry's foot as we tried to move back out of the way in the now overly-crowded space. Nixon paused briefly and apologized to Jerry as he shook his hand, then quickly jumped into the vehicle.

It was over as quickly as it happened. That's police work for you. At a moment's notice, long hours of boredom can change to excitement or danger. Who would have thought?

Hyatt Regency Walkway Collapse

It was Friday evening, July 17, 1981, that I decided to go to the Hyatt Regency Hotel located at 2345 McGee in Kansas City to watch a dance contest. I had attended a couple other dances, which were becoming quite popular, and had even promoted it among friends. The dance was to start around 7 p.m. that evening. I believe there were more than 1,500 persons who also had gathered in the atrium to participate in or watch the dance contest. Construction of the 40-story Hyatt Regency Hotel had been completed in 1980.

That night the place was really packed. My ex-wife, Kathy, and I were there with a small group consisting of a friend of mine, Rocky R., his wife, and his parents, Pascal and Donna. We ate at the terrace restaurant on the second level. When we finished eating, they announced the dance contest was about to begin. We hurriedly paid for our dinner and intended to head toward the upper walkway on the third floor. As luck would have it, my buddy, Rocky, paid with a $100 bill. This was about 7:05 p.m. The cashier apologized and sent a waiter to get change. While Rocky was waiting at the cash register, his wife, parents, and Kathy stood at the bottom of the escalator to the third floor. I stood nearby at the top of the second floor escalator looking down at the dance floor.

They had cleared the floor for the contestants by moving people back under the alcove. I noticed the second floor and the fourth floor walkways were crowded with onlookers. The dance contest had just started. There was still space on the third floor walkway nearest the escalator, if we hurried.

Suddenly, there was a tremendous cracking sound above. As I glanced up, I could see the fourth floor walkway start falling. I remember it striking the lower second floor walkway suspended below it and they both went crashing down on all the people below. I recall hearing a loud "ah" from the crowd, which was more like a gasp in unison. I stood for a second or two in disbelief as the crowd moved away from the damaged walkways and then immediately moved back toward them to try to help the unfortunate.

The room was filled with a white billowing cloud of drywall dust, slowly settling to the floor and covering everything below. I could hear the sound of running water across the room from a second- or third-floor broken pipe. The water was quickly pooling in the recessed lower floor. It was surreal. Later, I remembered thinking there were two types of people there; those who were injured and those who wanted to help.

As I bolted down the stairs to locate a phone, I observed an elderly man stand up on the south end of the fourth floor walkway, brush off his suit, and look around bewildered. He apparently had ridden the fourth floor walkway to the lobby floor. I remember seeing a service desk below and behind the escalator. As I rounded the corner at the bottom of the escalator, I observed an elderly man sitting at a desk with a phone in one hand trying to make a call. His hands were visibly shaking. I yelled, "Police officer, I need to use the phone." He immediately threw it down on the desk like a hot potato.

I called the police dispatch supervisor, Judy Batcheller, to advise her of the Hyatt walkway collapse. I recall taking a deep breath to settle myself and then talking with Judy. Apparently, other calls were being received by dispatchers; I could tell from the excitement while I was talking to Judy. I advised Judy that we needed several ambulances, and heavy equipment would be needed to help remove the collapsed walkways from atop all the victims.

I later heard that the tape of our conversation was played on the radio or television. I estimated about 100 people were injured or killed, without having any real idea how much of the crowd had escaped injury from the falling walkways. Clearing the dance floor before the dance started and moving people under the alcoves had unknowingly saved many lives.

After the call to the dispatcher, I headed back toward the fallen walkways to try to help. I noticed a local TV cameraman frantically trying to reload his shoulder-held camera. I remember the bright flood lights of the camera as several Good Samaritans joined in an effort to lift a section of the fourth-floor walkway off people we believed to be trapped underneath. It was too heavy to lift. I heard later the walkways were 120 feet long and weighed about 64,000 pounds. I recall a Kansas City Royal baseball player that I recognized at the time among the group trying to help lift a slab of concrete. The walkways were pretty much reduced to damaged cement slabs with shiny brass colored rails. The glass sidewalls were broken and splintered, making the area treacherous to navigate.

At some point, I realized I had abandoned my friends and Kathy. I located Rocky, his parents, and Kathy. Fortunately, they were all okay. They decided to head home and agreed to take Kathy with them. I decided I wanted to stay to try and help rescue the victims who still were trapped under the debris.

I noticed an arm sticking out beneath a lower walkway, moving back and forth in a waving motion. I figured the guy was alive and letting us know where he was under the debris. After a few minutes, the arm quit moving and I realized the suffering was probably over for the gentleman.

I saw a woman crushed near the waist between the fourth- and second-floor walkways, frozen in a vertical position. A man was lying on his back near the bottom of the escalator. He was alive but unable to move because of a back injury. His wife was standing near his side, wanting me to help move him away from the possible path of the remaining walkway located about 50 feet above them. I told her it would be best not to move him and that I would stay with him. I reassured them both that the walkway probably would not fall and would barely miss him, and that moving him could be more damaging to the person. We both stayed with him.

At some point a medical person arrived to care for the man. I then moved toward the walkway again. One of Kansas City's Finest met me there. He was climbing over the walkway debris. I told him to get off the slab of cement, because people were under there. He quickly jumped down to the floor. I thought they were all crushed like the man with a waving arm. I wasn't aware that the underside on the walkway was concave by design. That is probably why some survived the crushing blow from the walkways falling on top of them.

The place was soon crowded with police and other emergency personnel. I headed to the KCPD dispatcher's office at 1125 Locust. There I wrote a summary of what I had observed happen while it was fresh in my mind. I left to pick up Kathy and headed home, totally exhausted.

For weeks afterward, I felt tired and lethargic. I later learned it was probably stress, related to the trauma I had experienced and the horrific event that I had witnessed. I later heard that a total of 114 people were killed and that over 200 people were injured in the Hyatt Regency walkway collapse.

It was about three years after the incident before I returned to the Hyatt Hotel complex. I didn't have any anxieties about the Hyatt, but just didn't have a reason to revisit. I had heard about the Skies, a rotating restaurant located atop the Hyatt Regency Crown Center, and I wanted to check it out. It was a beautiful sight, looking out of the windows of the panoramic view of downtown Kansas City.

Police Officer Columbus (Leon) Cook, taken in his first year as a KCPD officer in 1966. (Courtesy of the KCPD)

Chapter 16

Columbus L. (Leon) Cook

Retired Sergeant, KCPD, 1966-1991

The Hyatt Regency Hotel Walkway Collapse

I served on the KCPD for 25-years and had the opportunity to work many different assignments. These assignments allowed me to witness many things, some good and many bad, some happy and some very sad. I think one of the most humbling and devastating scenes I ever witnessed was the collapse of the Hyatt Regency skywalks on July 17, 1981. At this time, I was assigned as a traffic enforcement squad supervisor. The traffic unit in 1981 was located at 28th and Main, only a few blocks from the Hyatt Regency Hotel. I worked off-duty security for the Hyatt Regency and had worked many of the Tea Dances, but that day I was on a golf trip to Excelsior Springs and Officer James Aichele was working the Tea Dance in my place.

Mike MacMahon and I had played 72 holes of golf and were on our way home just south of Liberty, MO when several police motorcycles passed us with emergency equipment blaring. We turned the radio on and heard what had transpired and continued on our way home. I arrived home around 8:30 p.m. I took my shower and sat down to eat dinner when the phone rang. It was my Captain informing me to report immediately to the Traffic Division, where I arrived about 9:45 p.m. At that time, I and the members of my squad relieved the day shift and several district officers, who were working the traffic perimeter. The perimeter was secured and I reported inside the Hyatt Hotel to assess the need for further personnel. I entered the lobby through the kitchen area and heard the steady stream of water still pouring from the broken pipes, and the cries of the injured still awaiting for the rubble to be removed from their broken bodies. The stench of death was in the air and many of the ones trapped were already dead and many more knew it was just a matter of time. There was a delay due to a fear of the front building wall collapsing. An entry needed to be established to get the recovery equipment in the lobby. That concern caused a very long wait and I am sure, to the injured parties, it seemed like an eternity.

The Fire Chief was directing the recovery activities with the assistance of a construction crew supervisor and a structural engineer. All officers on the scene were helping comfort the injured and trying to reach their loved ones, while trying to calm the relatives and friends arriving at the scene. I am sure that anyone who spent 25 years on the Police Department encountered several unbelievable situations, but, for me, this one tops them all. You could hear many victims begging for help, but there was no way to assist them due to the volatile situation with the front wall. This went on for what seemed to be hours, but in reality the last survivor was pulled from the rubble around 4:00 a.m. on July 18th.

Once the last survivor was pulled from the site, several of us went through the lobby checking the rubble for any personal property. This was cataloged and recovered by police personnel, to be given to survivors and or their families. During this search, many body parts were discovered lying under the debris. These were gathered and placed with the bodies in the make-shift morgue at the scene.

I had been over these skywalks many times thinking how could a walkway with three bolts support the concrete, plus the weight of the pedestrian traffic on them. When you entered the walkway, you could see daylight between the walkway and the floor; it was attached to long rods with the three bolts in plain sight. This design flaw was discovered and was determined to be the main cause of the collapse. I worked off-duty for the Hyatt a couple more years, but that night is definitely the most memorable of them all. Seventy-two holes of golf and the Hyatt Regency experience was very tiring. However, due to the gravity of the situation, I didn't feel the exhaustion until I arrived home and finally sat on my sofa. My ordeal started at 5:30 a.m. on the 17th of July, and I finally returned home at 3:00 p.m. on the 18th of July.

Columbus L. (Leon) Cook

This photo depicts Sergeant Leon Cook, in full motorcycle uniform in the 1980s. (Courtesy of the KCPD)

Pictured above are my brother-in-law, Bob McConnell, and my sister, Darlene McConnell that was taken in the 1980's.
(Family photograph)

Chapter 17

Bob McConnell

Retired Director of Jackson County Board of Realtors

A Miracle that Came Out of the Hyatt Walkway Collapse

With all of the sad things involved in the Hyatt Regency tragedy, which happened in Kansas City on July 17, 1981, my wife and I were blessed with what I called, and still call, a miracle that happened the night the walkways came down on all those helpless people.

At that time, I served as the director of education of the Eastern Jackson County Board of Realtors in Independence. I was actively teaching real estate pre-licensing classes to assist the public in obtaining a license from the Missouri Real Estate Commission to practice real estate in the state of Missouri. We had schools in Kansas City, but also in Clinton, Warrensburg, and St. Joseph.

One of my instructors at that time was James "Sam" Cottingham, a former city attorney for Independence. Sam taught real estate law to the students. Unfortunately, he was one of those victims on that tragic night.

On the Wednesday before the incident, Sam called me and said he and his wife Norma would like us to go with them to watch a dance contest at the Hyatt on Friday night. Darlene and I were really excited because we had never attended one before, and we knew you could never say no to Sam. He was truly a wonderful person.

On Thursday night, I received a telephone call from another of my instructors, named Allen Richey. He said he just could not make it to St. Joseph for the scheduled class the following night, Friday, because he had the flu so bad it was keeping him in bed. Allen was a wonderful instructor and had never called in sick for all the years that he taught for me. I had no one else to turn to because the only persons who could teach the law course were Sam, Allen, and me. So, knowing Sam was going to the dance, it was on my shoulders to cover for Allen, which I did.

The miracle was that I was not at the dance. Knowing myself, I would have been right with Sam getting drinks for ourselves and our wives when the walkways fell. I later learned Sam had been pulled from under the collapsed walkways and that he had been identified only by his college ring he had been wearing. His wife, Norma, was not injured during the collapse, and I am grateful she was not one of the 114 victims who died that dreadful night of the tragedy.

Strange, though it may be, for years after when I drove by the cemetery in Independence where Sam was buried, my radar detector alarm would go off. As much as I searched, I could not see any police cars in the area. I wondered if Sam was trying to tell me something.

This photo is the wedding ceremony of Jon and Bonnie Perry in Kansas City during the 1968 riots. Pictured above in the photo are, L-R: Kathy Gilroy, Mary Riggs (little girl), Carol Kotsifakis, Lee Alison, Bonnie Perry (Bride), Jon Perry (Groom), Clinton Perry (Little boy), Tim Moore, and Bob White. (Family Photo)

Chapter 18

Jon D. Perry

Retired Sergeant, KCPD, 1968-1993; Currently employed with Virginia State Police

In the Wrong Line

I returned from Vietnam in November 1967, and planned to live off my unemployment. I sold the Air Force 16 days of leave and discovered that I could not sign up for my unemployment until those 16 days were up. The day finally came, and there I went, to the unemployment office. When I walked in the door, I noticed two lines, one long one and one short one. I chose the long line, which turned out to be the wrong line. The closer I got to the person at the counter, the longer the other line became.

When I got to the person in the window and told her that I wanted to sign up for my unemployment, she told me I was in the wrong line and I needed to be in the other line, the one that was now long. I got in that line and eventually made it up to the counter again, and she gave me a series of forms that I had to fill out.

When my name was called, I went behind the counter and met with another lady who asked me a series of questions, including what I did in the military. I told her that I was an air policeman. She said the KCPD was hiring and I should go over there and put in an application. Again, I had no intention of working; I just wanted to live off of the fat of the land for a while.

At the end of our meeting, the lady told me that she would see me in a week. I asked her, "Aren't we missing something here?"

And to that she said, "What"? I said "A check, money?" She said, "Oh, you don't get that until you have applied for X number of jobs. Return in a week."

To that I said, "Who did you say was hiring?" and that is how I joined the police department.

I was hired on January 13, 1968, and had to wait until February for our academy class to begin. Two or three of us were hired at the same time, and we burned the month working in the Records Unit, fumbling around with reports and waiting on people. We finally made it to the academy, which, at the time, was housed at 42nd and Indiana. We had made it through all but the report-writing section, which was the last section of training.

My wife, Bonnie, and I were engaged at the time and the wedding was scheduled for Saturday, April 13. Bonnie worked downtown at Hartford Insurance Co., and we had planned to meet downtown for lunch and then go to the Jackson County Courthouse to pick up the application for our marriage license.

At that time, there was a three-day waiting period, so we had to get the license on that date. Early in the day, we were listening to reports that started coming over the police radio about rioters marching toward City Hall. Members of my class began trying to talk me out of going downtown, and I told them that I had to go because of the three-day waiting period and the wedding being scheduled for the 13th.

We then began listening to where the rioters were and, planning a route for me to take to get downtown, I began calling Bonnie at her work. There was no answer. I found out later that due to the situation, the insurance company had let everyone go home to get out of the area. Of course, this was before cell phones. Because I could not get in touch with her, I was afraid that she would be waiting on the steps of the courthouse as we had originally planned, so there I went.

I was in full police uniform, but I was driving my 1963 Corvair (don't laugh). I went the circuitous route to avoid the rioters. I was driving north on Main and I looked up to see a wall of people running toward me. They were stretched completely across the street and seemed to be three or four people deep. As they approached my car, they parted, ran around me and then on down the street. Following the crowd were about three plainclothes policemen with their guns drawn.

I continued to drive north on Main, turned right onto 12th Street, and headed toward the courthouse. As I approached Oak Street, there was a barricade across the street with a uniformed policeman blocking traffic. I pulled up to him and he looked into my vehicle and asked where I was going. I motioned to the other side of the barricade. All around the courthouse, people were protesting. The policeman told me that he would not go in there if he were me, and I told him that I thought my wife was on the steps of the courthouse. With that, he lifted the barricade and allowed me to drive through. Again, people parted in front of me, which allowed me to drive ahead. Some looked in and saw the uniform, and I guess they thought that the police department had pretty much hit rock bottom, putting their officers on patrol in Corvairs.

I drove straight east on 12th Street and out the other side without locating my wife. At that time, her red hair would have stood out. I now realized that she probably had gone home. I met her there and we went to the Jackson County Courthouse, located in neighboring Independence, instead.

During the period that the riots lasted, a curfew was placed on the city. Anybody discovered outside after dark would be arrested. Well, we had our wedding rehearsal and dinner on Friday night, April 12, and the curfew created problems.

Bob White, now retired from the KCPD, was one of my groomsmen and he and I escorted everyone home after the rehearsal dinner to keep our wedding party out of jail. Both Bob and I had to work on Friday night. We were working midnight to noon (twelve-hour shifts) in the jail. I was allowed to go home at 5 a.m. to get ready for the wedding, which was at 2 p.m. on Saturday. They made Bob work until noon, so he did not get any sleep. After our wedding on Saturday, we went to our new apartment at 4125 Paseo.

Bob's wife had painted a large bull's-eye on the top of our little red Corvair in white shoe polish and I never could get that thing off the top of that car. When I sold it to some lucky buyer, it was still there, thankfully a little fainter than when Jackie had painted it.

This was the beginning of my police career. I cannot tell people that I joined the police to save the world, but rather I joined so I would not have to stand in that damned line at the unemployment office again!

Metro Drug Squad

I was assigned to the Narcotics Unit from approximately 1979 to 1984. Then, Captain Lloyd Cooper called and asked if I would be interested in working in the Metro Drug Squad. I was a sergeant, and apparently there had been some recent problems with the supervision. During our conversation, Captain Cooper shared with me the sensitivity of the assignment, especially with the nature of the metro capacity of the squad. I accepted the assignment with some trepidation, since I had never worked in narcotics as a detective, but I thought it would be fun, and that was always an issue with me.

I inherited a squad that included Mike Hand, Doug Clark, Mark Himmel from the Platte County Sheriff's Office, Mark "Thumper" and some others. When I went to the squad, there was a two-year limit on the assignment because of the nature of the job. During my tenure, we negotiated with management and got that time restriction removed, with the stipulation that we would go to see Dr. Marshall Saper, the department psychologist, every other month. I spent two years with the Metro Drug Squad and the remaining two years with the Narcotics Unit after the Metro Drug Squad was disbanded, for whatever reason.

I believe it was on a Saturday night when we were in the office, thinking of something to do. We received a telephone call from a snitch who had worked in the past with a detective on another squad. The caller said he was working in a bar on Troost and a person had come in asking if anyone wanted to purchase some heroin. At the time, we were not buying a lot of heroin, and the informant did not know the name of the subject.

I sent Detective Gregory Russell and another detective, possibly Steve Green, out to the bar to see if they could hook up with the subject and see if we could make a purchase. Because it was a slow night, I recall assigning the entire squad to this deal. We pretty much followed Greg and Steve to the bar and then waited until they came out and contacted us to let us know how it went.

When they came out of the bar and we met up, they told me that they had made contact with the subject and he had given them a gram sample. It field-tested positive, as I recall. The crook informed Russell and Green that he had entered this country illegally through Baja, Mexico, and had brought a large quantity of "pure heroin" with him and now wanted to sell the entire load. As I recall, Russell and Green informed the crook that they could not afford the entire load but would be interested in half a pound.

The following Monday, we took the sample to the DEA for testing. When we got the results of the test, we were informed that it was 98 percent pure and they had mathematically diluted the gram sample down to street strength. Of course, we worked the case with the DEA because they always had the money for large purchases like this. The DEA agreed to front the money for a half-pound purchase; I think it was $50,000. Needless to say, the money was not going home with the crook; he was going to jail.

When Greg contacted the crook again, we agreed to make the purchase at the Landing Shopping Center at 63rd and Troost. On the day of the deal, I had arranged for one of our helicopters to hover high over the shopping center and, in addition, had arranged for many of our undercover officers to be nearby.

A buy-signal was arranged, so that when Greg made the purchase and we saw the signal, the other officers were to move in for the arrest. I informed all the officers assigned to the operation that this crook would not leave the parking lot with the money. I had signed for the money and was not going to take the chance of having to repay the federal government. The crook showed up as planned, and Greg and Steve made the deal. The signal was given and, as planned, all of our people moved in and made the arrest without incident.

The crook was taken to the DEA office, where he was debriefed and given an opportunity to roll over on his suppliers. He agreed, since he had brought the heroin in illegally through Mexico. We found out that his contact was in Thailand. The case went all the way back to Thailand, and arrests were made in that country.

As a side note, while I was a supervisor, I prided myself on never asking a subordinate to do something that I would not do. I bought a little dope occasionally to see what my undercover officers went through or at least get a feel for what they were doing. Having said that, Greg Russell and Steve Green, both being black undercover officers, regularly went into places that I was not sure I would go.

On another deal, Greg approached an apartment building and made contact with the watchman to meet a drug dealer. The watchman took Greg in the building, searched Greg for a gun and "kills kit," and then put him on an elevator and sent him up to an unknown floor. Our source of information on this deal did not know on which floor the dealer was located, only that someone would send him up. As Greg got out on the unknown floor, he was taken to a room where he was locked in. He was told the crook would come to the room and see what Greg wanted, then leave to get the requested drug, and return to make the sale. At the conclusion of the sale, Greg would be allowed to leave the building by riding the elevator down and walking away.

Before this purchase was made, I asked Greg what he thought, and he said he would go in and make the purchase. We had been trying to get into this group for a long time, and this was our opportunity. I told him that I would do the surveillance and asked how much time he wanted before I called the Tactical Unit to come in and get him out. I think we agreed on 30 minutes, and I told him that in 31 minutes I was calling the tactical team.

When Greg disappeared into the building, I was watching the digital clock on the dash of my police vehicle. I have never liked digital clocks since this experience. I watched the minutes click down. As the elapsed time got to 25 minutes, then 26, my pucker factor had increased to about 9.9 and I went to the nearest pay phone and called the dispatcher.

As I was waiting for the tactical sergeant, Greg came walking out of the building. I cannot tell you how happy I was to see him. As I recall, we made one more purchase as described, but this time we had more information about the location inside the building, along with who the crooks were. I know from my experience in the Narcotics Unit that the offenders never got enough time in prison consistent with the amount of risk we took. All of the undercover officers who worked for me did a fantastic job, and I continue to have the greatest amount of respect for all of them.

Law Enforcement Satellite Teleconferencing Network (LESTN) is Born

I had been assigned to the Regional Police Academy for a little over two years and was the supervisor of instruction. At this time, the academy was housed at Penn Valley Community College. As I look back on my career, this was one of the more gratifying assignments that I had.

After two years as the supervisor of instruction, I was reassigned to the Video Seminar Unit within the academy. Our commander, at the time, was Major Richard Fletcher. Previously, I had briefly worked for Major Fletcher in Internal Affairs, so we knew each other and had a mutual respect.

I had one subordinate and that was Officer Bob Bennett. Bob knew what he was doing with the video stuff and I knew the seminar part. I pretty much stayed out of Bob's way and allowed him the opportunity to use his creativity with the video program. There was a little-known city ordinance that required telecommunications between city organizations, and it was Bob's responsibility to follow up on that and establish this communications system. After a short period of time, we hired a civilian employee, Chip, who was extremely well-versed in the project at hand, and was very instrumental in setting up this communication system.

I remember one afternoon while the three of us were sitting and discussing our unit; Chip piped up and asked if we had ever considered the possibility of getting involved with teleconferencing. I had no clue what he was talking about. Chip explained the process, and the Law Enforcement Satellite Teleconferencing Network (LESTN) was born. Basically, the project consisted of renting a transponder on a communication satellite and then producing a presentation. We'd publish the date and time of the teleconference (presentation) so law enforcement agencies around the world could tune in.

Bob, Chip, and I quickly realized that the KCPD could not pull this off by ourselves, so we contacted Tony Triplett at the Kansas City FBI office. After explaining the teleconferencing project to Tony, he was sold on the idea. Then our job was to sell the project to our respective organizations. Tony was able to sell the FBI on the project, and a relationship between the KCPD and the FBI was formed. The project was launched with the first teleconference aired in 1985, on the topic of "Hostage Negotiation." This topic was selected because of my involvement with the FBI negotiators at the FBI Academy in Quantico, VA.

Several teleconferences were aired over the next several years. Bob, Tony, and I chose Larry Welch, then director of a training academy in Topeka, Kansas as the moderator for the teleconferences.

When we were preparing the first teleconference, we wanted to identify someone to kick it off who represented both the federal and the local level. One name quickly jumped out of the memory bank: former KCPD Chief Clarence Kelley had retired as director of the FBI and had relocated back to Kansas City. Tony stayed in contact with Chief Kelley, and he quickly agreed to do it. We decided that we would record Chief Kelley, rather than have him do it live. He agreed to this and wrote out his remarks. On an agreed date, we picked him up for the taping of his comments. We picked him up in time to be able to take him to lunch at one of his favorite restaurants, Ross's Grill, just north of the Plaza.

While sitting there for lunch, I wished someone would have walked in that I knew so they could have seen me. Chief Kelley began telling war stories. He told about the time he was a fairly new agent and assigned to do a "black-bag job" on an organized crime member's house. He gained entrance into the residence alone, and then began looking for the place where he had gained entrance, but could not find it. He never said if the bad guy was asleep upstairs or not, but he did say that business picked up and he still couldn't find his way out.

After our initial teleconference was launched, Tony received recognition for his participation in the project. I think he received $250 for his efforts. As a direct result of our bypassing the police department's executive committee, Bob, Chip and I received no recognition for our effort.

As a matter of fact, Major Fletcher was transferred somewhere along the line and another major took over at the academy. I was called into his office and he gave me the "We're in the same boat, but we are not all rowing in the same direction" speech and I informed him that he should transfer me to get somebody in the boat rowing in the same direction as everyone else. I was reassigned to East Patrol Division, Watch 1. After receiving this assignment, Chief Joiner contacted me and asked me where I wanted to be assigned. I told him that East Zone Watch 1 was fine.

I had been at East Zone for some months when I received a phone call from my good friend, Mike Napier, then special agent with the FBI. During this call, Mike informed me that the FBI was going to invite the Kansas City Police Department to participate in the psychological profiling program and that I should put in for it. Mike briefly described the program and casually mentioned that, if I was accepted, I would be gone for a year, studying at the FBI Academy in Quantico. Well, you know how after you have been awakened and begin to think about something, you cannot go back to sleep, and you talk yourself into it?

My wife came home from work and I explained my telephone call from Mike. I casually mentioned that I would be gone for a year studying the technique. Keep in mind that we had twin boys who were 14 and a daughter who was 18. After I explained the program, she thought about it for about five minutes and said, "If it will help your career, do it."

After my wife agreed to the assignment, I made my interest known to the command staff and when the invitation came through, I think I was the only person who expressed interest. The fact that one had to be away from home for a year was a deal-breaker for most of the folks. After being selected to be the department's representative, I was reassigned to the Homicide Unit for approximately two months before my departure. I was provided with a department vehicle, gas credit card and $1,200 for the year, in addition to my regular salary. I left Kansas City on January 1, 1988, to spend a year at the National Center for the Analysis of Violent Crime (NCAVC).

I was also given one airline ticket per month. I could fly back home for a weekend visit or my wife could fly out. I completed my one year of training, and came back to the KCPD where I was assigned to the Violent Crimes Unit. I remained in that unit until I retired on January 16, 1993. I left at 25-years exactly to the date I hired on because I thought I would be more employable at age 48 with 25-years of service than if I retired at age 53 with 30-years of service.

Virginia State Police

Upon retiring from the KCPD, I was hired by the Virginia State Police (VSP) where I completed approximately 13 years of full-time service. Then I was informed that they needed a psychological profiler who would hit the ground running, working cases around the Commonwealth, a job I now perform on a part-time basis. I have had a wonderful career with the VSP, and have ended up living here in the state to this very day.

Jon Perry was just promoted to sergeant in 1976. He is standing in front of the Argyle Building in Kansas City. His aunt, to his left is Gertrude Phillips. His mother to his right is Elizabeth Perry. (Courtesy of the KCPD)

Jon Perry went to work with the Virginia State Police (VSP) after retiring from the KCPD. He served 13 years full-time with the VSP, and is currently working part-time with the VSP as a Psychological Profiler.
(Courtesy of Virginia State Police Department)

This is a photo of Police Officer Ben Eyre that was taken in 1971. (Courtesy of the KCPD)

Chapter 19

Ben C. Eyre

Retired Officer, KCPD, 1971-1996

When I was about six or seven years old, my mother would tell me when I got into mischief that the police would come and take me away, so I was always afraid of the police during my youth.

One night, my two older sisters took me to the Nu-Way Drive-In at Meyer and Troost for a hamburger. Lo, and behold, a cop pulled in next to us. This made me scared because I had been acting up. My sister told me to straighten up or she would get the cop to come after me. She called him over and I hid on the backseat floor. He leaned in and said "Come on over and see my police car." Well, I was so scared I started crying; I thought I was going to jail. But he was very nice and told me I was not going to jail and to come and see the inside of his police car. So, I went and sat in the front seat and he explained all about how the siren and red lights worked and all about the shotgun.

After we left the drive-in, I was so impressed that from that day on I kept telling everyone that someday I would become a KCPD officer.

I had another incident when I was visiting the police headquarters building on a trip with the Cub Scouts. I wasn't feeling very well, and I got sick and threw up on the floor. A police sergeant took me to the bathroom and cleaned me all up. He told me to not worry about getting sick, and, again, I really respected the police. Ever since those two incidents, I had always wanted to be a policeman.

I was born in Kansas City at St. Luke's Hospital and graduated from Southwest High School. After a stint in the U.S. Marines, I heard that the KCPD wanted to hire around 300 new officers because of an E-Tax being passed. I joined the department on November 1, 1971, and was in the ninth academy recruit class.

In February 1972, I was assigned to the Metro Police Station, where I remained until March 1976. I was then assigned to the East Patrol Station until November 1984, and the South Patrol Station until 1986. Eventually, I transferred to the Traffic DUI squad, until my retirement on December 16, 1996. I completed 25 years with the KCPD.

Iron Skillet Disturbance

It was in August 1974, at 6:30 a.m. when I received a disturbance call in the 6800 block of Askew. My radio number was 233 and my immediate supervisor, Sergeant Winston, volunteered to make the call with me because he was closer than the other district car. Upon our arrival, we encountered a black female at the front door who was crying and bleeding from her nose, down her face, onto her nightgown. When we got inside, we came in contact with a tall black male who was standing by the dining room table in his pajama bottoms, holding an ice pack on his forehead. He began yelling that the black female, who was his wife, had hit him in the head with an iron skillet while he was asleep and it startled him, so he got out of the bed and punched her in the face.

She interrupted that she had gotten up and started to check the mail that she had brought in from the night before. Upon opening the MasterCard bill, she saw a $15 charge for a local hotel room in Kansas City and why would he need to stay at a local hotel? Well, you might guess why and you'd be right!

At this time, we separated the two, and I took the husband into the living room and asked him (biting my lip not to laugh) why he didn't pay in cash. He replied that he only had $4 left and this lady was so fine he did not want her to get away, so he used his MasterCard. He said, "Officer, I have watched the mailbox for the past three weeks for that bill to come, so I could get it and pay it before my wife would find it. Well, yesterday I had to work a double shift and when I came home, I was tired and forgot to check the mail, and she found it, and you know the rest of the story." The husband refused treatment, and neither wanted to press charges against each other, so he decided to pack his bags and leave.

Drunk Driver

It was in the summer of 1977, about 4:30 p.m., and I was on the evening shift, working radio number 325 at East Patrol. I was driving eastbound on 17th Street from Topping and as I was approaching a hill, an unknown car came at me head on.

I swerved to the right, going off the roadway, and, as the vehicle passed me, it missed hitting my car by inches. I quickly turned my patrol car around and turned on my lights and siren. Upon getting the vehicle stopped close to Hardesty, I exited my car.

The driver was just sitting calmly behind the wheel. I yelled for him to roll down the window and, as he did, I smelled liquor emanating from his vehicle. He said to me, slurring, "Are you going to give me another ticket?" I yelled "Another ticket? I haven't given you one yet!" "Yes, you did," he said, "about a half hour ago."

He handed me a yellow copy of a traffic citation from an Independence police officer from about a half hour earlier. He was arrested for driving while intoxicated and taken to East Patrol and given a breathalyzer, where he blew a .25 percent on the machine, which is extremely intoxicated.

Drunken Driving Nurse

It was an August night in 1990, and Officer Groves heard a CB call that a small silver car was driving northbound in the southbound lanes of I-435 at 95th Street. I was on I-470, just about one mile away, and caught up to Groves and Officer Thompson, who were catching up to the car just past 87th Street. All three of us had our red lights and sirens on, but we were in unmarked Chevrolets with the headlights flashing, as well as the red light in the back and one on the dashboard.

The car in question was being operated by a white female, and we had to do something to stop her. I saw a spot to cross the Interstate and went for it, crossing over into the southbound lanes ahead of her, leaving my flashing headlights on. I exited my patrol car with my flashlight and the lit-up red cone on the front. I got the silver car to stop and then stood in the middle of the freeway and started waving to stop all traffic coming toward me. The next vehicle coming over the hill in the same lane as the silver car was a semi. Officer Thompson left his vehicle on the northbound side and came over to help me get the female out of her car. She was barely able to stand, because she was so intoxicated. She was taken to Metro Patrol, where she blew a .23 percent on the breathalyzer and told us she was a registered nurse.

This photo of Police Officer, Keith Gregory was taken in 1966.
(Courtesy of the KCPD)

Chapter 20

Keith L. "Rocky" Gregory

Retired Sergeant, KCPD, 1966–1996

I was born in San Diego in 1943. My Dad always told me, "If you had been born 20 minutes earlier, you would have been Mexican." I'm not sure what my parents were doing south of the border with my mother so pregnant, and I can't ask because they've both passed on.

I went to Hogan High School and graduated from De La Salle Military Academy in 1960 at age 17. I joined the Air Force three months later and spent three-and-a-half years in Spain. When I got out, I went to college for two years and also worked at Safeway grocery store at Linwood and Gillham, in midtown Kansas City. One night, as we were closing, a salt-and-pepper team of robbers came in and held us up.

I was complaining to Roark Wagner, Officer Charley Dale's brother, and a friend of mine for years. Our dads worked together, and Roark and I went in the Air Force together. I told him about the robbery, and he told me that the police department was hiring and that if someone was going to point a gun at me, then I should have one to point back, so why didn't I join? I joined the KCPD on September 1, 1966, and retired from the department 30 years later.

A Funny Story

I was working dog watch out of the old South Patrol Sub-Station, which was located at 107th and Blue Ridge. One night, about 12:30 a.m., I received a call and was told to make it a "Code One," which means red lights and siren.

I arrived at the scene at the same time as an ambulance. The two paramedics and I raced up the steps to the house and in the open front door. Upon entering the house, we encountered a little 75-year-old lady in her nightgown, talking on the phone. She pointed to a rear bedroom located to her right. We saw a body lying on the floor that turned out to be her husband. He was lying on his back, wearing only an undershirt.

The two paramedics rushed into the room to try and assist the man while I remained with the little old lady who was still talking on the phone. She was apparently talking to her daughter, as the conversation went something like this: "Yes, I think Dad is gone. He grabbed his chest and fell to the floor. I called 911 and the police and ambulance just arrived." There was a pause, and then she said, "I don't think that is any of your business."

At this point, I began to put things together and realized what this old couple had been doing. It became rather difficult to keep a straight and sympathetic face. Her conversation continued. "I still don't believe it is any of your business, but if you must know, Dad and I were making love." By this time I was biting my tongue to keep a straight face. She then hung up and turned to me.

This little 75-year-old lady, with tears streaming down her face, looked me straight in the eye, and said, "Yes, officer, we were making love, and then Dad got up to go to the bathroom. He collapsed in the middle of the floor and I knew right away he was gone." She continued, "But at least he died happy!"

I think at this time blood began to seep from my mouth from biting my tongue so hard. The paramedics joined us and confirmed what the lady already knew. Family began to arrive and we finished the call in a routine manner. But I will never forget that little old lady as long as I live.

1968 Riot Story

It was the second night of the "civil disturbances" of 1968, better known as "the riots." All officers were working twelve-hour shifts and we were waiting for the governor to activate the National Guard. I reported to work that night at Linwood and Paseo, at the Scottish Rites Temple, which was being used as the command post and staging area.

I had been riding a line beat from 27th to 39th on Prospect. I had at least one bullet hole in my car, just below the driver's door handle, and I was determined to be ready if any more bullets were directed my way. I was armed with my department-issued Smith and Wesson .38 revolver and had a pocket full of extra shells. The vehicle was equipped with a Remington 12-gauge shotgun, and I had extra shells for it in my other pocket. I also had secured an M1 carbine with two 30-round clips taped back to back. I was ready.

Upon arrival at work that night, I was informed that I would have three National Guard soldiers riding with me for the entire twelve-hour shift. They would be armed with M1 rifles. I reported to my car and was introduced to the three soldiers. Their names have since escaped me, but I do remember that there were two black gentlemen in their 50s and one young country boy from the Boot heel of Missouri.

We all got in the car and started eastbound on Linwood with those lovely M1 rifles sticking out of all four windows. We were ready. As we approached Prospect, I turned to the black gentleman sitting next to me, and said, "Sir, you have probably already done this, but if you haven't, you can load your weapons now, we are at our assigned beat."

This gentleman looked at me, and in a soft voice said, "Officer, they gave us guns but they never gave us any ammunition. We have no bullets to load." At this point, I think I screamed "What!?" I said several other things at that time, which are largely unprintable. Needless to say I questioned the intelligence of the leaders of the National Guard who would put their people in harm's way without any way to protect themselves. Fortunately, after passing over the shotgun to the gentleman in the front, we finished the night with no serious incidents.

27th and Prospect

It was the fifth or sixth day of the "civil disturbances," and I had finally gotten to work days. The command staff had decided that we should change our approach from looking like Pancho Villas' bandits and made everyone take off the crossed bandoliers of ammunition most of us were wearing. We were also told to leave our M1s and rifles in the trunk unless fired upon.

I still had the same line beat, but the National Guard had gone home and I was given a partner for the duration. I cannot remember who was with me at the time, but we got along fine. On this particular day we were approaching the noon hour and my partner suggested we find somewhere to eat.

Earlier in the day, at roll call, the desk sergeant suggested that it would further the cause of peace if we interacted with the populace, whenever possible. I turned to my partner and asked him if ham and beans and cornbread or possibly a hot dog would do for lunch. He said yes, so I drove to 27th and Prospect to a place I knew of. I had heard that it was a pool hall run by a lady who served the best ham and beans and cornbread on Prospect.

When we got there, my partner said "You're not going in there, are you?" We walked in to the pool hall, and you could have heard a pin drop. My partner and I walked over to the kitchen window and ordered our food, and I turned and said, to no one in particular, "Who's up for a game of partners?" and put my quarter on an empty table.

I'm not sure to this day why a couple of guys actually stepped forward and played us or why we were not hassled while we ate after the game. After five or six days of rioting and shooting and burning, here were two crazy cops sitting in their midst, playing pool and eating as if nothing had ever happened.

After we finished our meal, we said our farewells and went back to our line beat. My partner told me at the end of the shift that, if it was all the same to me, he would prefer to ride with someone who didn't have a death wish and was just a little less insane!

Police Officer James Post. Academy photo, 1965
(Courtesy of the KCPD)

Chapter 21

James G. Post

Retired Sergeant, KCPD, 1965-1990

How It All Started

My Dad was a Kansas City, Kansas, police detective in the early 1950s, so the seed was probably planted then. After high school and a year at Kansas City Junior College, I transferred to Central Missouri State University in Warrensburg and started taking some criminal justice courses. To pay for college, I had to return to Kansas City to work weekends and, on school breaks, I worked midnights at a Phillip 66 station just south of the airport. The regular night attendant was a retired deputy, so the KCPD officers spent a lot of time there because it was about the only business open all night in Platte County back then.

    I became friends with some officers who were only a couple years older than me at the time. It should be noted that, at that time, the shifts rotated every thirty days, and to say there was a lack of activity on dog watch would be a gross understatement. Those NPD guys went days without a call for service, particularly on the first watch.

    As we became friends, I started riding with these officers. I already had the desire for public service, having experienced some of it with my Dad. I also had seen the boring side from the textbooks at CMSU. Those coppers filled in all the remaining blanks for me. I learned that law enforcement was not only personally rewarding and satisfying on many levels, but also a lot of fun. I first experienced Arthur Bryant's BBQ (a famous BBQ place in Kansas City) with these great guys, as well as hearing about pursuits, war stories, and all the assorted bitches and complaints, too. My primary mentor was Gene Krogman, who went on to have a great career as one of KCPD's first K-9 officers.

Once I approached the magic age of 21, I applied. I flew through the process until the oral review board, where I was immediately intimidated by a room full of brown-uniformed PD brass. They were complimentary about my motives, background, and education, but balked when they learned I held the dreaded "1-A status." For those who do not remember the military draft, a 1-A classification was Numero Uno on the eligibility hit parade, the next to go. The panel spokesman said something like, "Come back after you're married or have served, and we'll take you."

Dejected over being rejected, I joined the U.S. Army Reserves, did my six months at Fort Leonard Wood and, for good measure, got married, too. I was then accepted to the KCPD, hired effective October 1, 1965, and entered the academy as a member of the 100th recruit class in the department's history.

But that number would become a plague to all of us a few months later. A reporter from the Kansas City Star conned Chief Clarence Kelley into letting him enroll in our class to write a series of (presumably positive) informative articles about police academy training. We soon knew something was amiss when the reporter only attended the controversial classes, such as riot training, crowd control, baton training and, naturally, firearms training. After graduation, the bombshell articles started to drop. We were labeled "The All-White 100th" in a series of critical, inflammatory articles, after which, the academy commander was transferred.

The reporter was to have a short career in Kansas City, as well, but the damage was done. One of the first buildings to be torched in the riots three years later was, predictably, the police academy.

My Retirement

I retired in 1990, after 25 years. I actually used my "V" (vacation) days so I could leave early to start my "new career" at a Kansas City high school as a security officer when school started in the fall. What a horrible nine months that turned out to be. I soon learned the student's word was always taken over security, particularly if they had the parents backing ("My Johnny said he didn't do it...").

I was called into parent/student/administration meetings (without advance notice) and didn't have a friend in the room, while the kid, the parent, and the school bosses each took a shot at me.

My reports were questioned, scrutinized, and returned to be rewritten to support the school and/or the student more favorably. I pointed out I had never had a report returned in 25 years at the KCPD, but no matter. I also learned that the athletes were strictly hands-off, immune to discipline, and could openly violate school policy. Security was impotent, and I was relieved when my nine-month tour ended. I've had many, many wonderful experiences in the last 20 years of retirement, but that first job was not one of them.

Police Cars Have Been Good to Me

For the last 45-plus years, police cars have been very good to me. During the first 25 years, they got me to the action on time, got me to the hospital on time (so I didn't have to deliver in the backseat), kept me warm and dry (most of the time), and saved my butt in a few serious crashes. Sure, I got stranded a few times with total electrical meltdowns and flat tires, and got hot when we had to turn off the A/C (to pull up hills) in those damn Ford Fairmonts. I had a few unkind letters placed in my personnel jacket for pushing the envelope too far and bending a few of them, but I only lost one chase (my first one) because no one warned me to let go of the "mike" in a chase. With every turn, the cord got shorter and shorter until my face was in the steering wheel. Those old canvas seat covers were hemorrhoid-makers, and we sure lacked a lot of modern-day conveniences, such as power windows, AM/FM radios, power brakes and steering and, lamentably, cup holders.

The last 20 years have improved my appreciation for police cars and my respect for those honorable machines that provide safe havens for the men and women of law enforcement. Always being a car guy, my tastes range from customs to hot rods, muscle cars, off-roaders, pickups, sports cars, dune buggies, low riders, you name it. A year before retiring, I bought my first used squad car, a 1986 Crown Vic, that had seen service with the Wyoming Highway Patrol.

A few months later, I had the opportunity to drive it to Cheyenne and meet the trooper who had driven it. He asked me "When you got it, was the hood scratched and was there a dent in the front bumper?" I said "Yes, I had the hood painted, but never fixed the bumper.

Why?" He grinned and said "That dent happened when I finished the pursuit of a bank robber by knocking his car off the Interstate, and the scratch came from me pulling him out of his driver's window and dragging him across my hood." Well, I was hooked on police cars then and there and haven't looked back. These cars all have stories.

I've probably owned a hundred or more cruisers in the last 20 years, but I still have that old Crown Vic. I bought it when it was a scant three years old, and now it qualifies for antique tags. From that first purchase, I created a local police car club that has grown into the only international organization dedicated exclusively to police cars, with members in Canada, England, Germany, Japan, and Australia, and throughout the United States.

Because of this hobby, I was hired to design scale model, die-cast police cars and have the honor of having my picture (in KCPD blues) on the back of each package. I have written and published a book on restoring police cars, and I have written a quarterly article in a police magazine for over a dozen years. My wife and I operated a police car museum for six years in the Arkansas Ozarks, and I've worked on movie productions as vehicle coordinator. I've had some of my police cars in commercials and movies, and one of my cars now resides in the Ronald Reagan Presidential Library, of which I am very proud.

Because of my magazine employment, I've been able to drive all the new police car prototypes over the years, including Camaros, Caprices, Mustangs, and the HEMI Dodges. Although my car collecting has slowed down somewhat, and I've returned to my roots (buying cars I had years ago), I still have these cruisers: the Crown Vic that started it all and a 2010 HEMI Charger. Looking back, I wouldn't change a thing...well, maybe some of those accidents that got me on Sergeant Jim Rowe's list!

After we closed our museum, we moved into a log house and I built an adjacent 60x80 metal building that incorporates my office, a large game room, a smaller museum, and car storage. However, I've sold enough cars now that I don't really need all the space anymore.

My book was co-authored by Ed Sanow and is titled Police Cars: Restoring, Collecting and Showing America's Favorite Sedans, published in 1990. I am the automotive consultant and columnist for Police and Security News and my column is titled "The Wheels of Justice." I also freelance for Law & Order and Police Collector's News, plus I write the quarterly newsletter (The Rap sheet) for my car club.

Retired Sergeant Jim Post poses beside his 1970 restored Dodge Polaris. This squad car was used In leading area parades in Eureka Springs, Arkansas. This photo was taken by his wife near the Beaver Lake (Courtesy of Jim Post)

This photo was taken in 2005 of John Stewart, forensic specialist (on left) and Seth Cooper, KCPD crime lab chemist, at a meth-cooking crime scene. The air tank strapped to Cooper's back is a standard MSA self-contained breathing apparatus used to enter any unknown air quality environment. Stewart makes the quote, "We dare to go where even the angels fear to tread." (Courtesy of the KCPD)

Chapter 22

John R. Stewart

**Retired Detective, KCPD, 1970-1998;
Civilian Investigator, Forensic Specialist 2, KCPD
Metro-Meth Section, 1998-Present**

House Fire

While working my job as a police officer for the KCPD, I remember one of the bad times that occurred. It was around March 1973, sometime between 2 and 3 a.m., working the dog watch shift at East Patrol Division.

It was a pretty cold morning and, while on patrol, I met up with Officer Jerry Borchers, one of those kinds of guys who is easy to get along with and was just as immortal on the job as I thought I was: full speed ahead and fear no evil. I saw his patrol car in the parking lot at 39th and Bales, so I pulled up and parked my patrol car next to Jerry's.

I saw that he had purchased some chicken at 39th and Indiana and was enjoying every bite of it. As for myself, I couldn't stand the taste of chicken; give me a good old-fashioned McDonald's Big Mac and I would be happy forever. As Jerry and I were talking, in between his bites of his chicken, I heard a fire truck siren as it was leaving the fire station, just south of Church's Chicken.

Both of us saw the fire truck go rolling by north on Indiana. I always had a curiosity about where fire trucks were headed, and since there was no real action going on that night, I told Jerry, "Let's go follow that fire truck."

We followed the fire truck to about 33rd and Benton where it stopped by a two-story house that was engulfed in flames. Usually we would help out the fire crews by keeping road traffic from driving over the water lines and curiosity seekers far enough away from the scene that they didn't get in the firemen's way.

While there, we found out that a female had jumped off the roof area just below the second-story window and broken her leg when she hit the ground. A male, who also lived at that address, was standing outside in the front yard of the house, but appeared uninjured.

We also heard that there were three small children in the upstairs bedroom where the fire was burning. It was about that time Jerry and I saw a fireman take a large ladder off of the fire truck and carry it to the side of the house where he extended the ladder up to the second-story window, the room the children were thought to be in.

Jerry and I went up to where the fireman was climbing the ladder, and I noticed that the ladder was swaying from the weight of the fireman and the blowing wind. I grabbed the ladder with both hands to steady it while the fireman continued to climb the ladder. A few minutes later, a big billow of hot smoke flowed straight down on me. As I said before, young cops always think they're bulletproof and immortal, so I did not think much about all the smoke that gathered around me and Jerry at the time. Hindsight being 20-20, I should have known better. It didn't even occur to me that the fireman was wearing a Self-Contained Breathing Apparatus (SCBA) and I was not, which would later come back to haunt me.

The fireman went through the window and found the children; he brought them down the ladder one at a time. All three children appeared to be dead. This meant that Jerry was going to have to take the dead body reports. Being the senior officer on site, I told Jerry that junior officers take the reports. Of course, I think later in his career Jerry realized I had pulled a fast one on him and had him do the reports because I really did not want to.

By the time the ambulance arrived, the fire had been almost completely extinguished, so we followed the ambulance to General Hospital. When we got there, Jerry grabbed the required paperwork and followed the ambulance crew with the bodies inside. I entered a short time later and observed Jerry was busy meeting with Sergeant George Henthorn from the Homicide Unit, who was gathering information from Jerry for the reports that he had to write. As I watched them talking back and forth, I noticed that Jerry did not seem comfortable talking to the sergeant. I found out later that he thought the sergeant was an uncaring, callous ass who didn't give a damn that three kids had just died in a fire.

After a few more years on the job, Jerry figured it out: the sergeant was not being callous or hard about it; he was just doing his job. After a while, you learn to grow a thick hide and keep emotions out of what you're doing, especially when it comes to dealing with the death of children.

Anyway, as I watched the two of them bantering back and forth, I started getting lightheaded and faint. There was a hospital gurney near us in the hallway, so I hopped up to lie down. As I lay there, I told someone that I needed oxygen. No matter how many breaths I took or how deep I breathed, I felt as if I was not getting any air in my lungs. A few minutes later I apparently passed out cold on the gurney. This was a bigger deal than I had bargained for. The dog watch commander, Captain Leroy Swift, had arrived just as I began to regain consciousness. Captain Swift had been briefed on the fire incident and he saw the obvious condition I was in and the possible danger involved. So, he transported me in his vehicle to Research Hospital for an examination and treatment. This was where the police department surgeon worked at the time.

They got me into a room and pretty soon a male nurse came in and took all of my vitals. I was still feeling dizzy and lightheaded so I told him that I needed oxygen. They placed the oxygen mask on me and later told me that I had suffered smoke inhalation. By that time, I was so weak and tired I could barely keep my eyes open.

Later that evening, an intern came in and woke me up. He was holding a hypodermic syringe with what looked like a five-foot long needle on the end of it. The intern told me they had to draw blood from me, so I held out my arm and told him to go ahead and take it. I swear I saw a sneering grin on the intern's face, and the next thing he told me was that, in order to determine my blood gas levels, he had to draw the blood with the syringe from one of the femoral arteries located in my groin.

He stuck that sucker in that artery and I screamed. After he got the needle out, he left the room without telling me what exactly was wrong.

On the second day in the hospital, my curiosity shot way up

when the intern walked in the room with a heart machine to monitor my vitals. He strapped it on me. I asked him what this was for and he told me again that I had suffered smoke inhalation; however, he also told me that I had cyanide poisoning from the lead-based paint that burned at the fire scene. I then got a little upset about it and rudely stated to the intern, "Now you tell me what's going on."

Of course, I learned to never piss off an intern. It seemed like every four hours that intern came back into the room and stuck that needle in me to check my blood gases, grinning the whole time he was doing it. (I did forget to mention that the whole time I was in the hospital, my wife and friends would come and visit, so it was not as lonely as I make it sound.)

Finally, on the third day, the doctors came into the room and told me that I could leave. It seems before I went into the hospital, I had dark hair, and Jerry, to this day, kids me about my hair turning gray after my fire experience on that cold morning of March 1973. At least I can kid back at Jerry because he had to take the dead body reports that night. Guess what? I think over the years his hair has turned grayer than mine.

Major "Super-Lab" Investigation

In 1985, after some 15 years in patrol, I tried out for the Investigation Bureau, made it, and became a detective. I started out working in the Vice Unit, which was not really as bad as you would think. I had some good times and laughs with my vice partners back then. About a year and half later, I was assigned to work with the Organized Crime Drug Enforcement Task Force and spent about two years working Jamaican drug cases.

The assignment later developed into the Financial Investigation Squad, and we worked several cases involving money laundering and high-level drug dealers in the Kansas City area. Between 1991 and 1995, I was assigned to the KCPD Juvenile Unit, after which I was reassigned to the Drug Enforcement Unit. It was there that Detective Pat Shea and I were assigned to work all clandestine methamphetamine laboratories in the Kansas City area.

After about a year of working lab cases, we were put through the federal government's Drug Enforcement Administration's school for clandestine laboratory investigations and safety training. Apparently, someone on the department figured out that if we blew ourselves up in a lab for lack of proper training, the department would be liable to pay a good chunk of change to our widows.

Around 1998, Shey and I transferred from the Drug Enforcement Unit to working with the federal government in a newly developed unit called the "High Intensity Drug Trafficking Area, Joint Jurisdictional Metropolitan Methamphetamine Task Force." From that day on, we would respond to meth lab calls dressed up in our little white personnel protection suits and air tanks when we went in to gather evidence of manufacturing a controlled substance for court cases, along with cleaning up all the hazardous waste involving meth labs.

In 1998, I retired as a detective and came back to work three days later as a civilian Forensic Specialist Two. I referred to my new position as a "glorified Crime Scene Investigator." In 2000, I did get trained by the department as an actual CSI and was assigned to the Metro Meth Task Force.

Of all the clandestine laboratory cases I responded to over the years, one of the most notable cases I worked was in September 2007. A guy by the last name of Leonard lived at 4800 N. Northwood on the outskirts of Riverside, MO in Platte County. The detectives in the unit received information that Leonard was operating a meth lab at that address, so a bunch of us guys went out there to do a "knock and talk" on his house (a fancy way of attempting to gain entry into someone's house to look for evidence of wrongdoing, without a search warrant.)

When we got to the address, we could smell chemicals coming from the garage. We knocked on Leonard's door and we heard noises coming from inside, but no one would answer the door. A couple of the detectives found what they determined was a stolen tractor in the back yard of the house, so they decided to go get a search warrant for the house involving the stolen tractor. When two detectives left to write up the affidavit for the warrant, we all just waited for about 30 minutes. Meanwhile, we set up guard parameters around the house to prevent anyone from fleeing before the warrant could be obtained.

Just then Leonard came out of the sliding glass door on the back of the residence and fired several gunshots at three detectives standing outside and then ran back inside. We found out later that he had what was called a "clacker" (military jargon for an electrical-charge generating device) that was attached to a cord. When he started to run outside of the house, the cord, which was connected to what we later learned was a live military Claymore mine, had detached from the clacker in the house, and he had gone back inside to reattach the cord to the clacker.

The Claymore mine had been set up by Leonard to blow up a police department Tactical Response Team (informally called a "SWAT Team") if and when they attempted entry at the front door of the house. The girlfriend who was with Leonard in the house at the time told him to not do that, so he turned the mine toward the garage that was adjacent to the residence.

As he left the house, he triggered the device, which blew up the meth lab in the garage. Most of us were about 100 feet from the garage when it went off, and we watched the roof of the house blow about thirty feet into the air. As Leonard ran from the back of the house, he, and the detectives who were chasing him, continued to shoot wildly at each other. However, when the roof blew off the house, everybody except Leonard just stopped and watched as the roof came back down. Leonard was able to get away from the scene via a Jeep he had parked near his house which he drove along a prearranged path through a wooded area.

His escape was short-lived. He was caught a little while later when he wrecked his Jeep into a fence and was apprehended. Leonard's girlfriend, who ran out when he did, was arrested by the detectives at the scene. The garage and house completely burned to the ground, and law enforcement guards were kept onsite until the next morning, at which time the scene would be cool enough to allow officers to search it as a crime scene and recover any evidence that remained. This investigation lasted for about four to five months and we were able to identify several other persons involved in the conspiracy involving the operation of the clandestine meth lab.

Leonard had been operating the lab for about three months. This was one of the biggest labs ever discovered in the Kansas City area, as well as the first actual "super-lab" found in Missouri. Leonard was responsible for making about five to ten pounds of meth each day, a massive amount. This case went to trial in federal court, and Leonard was sentenced to one federal life term for shooting at a U.S. Marshal. The prosecuting attorney for Platte County filed state charges, which were three counts of shooting at the three detectives. He received three life-term sentences from the state of Missouri. All fifteen of the other state charges against him involved conspiracy to distribute meth.

Items Recovered from the Meth Lab Crime Scene

A trailer was located on the property which contained Acetone cans, chemical solvents, and meth lab operation equipment. One thousand pounds of lab waste was collected at the scene, including:

1. 58 empty 32-ounce cans of naphtha and seven empty one-gallon cans
2. 101 empty one-gallon cans and 232 empty one-gallon cans of Acetone
3. 118 empty 1-gallon cans and twenty-five 32-ounce cans of Toluene
4. 1,000 gallons of chemical solvent
5. 4 one-gallon jugs of hydrochloride acid
6. Methamphetamine and amphetamine
7. 5 semi-automatic pistols and one revolver
8. A 12-gauge shotgun
9. Four rifles and three assault rifles
10. A chemical flask, heating mantle with a broken 2,000-ml flask, a reaction mass that contained phosphorus, iodine, and pseudoephedrine which was recovered and was possibly cooking at the time of the explosion and fire
11. 75 total solvent cans which contributed to intensify the fire in the garage
12. 55-gallon barrel, two-thirds full of Acetone
13. 22,000-ml, round-bottomed, chemical flask

Neighborhood Meth Lab Static Display

Of course, not every day is as exciting as that day was, so to fill in some of the downtime we might set up a neighborhood display.

My partner, Kristine Davis, and I were often asked to go to different neighborhoods or community events and set up a fake meth lab display. This was used to educate people so they would know what the meth lab would consist of, how the meth was cooked, and the typical chemical smells associated with a clandestine meth lab.

Sometime in 2009, I recall a neighborhood requested our unit to set up this display for them during their block party around 16th street in Kansas City. After setting up the display, citizens came over to look at the display to see what meth labs looked like. While we were talking with the citizens, I saw Mayor Mark Funkhouser walking by our set-up. We asked if he wanted to be in a photo shoot with us and, to my surprise, he agreed. The mayor seemed very interested in the static display and he thought it was a good idea to show neighborhoods what labs looked like.

The most common smells around a meth lab is usually an acetone smell like fingernail polish. It can also have a very potent iodine smell. When we investigated a lab, we wore protective clothing with special Nytril chemical gloves and masks with self-contained breathing apparatus. We also had air meters to test the air quality.

The chemist will determine if it is safe for people to go in without the breathing apparatus. The average small meth lab takes about four hours to work to clear the scene. We were always on call, 24/7, and we responded no matter the location or type of weather. A person can oftentimes see a reddish or purple-reddish coloring on the outside of a house if someone is operating a meth lab inside.

When breaking down a meth lab, we usually take the bulk items outside. We would inventory them and leave them outside the recovery site for a special local hazardous waste pick-up company to respond and haul the bulk items away.

We only recovered small sample bottles of the chemicals and powders for the chemist to analyze at the lab. Under no circumstances did we just leave hazardous waste sitting on the side of the road when we cleaned out a house. We waited until the bulk items were picked up by the hazardous waste truck. They were required to handle hazardous waste in accordance with EPA guidelines.

This is a photo of a neighborhood Meth-Lab Display. Standing L-R, Forensic Specialist 2, Kristin Davis, Forensic Specialist 4, Seth Cooper, K.C, Mayor Mark Funkhouser, Forensic Specialist 3, Jason Cooper and kneeling in front, Forensic Specialist 2, John Stewart. Kristin and Stewart both work full time with the KCPD Metro Meth-section and Cooper and Kennedy both work out of the KCPD Crime Lab as chemist. (Courtesy of John Stewart)

Chief Warrant Officer, Jack Livella, being promoted to CWO4 at a ceremony at Richards Gebaur AFB in Belton, MO. CWO4 William Price is pictured pinning the rank on Livella, while the 493rd CID Unit Commander, LTC Lawrence Sheppard, is on the right. (Courtesy of 493rd MP Detachment (CID) Reserve Unit)

Chapter 23

Jack Livella

Retired CWO4, U.S. Army Reserves (CID)

I was born in Johnstown, Pennsylvania in 1940. My father worked in the steel mills and I didn't want to end up like he did, so I, along with some of my high school friends, decided to join the Air Force after graduation in 1959. I really wanted to join the Marines, but I knew they would throw me into the water and I had never learned to swim. That's why I joined the Air Force for what I thought would be four years. I ended up spending eleven years, instead.

While in the Air Force, I became interested in law enforcement. I was stationed in New Mexico and started taking college courses at Roswell Community College. There, I met a student who became a friend of mine. He was a special agent with the Air Force Office of Special Investigations, commonly known as (OSI). He suggested I apply for the OSI because he knew of my interest in law enforcement. I applied for and went through the exhaustive process and school that the Air Force required and was accepted as a special agent, where I remained for about a year and a half. I was a staff sergeant at that time.

I later found out that the Army was recruiting OSI agents to cross-train into the Army to become criminal investigators, commonly referred to as CID agents. OSI agents could transfer into the Army and be appointed as warrant officers, so this was an easy choice for me to make. I went through all of the Army's testing and requirements and was selected to join the Army CID as a warrant officer (WO1).

On September 9, 1970, I was discharged from the Air Force, and the next day I was sworn into the Army as a WO1. I was immediately sent to the CID school at Fort Gordon, Georgia. After graduation, I became a fully accredited CID agent and, in November 1970, I was assigned to Fort Riley, Kansas.

I reported to Fort Riley and met the operations officer, whose name was Tom South. It was close to lunch that first day, so he invited me to go with him to the Officer's Club. We were just walking out the front door when the on-call duty agent received a phone call that a dead body had been found in a field. Because it was a major crime scene, all agents responded.

It had been a cold week and there was a little snow on the frozen ground. We arrived in the area and began a search. The body obviously had been there for a week or more. Wild animals appeared to have chewed on the body and had done a good job of disfiguring the face and hands. The body was that of a white male, but this was all we could determine. During the area search, about 100 yards away from the first body, we found another body. It appeared that the second body had also been there for about the same amount of time. This also was a white male, and the face and hands had been disfigured by animals like the first body. Identification would have been impossible based on those characteristics; a more complete investigation had to be conducted.

This investigation of the scene went on all day and the bodies eventually were taken to the morgue. It was determined that both victims had been shot and killed off-post and later dumped onto the ground of the training area on the post. A background investigation showed both victims were Army soldiers and noted to be very good pool players, or "pool hustlers." That may have been the reason they were killed because they hustled the wrong people in the nearby area of Junction City.

An autopsy is not a pleasant thing to observe, and I've watched several. The thing I remember most about these autopsies and others is the odor that emanates from the body when it is cut open. If you have been around a wet chicken that has had its feathers plucked, it smells the same way. I remember my mother boiling a chicken in hot water and plucking the feathers, and that odor is the same as in every autopsy that I have been present for.

The investigation continued for several weeks and no suspects were developed. Eventually, the jurisdiction was assumed by the FBI, because the victims were Army members and the crime was discovered on a government reservation. CID continued to assist them as a cooperating agency. To my knowledge, this crime was never solved. I still remember the names of the victims and I see clearly in my mind those bodies because this crime happened on my first day assigned as a CID agent. I remained at Fort Riley from 1970 to December 1971.

From December 1971 through fall 1972, I was reassigned to Vietnam and spent some time with the 8th MP group at Qui Nhong near the North Vietnam border. We had some great facilities and every agent even had his own Jeep. We worked a lot of black marketing and drug cases, mostly heroin, and cases where officers were killed by their own men.

After that assignment ended, I was sent back to Fort Riley. I directed the narcotics section there and worked closely with a member of the Kansas City DEA. They were building local cases through a military confidential source that I could assist with. The Kansas City Task Force agent, Park Kaestner, was aware that I was getting out of the Army soon, and he asked me if I would be interested in working with him at the KCPD Task Force.

After I was discharged, he set up an interview and I was selected. I was actually hired by the Kansas Attorney General's office. Vern Miller was the Kansas attorney general at the time. Kansas paid my salary, but the state was reimbursed by the Justice Department. I spent almost three years with the K.C. Task Force. I worked with Kaestner in Junction City on several cases because he had military confidential informants in that area. My time with the DEA task force ended in 1975, and I then learned there was an Army Reserve (493d CID) unit in Kansas City.

One of the most enjoyable assignments, while being in the Reserves, was the protective service missions. The Army CID is responsible for the security of the Secretary of Defense, the Chairman of the Joint Chiefs of Staff, and the Army Chief of Staff. These officials have the same security that the president has, except through the CID. The CID agents attend training schools conducted by the Secret Service. I was fortunate to provide security for Secretaries of Defense William Perry and Les Aspin, and retired Army General Norman Schwartzkopf.

I remember one assignment in Mexico City, protecting Secretary Perry, and at that time I had a full beard. I did not want to shave that beard off for an assignment that only lasted three or four days. But someone in the inner circle on Perry's staff had commented to Army headquarters about it, and that was my last protective mission. I think the word came down from the CID in Washington that Reserve Agents were not permitted to have full beards when they were on protective details.

Another enjoyable mission that I went on as a Reserve CID Agent was before I went to Mexico. The defense secretary of Colombia was on vacation in Miami with his family and became very ill and had to be hospitalized. At that time, a prominent drug dealer, Pablo Escobar, was highly active and the government of Colombia was worried about his safety. This duty fell to the responsibility of the CID, and I was assigned, along with Larry Overfield and one or two other agents.

We were in Miami for a week and worked every day on twelve-hour shifts. That was my first trip to Miami and the first time I had seen bikinis that barely covered anything on a woman. I thought I was in a foreign country because nobody spoke English. But, we had accommodations that were top-notch.

During my time in the 493rd CID, I advanced in grade from CWO2 to CWO4. When promoted to CWO4, LTC Shepherd was the unit commander. My grade was pinned on me by CWO4 Joe Lyles and CWO4 Bill Price, who had retired from the KCPD as a sergeant. I retired as a CWO4 in 2000, at age 60.

Kevin Eckhoff was a member of the 493rd CID Unit based at Richards-Gebaur AFB. In this photo, he is serving an extended assignment in Washington D.C. He is holding an H&K MP5 assault rifle, getting ready to protect Deputy Security of Defense Paul Wolfowitz. Photo was taken in 2001, during the President Bush administration. (Courtesy of Kevin Eckhoff)

Chapter 24

Kevin D. Eckhoff

U.S. Army Military Police, 1974-1977;
CWO3, U.S. Army CID (Army Reserve), 1986-2003

As a kid growing up, all I ever really wanted to be was a cop and join the military. In September 1974, at age 18, I got to do both. I enlisted in the U.S. Army and, after basic training at Fort Polk, Louisiana, I was sent to Fort Gordon, Georgia to attend the Military Police (MP) School.

MP school lasted for eight weeks, and then I was off to my first assignment at Fort Riley, Kansas I was assigned to the security detachment at the Army Retraining Brigade (USARB). It was there that I spent the remainder of my three-year tour. It also was in the Army that I grew up, both physically and mentally. When I enlisted, I was 5'7" tall and weighed 120 pounds. I was not the typical MP, but USARB was a minimum-security correctional facility where soldiers who had been court-martialed were given one last chance to return to active duty. It was run like basic training, including drill sergeants.

The big difference was these soldiers were still treated like prisoners, and they were under a "one-strike-and-you're-out" policy. Anyone who has been around prisoners knows that they "eat their young." I was blessed to work with a detachment of MPs that always had each other's back and we always, always worked with a partner. By the time I received my honorable discharge in 1977 I had attained the rank of sergeant and was assigned as a

Military Police Investigator. I also had grown to 6' tall and weighed 175 pounds. So, yes, I really had grown.

What was next? By the end of my three-year tour of active duty, I was pretty sure a full-time law enforcement career was not what I wanted. Through the use of my GI Bill and part-time work, I put myself through college. In 1982, I graduated from Central Missouri State University with a Bachelor of Science degree in marketing. I then attended the University of Missouri-Columbia to pursue a graduate degree in education. Unfortunately, my GI Bill ran out before I graduated.

Well, enough messing around, it was time to really get started on my career. I moved to Kansas City and found employment with a telecommunications contractor. It was here that I spent four years learning the telecommunications business from the ground floor. I then was hired by a national telecommunications company where I am still today after almost 22 years.

After a couple of years in Kansas City, I started to miss the military. As a veteran, you leave the military, but it never really leaves you. So, in 1986, I decided it was time to re-enlist. Only this time, I chose the Army Reserves, and I pretty much committed to having two careers, one civilian and one military. I also missed law enforcement, but not enough to pursue that as a civilian career.

Again, God truly blessed my life and I had the honor to be interviewed for an Army CID special agent position with the 493rd Military Police Detachment (Army Reserve). The 493rd was having a field training exercise (FTX) on the weekend I was to interview. So I, dressed in suit and tie, was interviewed by the special agents from the 493rd in a field tent, in the backwoods of Richards-Gebaur Air Force Base. It was apparent I was in the company of greatness and was being interviewed by professionals. These Army Reserve CID agents were leaders in their civilian professions: KCPD commanders, detectives, and police officers; federal investigators; future metropolitan police chiefs, as well as a variety of other law enforcement positions.

The interview went well, and I was accepted into the unit to train to become an Army CID special agent. The 493rd became my second family. While in the unit, I attended a variety of professional schools and training courses: CID Apprentice Special Agent course, Hostage Negotiations, Protective Services, Child Abuse Prevention and Investigations, and Advance Crime Scene. Over the years, the central focus of the unit was training both in investigative techniques and personal security missions. I came into the unit in 1986 as a Specialist Four (SP4). In 2003, when I retired, I was a Chief Warrant Officer Three (CWO3) and was the detachment commander. It was an amazing experience.

September 11, 2001, is a date that needs no explanation. Like most, my life and those of my family were profoundly affected by the events of the day. By that time, I had been married for 13 years to the love of my life, Karen, and we had a 9-year old daughter, Meghan. Several weeks later, 11 members of the 493rd, including me, were activated for a one-year tour and assigned to the CID's Protective Service Unit (PSU) in Washington, D.C. This unit was responsible for the personal protection for seven individuals within the Department of Defense. Our role was similar to what the Secret Service does for the president. Ninety other Army Reserve CID agents from across the country also were activated and deployed for this same mission.

It was time to leave the business world for a year and put on the Kevlar vest and sidearm. All those years of training had paid off and I was ready to hit the ground running. Upon arrival, I was assigned to the personal security detail for Deputy Secretary of Defense Paul Wolfowitz. This was the most rewarding year of my life, professionally, and the hardest year personally. Karen and Meghan are my heroes. The families of those serving make a huge sacrifice.

Rule No. 1

In motorcade operations, the vehicle directly behind the vehicle in which the protected VIP is located, usually an armored limousine, is called the chase vehicle. The chase vehicle is usually manned by two special agents, both armed. Rule No. 1 of chase operations is that no one and I mean no one, gets between the limousine and the chase vehicle. This often means running bumper to bumper with the limousine in all traffic conditions, no matter the speed. Oh, by the way, it is bad form to run into the back of the limousine.

October 27, 2001, only 10 days after arriving in D.C., started off like most days in Washington. My partner, Jim Lowrie, a Reserve CID special agent from the Philadelphia area, and I had been assigned the day-shift residence watch at the deputy secretary's house. Our shift ran from 10 a.m. to 10 p.m. Most days on residence watch, you were protecting an empty house, but nevertheless, it was an important protective services function.

About 7 p.m., we received a call from his personal security officer (PASO) that they were bringing the deputy home, so we prepared for the arrival of his two-vehicle motorcade.

At that time, the standard protocol upon arriving home was for the two agents on residence watch to assume full protective services responsibility for the deputy. The motorcade would then depart until the next day, when they would again pick him up to go to the Pentagon. Because of September 11th and the heightened security measures required, the Protective Services Unit had to supplement their vehicle pool with rental cars. Unlike their regular pool of vehicles which were all equipped with the standard police equipment, including radios, lights, sirens, etc., the rental cars were just that...standard. Residence watch had two vehicles, both standard rentals; one an SUV, the other a Toyota Corolla.

After arrival, the deputy went into the house, and the PSO approached Jim and me. He told us that the deputy was going to drive his car over to an acquaintance's apartment, and one of us needed to follow him. So Jim and I decided that Jim would remain at his post and I would perform the chase function in the Corolla and follow the deputy, who was driving his own car.

Within minutes, the deputy came out of the house and, without saying a word, jumped into his car. My vehicle was parked across the street facing north, and his car was in the driveway facing west. I was at an immediate disadvantage because I did not know where his final destination was. He backed out of the driveway and, you guessed it, headed south in a hurry. If you have ever driven in D.C., you know that the streets are laid out like a giant spider web.

Rule No. 1 of motorcade operations was immediately breached. I was forced to do a rapid U-turn while watching him make a right turn and disappear down the street. Within seconds, I was on the same street and was able to spot him about two blocks ahead of me, but he obviously was unaware of Rule No. 1. It almost seemed like he was trying to lose me.

Now was not the time to panic. It was time to focus on my mission of his protection. In D.C., many of the main residential streets are four-lane during rush hour, but street parking is allowed during night hours and weekends. This effectively turns sections of these four-lane streets into two-lane streets. Remember, I wasn't performing this chase function in an unmarked law enforcement vehicle. I was chasing him in a Toyota rental car. I was dressed in civilian clothes, with only my badge and credentials to identify myself as law enforcement. I could lose the deputy, and I certainly could not afford to be pulled over by a Metro police officer for speeding.

In motorcade operations training, they did not cover this scenario. I just keep remembering Rule No. 1 as I drove a ridiculous speed, at times over 70 mph, on a city street. I was slowly gaining on him, but still about a half-block behind. Oh, great, here comes one of those famous D.C. traffic circles. Yep, my string of not-so-good luck was continuing.

After the traffic circle, there now were two vehicles between us. Rule No. 1, Rule No. 1, I had to catch him. I only wish I knew where he was headed. My luck was changing. Ahead was a city block with no parked cars. It was time to make a move on car No. 1 and make a mad pass using the right lane as a passing lane.

The deputy's sense of urgency had not abated, so, once again, he was starting to widen the gap between the two of us. I still had one more car to pass to catch up with him. You have got to be kidding me, here comes another traffic circle. Oh, well, it is time to make my move using the traffic circle as a passing opportunity. It worked and there no longer were cars between us.

By now, the adrenaline was really pumping and I seemed to be rapidly closing the gap. Just as I closed the gap to a car length, he made a left turn. Fortunately, there was no oncoming traffic and I was able to make the left turn with him. Almost immediately, he again turned left, and we pulled into an apartment complex parking lot.

I noticed a white SUV limousine parked in the lot, with several unmarked law enforcement type vehicles behind it. What was going on here? That was not one of our limousines. While the deputy was pulling into a parking spot, I was approached by a gentleman in cowboy boots and a sports coat. I immediately recognize the Secret Service lapel button he had on. He introduced himself as the PSO for Liz Cheney, Vice President Richard Cheney's daughter.

The deputy then approached my car and apologized for the rush. It seems he was running late for dinner with Liz, her husband, and some of his friends. What started out as a routine day certainly did not end up that way. I spent the rest of the evening in a Secret Service vehicle drinking coffee with Liz's protective service detail and watching the outside of the apartment. I learned a good lesson from this experience. Most importantly, don't panic and maintain focused on the mission. The other, make sure and ask questions before the mission, even if they might sound stupid.

I still don't know what I would have done if a Metro officer had attempted to pull me over. My plan, which was not the greatest, was to hold my badge out the window of the car, keep following the deputy and hope I did not get shot. Ultimately, his security was my mission, and ultimately the mission was successful.

"Excuse Me, Mr. President!"

In April 2002, I was designated as a PSO for the deputy secretary. The PSO is directly responsible for the deputy's personal security. He rides in the right front seat of the limo, and his sole function is to shadow the deputy secretary and escort him when he is in public. This generally takes place when he is out in public and not in a secure environment. Once he is in a secure place, such as the Pentagon, Capitol or White House, the PSO drops off into the background and waits for the next movement back into the public.

It was April 19, 2002, and like every morning of duty with the deputy, it started early. Upon arrival at the Pentagon, the first order of business was to obtain the deputy's daily schedule. It was important for the security team to have a copy of his schedule so we would be aware of any movements we would be making that day outside of the Pentagon. It also allowed us to make all of the proper security arrangements for a swift and smooth movement.

Most of our day in the Pentagon was spent in our office because we did not escort the deputy while he was in the building. The Pentagon was a secure facility and there was no need for us to shadow him. As soon as I saw his schedule, I knew it was going to be a big day for me personally. The deputy was scheduled to attend a meeting of the National Security Council at the White House. That meant that, for only the second time in my life, I would be stepping into the White House.

Later that morning, we left the Pentagon on schedule and took the short 5- to 10-minute ride to the White House. Upon arrival, the limousine was allowed into the parking area between the Eisenhower Executive Office Building and the West Wing of the White House. As the PSO, I escorted the deputy into the West Wing. Once through the doors, my job effectively was over until it was time to depart.

Just inside the doors of the West Wing is a small reception area with a desk manned by a uniformed member of the Secret Service. This reception area is just outside of the Situation Room, where the National Security Council meets. The White House cafeteria also is accessed from this reception area. This reception area had several sofas and chairs, which usually were occupied by the members of the different security teams that had brought their respective boss to a meeting. Oftentimes, those security teams represented such agencies as the CIA, FBI, and State Department, as well as other members of Army CID who had escorted Secretary of Defense Rumsfeld, Chairman of the Joint Chiefs General Meyers, or Vice-Chairman General Pace.

This reception area was a great place to people-watch because of its proximity to both the Situation Room and cafeteria. Anyone who was headed for either of these locations had to come through the reception area first. That was what made this day special for me. I knew that President George W. Bush was going to have to come through this small area to lead the meeting of the National Security Council. I was finally going to get to see the president up close. For some people, this may not be a big deal. For me, it was huge! As a member of the military, he was my commander-in-chief.

Within minutes of our arrival, the Secret Service officer gave those of us in the room the word that the president was on his way down. We all stood up in preparation. I happened to be standing at the corner of two hallways; one was rather short and headed to the north, the other was long and headed east into the White House. Since this was only my second time there, I anticipated him coming down the long hallway from the White House, so that is where I focused my attention. Suddenly, everyone stiffened, and it got very quiet. I then turned to the right a little more, and the president was standing right beside me, within inches.

Not only that, Vice President Cheney was right behind him. They had entered from the short north hallway and then moved on into the Situation Room. What I remember most about that moment was the president's demeanor and confidence. His posture was straight and he stood tall. Not in an arrogant way, but in a way that communicated his position as the leader of the free world. Thank goodness I did not turn too rapidly, or I would have bumped right into him. That would have not been good. One of two things then might have happened: either I would have been apologizing profusely, or trying to understand why there were three Secret Service agents on top of me with handcuffs.

The morning only got better. While waiting in the reception area for the meeting to be over, a young Navy sailor, his wife and two small children came and sat down in the reception area. The sailor was a steward (cook) in the White House cafeteria and was going to re-enlist in the White House with his family present. The sailor stepped away to visit with some friends, and his wife took the youngest to the restroom. That left their oldest son, probably 10 years old, setting on the sofa next to me while his parents were away.

While sitting there, I noticed he had a cast on his arm. Suddenly, the door to the Situation Room opened, and President Bush walked out by himself. The first thing the president noticed was the young boy on the sofa. He immediately walked to the boy and said, "Who is this young man?" He then engaged in a conversation with the boy and asked if it would be all right if he signed his cast.

What an amazing thing to witness! There were no cameras present and no media. This was not a staged event. He could have just as easily walked by and gone about his day. But no, he took the time to engage an obviously stunned young boy in conversation. I'm sure it is a day the boy will always remember. I know I will because I witnessed an act by a president that showed he really cared. It is too bad that the parents were both away and missed the entire event. It still seems surreal to me.

Seven months earlier, I was in an office working at my civilian job. Now I was standing next to the president in the White House, and I had a front row seat on history. As I said earlier, this year on active duty was the most professionally rewarding experience in my life. Nothing else will ever compare. Because of my position, I had the opportunity to go places and see people that most only see on TV. I stood next to presidents and other world leaders. I knew the deputy secretary of defense on a first-name basis. I called him "Sir" and he called me Kevin.

On my last official day of duty before returning home, his staff scheduled an office call for me with the deputy. At the appointed time, I arrived in his office. His secretary then placed a call to Karen at her workplace. The deputy got on one phone and asked me to get on another extension in his office. He thanked Karen and Meghan for their sacrifice by allowing me to serve him. It was very moving.

Several weeks later, we received an 8x10 photo that was autographed with a message for Karen and Meghan. I have nothing but the utmost respect for the former deputy secretary and the former president. I witnessed first-hand true professionalism and dedication. I also am truly blessed having Karen and Meghan as a part of my life. They stood by me and made a personal sacrifice that few understand. Finally and most importantly, I am blessed by a Savior who willingly died for me and protected me while I served.

Police Officer Joe McCune is training his K-9 dog, Ranger, at the K-9 Unit on Ozark Road in Kansas City. Photo taken sometime in 1984. (Courtesy of the KCPD)

Chapter 25

Joseph R. McCune

Retired Detective, KCPD, 1966-1992

Trust Your Dog (Partner)

It was around 1985, that I was working as a K-9 officer with my canine partner, Ranger. I was on routine patrol when we received a call from a district officer to meet him at a business in the downtown area of Kansas City. The patrol officer needed a K-9 crew to search a building downtown where they had received an alarm and had found an open window in the back of the building.

Ranger and I responded to the scene and entered through the back window. I soon found out that this building was a fur cleaning company. As was the practice, I yelled out for anyone to "Come out, or I would release the dog." After getting no response, I released Ranger from his leash and he immediately went over to a pile of furs on the floor. I worried Ranger was going to pee on the furs. I called him off and we went to the second floor of the building to work our way down.

After finding nothing on the second floor, we went back to the first floor and Ranger again went to the stack of furs and pushed his nose under the furs, then clamped his teeth onto the arm of the burglar who was hiding under the furs and pulled him out. During training with a new dog, the instructor always tells you to trust your dog. This was a case where Ranger had this suspect within 15 seconds, and I pulled him away thinking he was going to do something other than find the suspect. This goes back to what the instructor meant when he said, "Trust your dog."

Police Officer Balfour Rast. Academy photo 1975
(Courtesy of the KCPD)

Chapter 26

Balfour J. Rast

Retired Detective, KCPD, 1973-1998

I was born in 1951, at St. Joseph Hospital, located at that time at Linwood and Prospect in Kansas City. I attended St. Stephen's Elementary School, then Palmer Junior High and Truman High School, all in Independence. I also attended college, but did not earn a degree.

I joined the U.S. Army in 1969, and served at various locations, including Vietnam. I really wanted to become a warrant officer and fly helicopters while I was in Vietnam, but the Army was heavy with pilots; I could not get this position.

Instead, after discharge from the Army, I hired on as a clerk/typist with the KCPD on April 5, 1972. I applied for law enforcement positions every time I got a chance, but was continually turned down. My persistence paid off, and I was accepted into the police academy on January 3, 1975. Once the department found out how hard I worked, I never had a problem going anywhere I wanted on the job.

I had numerous positions on the job that included Patrol, Evidence Technician, Arson Bomb Unit, and even the Helicopter Unit that I had always wanted.

I married my current wife, Jeane Fracassa, in 1982. She was 21 years old and I was 31 when we were married. She is the daughter of Alfred R. Fracassa, who retired from the KCPD as a sergeant. At the time of his retirement, Al was working at the North Patrol Police

Station. He had a total of thirty years service on the department. My wife, Jeane, has now worked for the KCPD for thirty years, as well. She is the operations supervisor of the Communications Unit. We have one son, Alex, who is now 22 and going to college, with aspirations of working in the KCPD someday. I retired on Dec. 18, 1998, after 25 years of service.

Ruby's Soul Food Restaurant

Even after 35 years, I remember the armed robbery at Ruby's Soul Food Restaurant like it happened yesterday. On October 2, 1976, the call came out at about 5 a.m. Ron Rivera, a North Kansas City police officer at the time, was riding with me. He rode as a Ride-A-Long from time to time. He wanted to be a Kansas City officer and enjoyed the activities we saw, opposed to what he experienced in North Town.

We were sitting in a parking lot in the River Quay with Sergeant Charlie Boone. Charlie was reviewing a report of mine, as I recall. A call came over the radio of an armed robbery in progress at Ruby's, located at Truman and Brooklyn.

Ruby's Soul Food Restaurant was a place well known to KCPD officers, especially those in the Central Patrol Division. Ruby McIntyre, the owner, loved police officers, and loved having us around her café. We were good for business. The officers would come in to eat and sort of hold community meetings at the same time. Ruby was especially kind to the police, too. A plate of food was a sight to see. I was just a skinny kid at that time and, when I went to eat at Ruby's, she always filled my plate more than other officers because she thought I needed to put on some weight!

It took Sergeant Boone and me about three minutes to get from the River Quay to Ruby's, and we weren't the only officers responding. By the time I arrived, there already were about five or six other cars there. We could see through the window that the suspects had several patrons still in the restaurant. There were three suspects and they were all armed. If we entered the restaurant, we would have put a lot of people at risk if a gun battle ensued. Because we didn't want to have the patrons caught in crossfire, we took up positions outside to make arrests when the suspects left the business.

Sergeant Bob Arnold was the supervisor at the scene. He decided that he would try to coax the suspects out of the building because they were as much as captured. He pulled his patrol car to the front of the business and pointed it at the building. He turned on his car PA system and announced our presence and told the suspects to come out of the business, unarmed. The suspects had a better idea. One of them immediately closed the curtains to the front window. Then they moved to the back door of the business in an attempt to escape in that direction and out into the adjacent alley.

The patrons and Ruby decided this was the time to make their move and they all ran out the front door. Everyone got out except one elderly gentleman. Ruby broke her leg in the rush to escape. As the suspects reached the back door and started to exit, Officer Bill Munden saw one of them sticking his head out. Munden yelled to him that "You better go on out the front with your friends."

The suspect slammed the door and locked it. Several minutes passed with no activity. Sergeant Arnold called for an Operation 100, a term we used for barricaded suspects, with or without hostages, and we all settled in for the long haul. However, within a few minutes, all three suspects emerged from the front door of the business, with the old man as a hostage and shield. Sergeant Arnold was yelling at them to put their weapons down, and they were yelling the same back at us. They continued to move southbound along the sidewalk, the three of them holding the old man in front of them as a shield.

As the four reached the alley, another officer, who was originally in the rear of the business, pointed his service weapon at one of the suspects and pushed the suspect's weapon away. He told the suspect to drop his gun. Then the suspect did exactly the same thing to the officer and ordered the officer to drop his gun. They each did that about three times. The suspects turned and continued backing south along the sidewalk. I'm not sure what happened at that point, but the suspect who had his arm around the hostage's neck had suddenly raised his weapon and fired.

As the hostage fell to the ground, I took the safety off my shotgun and fired at the suspects huddled behind the hostage. Other officers also fired, and the suspects were immobilized. We separated the suspects from their weapons and took them into custody. I remember, as I was firing, I had already heard about three blasts from shotguns near me. I thought someone had shot the hostage, and that's what caused him to fall. I was pretty scared until I found out that the hostage had actually tripped on the curb and fell as the suspect holding him, began shooting.

About that same time, someone yelled that there were still suspects inside the business. Three or four of us started moving in toward the restaurant when another officer called out that the scene was clear. Two suspects were killed in the exchange of gunfire, and the third was wounded. I learned the third suspect lost a leg as a result of his wounds.

It's customary that officers involved in shootings are suspended pending the outcome of the investigation. Typically, in police-involved shootings, those suspensions last for at least a few days. After we spent hours writing reports and giving statements, we all were back to work the next night.

Attempted Rape-in-Progress

Another memorable occasion occurred in the late-night hours as I was patrolling the southern portion of the Central Patrol Division. I was driving north on Broadway, conducting building checks and looking for trouble to get into. I spotted what appeared to be a homeless man on the northwest corner of 39th & Broadway. He was shabbily dressed and unshaven, waving his arms trying to get my attention. I remember thinking, 'This is great, I'm going to spend the next hour dealing with this guy and have to transport him to the Helping Hand or Rescue Mission.' But I didn't want to ignore him in case something was going on that he wanted to tell me about.

As I exited my patrol car and approached the gentleman, I became a little nervous because he kept trying to get behind me. At first, I thought this was going to turn into a fight. I asked him what he needed, but he only made a grunting noise. I finally figured out that the man wasn't deaf and mute, but was trying to draw my attention to the Laundromat on the corner of 39th and Washington.

I glanced inside the Laundromat, but did not see anything. I kept trying to figure out what he wanted when we walked to the west side of the building. I looked through the window and saw a white female lying on the floor between several washing machines. A white male was standing over her, pulling the shorts she was wearing down to her ankles. It was obvious that this was not consensual and the female was very distraught.

I drew my service revolver and attempted to open the front door and quietly move to the suspect and take him into custody. To my surprise, a bell was attached to the door. The suspect jumped up and, while pulling up his pants, began to run for the rear door on the north side of the building. I identified myself and ordered him to stop. He complied. After taking the suspect into custody, my adrenaline was flowing pretty well.

Until that night, I had been assigned to 10-Sector, riding patrol in district 112, which was also my radio number. That night, I had just started working relief and was riding patrol district 132. I began calling for an assisting car. I kept using 112 as my radio number. The dispatcher on duty was a friend, and she kept answering me as 132. It took a couple exchanges like that before I realized she was actually answering me.

That's how it is in law enforcement: a few seconds of unbelievable exhilaration, followed by hours of monotony.

Helicopter Unit

From the time I started on the police department, my one dream was to someday make it to the Helicopter Unit. I fell in love with aviation during my stint in Vietnam. I would volunteer for field assignments just to get to ride in a helicopter. When I flew as a scout observer in Vietnam, the pilots would teach us to fly. It was only the pilot and the observer in the light observation helicopter and, if the pilot got injured, it would be up to the observer to get the ship back on the ground. I never lost the urge to one day be a pilot.

In 1989, I finally made it. It took about two years for me to begin my flight training, but it was worth it. We had a great section: John Young, Jerry Cox, Dave Reynolds, and me. Dave and

I were the newbie's and both got our pilot's licenses about the same time. John was an ex-Army Vietnam helicopter pilot, and Jerry learned how to fly on the department the same as Dave and me. John Young eventually moved on and Jerry Cox retired. John was replaced by Jack Shepley and Steve Faulkner came in to replace Jerry.

Jack was promoted to sergeant while working at the unit and was transferred back to the field when he was promoted. He was gone for a couple years and then returned as a sergeant. Steve was a K-9 handler before coming to the unit. We were a lot like combat pilots at the Helicopter Unit. It was still just the pilot and the observer in the police helicopter, so observers still got to do some flying so they could handle the ship if something happened to the pilot. Steve had put in his time as an observer and was coming to the time when he would start working on his license.

Helicopter Crash

It was the evening of December 1, 1992. I had conducted the helicopter preflight that night and already had flown my time for the evening. Steve Faulkner was my observer, so we were pretty much finished for the night. When it came time for the next flight, Dave Reynolds had a field officer who came out to ride along. We often took officers with us who wanted to learn the job and who aspired to an assignment in the unit. Reynolds was only in the air about 20 minutes—a short time—when his ride-a-long became airsick. Dave returned to the unit and because there was still time remaining for our flight requirements, Jack Shepley took over as pilot and Steve jumped in as the observer. They hadn't been up 20 minutes when a call came out that they were "going down" at 23rd and Topping. Everybody knew what that meant. They had some type of power failure and were not able to remain airborne. That also meant they had no power to put the ship anywhere they would have preferred to land.

Auto-rotation is the term applied to the emergency procedure for flying a helicopter when it loses power. The process is to disengage the rotor system from the drive train. Air moving through the rotor blades keeps them turning and you start looking for a suitable area to set the craft down. You don't have a lot of lift, but you still have some control over airspeed and maneuverability. Steve was running the searchlight, giving Jack some degree of visibility, and managing the radio while Jack maneuvered the ship.

The type of aircraft that we flew then was a model C, Schweizer 300. We used to fly the B model, and it used to be the Hughes 269, but the Schweizer Corp. bought the patent and it became the Schweizer 269, later named the 300. It has a longer stabilizer with the flat bottom. Without power, they fly like a rock. They have a steep angle of descent, and you don't get a lot of choice about where you can go. Put that together with the low altitudes we flew, and you don't get a lot of time to make a decision. From all appearances, Jack was shooting for an apartment complex parking lot. Unfortunately, they didn't have the altitude to make it that far. There was a wooded area just east of the apartments. Jack made his approach to the tops of the trees, but as he flared to settle through the trees, it turned out he was too high and with a 300, you only get one shot.

That night we lost two good officers. Both had families and both were devoted to them. Steve was really excited about beginning his flight training, and we were proud to have them as partners. That was the tragedy that sometimes comes with the job. There were so many other times when things were a lot better. Times when heavy rain caused flooding and we lifted people from the tops of their cars that were washed into a swollen creek; the foot chases and car chases that almost always resulted in apprehensions; and the bad guys we caught using the infrared camera. Those were the times that made the job worth all the bad that might come.

Balfour Rast is displaying the Model C, Schweizer 300 helicopter, also known as the 269C. The photo was taken at the Kansas City Air Show around 1992, at the Charles B. Wheeler Airport. This is the same type of helicopter that claimed the lives of Sergeant Jack Shepley and Officer Steve Faulkner on December 1, 1992. (Courtesy of the KCPD)

Police Sergeant Alfred Fracassa, his daughter, Jeane Rast, and Police Officer Balfour Rast. Sergeant Fracassa retired in 1992, with thirty years of service. Balfour Rast retired as a detective in 1998. Jeane Rast is still employed as the civilian operations supervisor in the Communications Unit of the KCPD (Courtesy of Olan Mills Studio)

This photo is of Captain Glenn Cherry, standing by a KCPD police vehicle. Photo taken in 1995, the same year he retired after 30 years of service.
(Courtesy of the KCPD)

Chapter 27

Glenn E. Cherry

**Retired Captain, KCPD, 1965–1995;
Civil Investigator, Environmental Protection Agency, 1997–Present**

I was born and raised in Kent County, Texas. I attended a two-room country school, with one outhouse for boys and another for girls. The school was closed after the 1945–46 school year. I attended high school in Spur, Texas, and graduated in 1950, at the age of 16.

I enlisted in the U.S. Marine Corps in 1951, at age of 17, and served two combat tours aboard the USS St. Paul off the coast of Korea. I was honorably discharged in 1954, at age 20.

On November 1, 1954, I became a police officer in Lubbock, Texas. I resigned from the Lubbock Police Department in June of 1965, and moved to Kansas City. On July 16, 1965, I was sworn in as a probationary police officer on the KCPD. On February 1, 1971, I was transferred to the Vice Unit as a detective, and on May 23, 1971, I was transferred to the Crimes against Persons Division (Homicide Unit). About a month later, CA Persons was reorganized, and a Rape Squad was organized under the supervision of Detective Sergeant Lloyd DeGraffenreid. Four detectives were assigned to this new unit: Charles Gunlock, Barney Gowin, Tom Sooter, and me.

Mack the Knife

A short time later, we recognized that a serial rapist was operating in the mid-city area. Part of his modus operandi (MO) never changed. He was a black male with a medium Afro hair style. He always used a knife to subdue the women, forced them to strip completely naked, covered their face with their clothing while he raped them, and then took their clothing with him when he left. As a result, women would always delay calling the police, while looking for something to cover up with before screaming for help.

Several times, we thought that we were making headway in finding "Mack the Knife," only to find that he had changed areas and the times that he would commit the rapes. At one time, he was abducting young women from mid-city apartment complex swimming pools during the daytime. As this pattern was identified, we started contacting apartment managers and warning them of the danger. During one visit, an apartment manager asked to see my credentials, and when I held them up, she grabbed them and refused to return them. It took about 30 minutes to get the credentials back.

In 1960, the No. 1 song in America was "Mack the Knife," sung by Bobby Darin. This song was taken from the "Three Penny Opera" which was popular during the 18th century. Ironically, the song was about a man who always used a knife, and his crimes included rape. We started calling the serial rapist "Mack the Knife," but we didn't know about the history of the song at that time.

Another time, "Mack the Knife" was committing rapes at night in the vicinity of the Nelson Art Gallery, located at 4525 Oak Street. A female officer from the youth unit was assigned to work as a decoy (at that time, females were assigned only to the youth unit and did not work in the field except on special assignment). The Rape Squad, along with one squad of tactical officers, was assigned to work in casual clothing, while uniformed tactical officers patrolled the area.

We did not have the miniaturized technology then that we have today. The female officer had a microphone under her clothing, but the receiver was about the size of a large dictionary. This was the era of the "love children," and I wrapped an old quilt around the receiver and made it look like a bedroll. That fit in perfectly with the area where we were working.

As the female officer moved around the Nelson Art Gallery area, she was approached several times by males who would attempt to "hit on her." None of these attempts turned out to be "Mack the Knife," but as she went from the east side to the south side one night, a black male ran after her but lost her in the darkness. During the week that the first female officer worked with us, we were unable to attract the serial rapist.

Another female officer volunteered to take on the decoy role. She appeared to enjoy the assignment and provided me a running commentary about the males who approached her. One night the undercover female officer was sitting on the steps on the east side of the Nelson Art Gallery building when a black male approached her. They talked for several minutes, and the black male embraced her and kissed her, but went no further. The female officer asked the black male to accompany her through the dark trees to the south side of the building. Once again, he failed to take the opportunity that had been provided for him.

The undercover female officer took the black male through the dark trees two more times before we sent an undercover male officer, under a pretext, to get the female officer away from the black male without tipping him off. As the black male left the area, he was allowed to drive several blocks and was stopped by uniformed tactical unit officers. During this stop, it was found that the black male had been convicted of rape, but there were no current wants or warrants on him.

After we secured the scene that night, we returned to the second floor of police headquarters for a critique of the night's actions. We had to release this suspect because we didn't have enough probable cause to file charges on him. It also was evident that he was not the serial rape suspect that we were looking for.

"Mack the Knife" changed the locations and times of his rapes once again, so we discontinued concentrating in the area of the Nelson Art Gallery.

One day the police dispatcher asked if anyone was in the area of 36th and Southwest Traffic way. We were informed over the air that a janitor in an apartment building had reported seeing a suspicious black male following a young female tenant into a building. The black male was observed to have grabbed the young woman with a knife to her throat, and had taken her to one of the carports at the back of the property.

With this information, several officers started toward the location of the apartments. Before anyone arrived at the scene, the black male had stripped the clothing from the young woman, covered her face and raped her. Once again, he took the young woman's clothes with him.

One tactical unit pulled behind a small store on the corner, and the officers got out of their car. Just as they did, "Mack the Knife" climbed a wooden privacy fence that separated the apartment complex parking lot from the rear lot of the store. For a moment, "Mack the Knife" was perched on top of the fence with the knife in one hand and the woman's clothes in the other, making a perfect target. There was absolutely no doubt that this was the suspect that we had named "Mack the Knife."

A tactical officer fired several shots at him but missed. "Mack the Knife" jumped back into the apartment parking lot and started running back toward Southwest Traffic way, but ran straight into the arms of two uniformed officers. "Mack the Knife" was taken to headquarters where he was booked for rape. During the booking, he identified himself as Gordon Ellis McRoy. He gave his age as 30, and gave a home address of Leavenworth, Kansas.

During interrogation, "Mack the Knife" never confessed to any of the rapes, but we believed that we could make cases on most of them. We had outstanding descriptions from the women, including one who was a student at the Kansas City Art Institute. This young woman had been in bed at home when "Mack the Knife" broke in and raped her. She drew a picture of her rapist, and when we compared his mug shot to the picture that she drew, there was absolutely no doubt that it was him.

But when we called the victims in for a line-up, only two women identified him: the woman he had raped when he was caught and a black woman. The woman who had drawn such a good picture of "Mack the Knife" could not identify him, but his fingerprints were identified at the scene of the rape. The reason that some of the women couldn't identify him in the lineup was that the suspect had been described by the women as having a full head of hair because he wore a stocking cap that covered his head. When his stocking cap was removed, he had a "chrome dome," and once the women saw his bald head, they immediately discounted him.

After the arrest of "Mack the Knife," we found that he had been living in the mid-city area with a young white woman from Gladstone, MO. Detective Gunlock and I interviewed the young woman and asked her how a Northland white woman had gotten together with a mid-city rapist. She said she was returning home to her mid-city apartment and, when she got out of her car, she scared "Mack the Knife." Detective Gunlock asked her what she meant. She stated that she had gotten out of her car and "everything was right with the world."

We took this to mean that she was high on drugs. She stated that she was just standing there enjoying the night when she saw "Mack the Knife" standing at the rear of the car. He immediately jumped back and crouched down, but she told him to come out and talk to her. Gunlock and I believed that he had intended to rape her, but she invited him into her apartment, instead. "Mack the Knife" was still living with her at the time of his arrest. There were many similarities between "Mack the Knife" and the more recent Waldo-area rapist. Both were living with one white woman while they raped other white women.

After the arrest, line-up, and interrogation, Gunlock and I were assigned to take "Mack the Knife" for arraignment at the Jackson County Courthouse. As we left headquarters, a photographer from the Kansas City Star took our picture and used it with an article describing the arrest. Gordon Ellis McRoy, aka "Mack the Knife," was tried, convicted, and sentenced to prison where he committed suicide. I can only wonder if he had become a rape victim in prison and couldn't handle what he had been handing out to those young women.

Police Officer Earle Hammond retired with the Kansas City, MO Police Department in 1994. He is now a fishing guide at Lake Pomme de Terre in the Missouri Ozarks. He is pictured holding a nice forty-four inch Muskie in 2009. Contact Hammond for great Muskie fishing at ehammond@positech.net. (Courtesy of Earle Hammond)

Chapter 28

Earle C. Hammond

Retired Police Officer, KCPD, 1965-1994
(K-9 Officer for 20 years)

I was born in Chicago in 1942. When I was in the fourth grade, my parents moved from Chicago, population four million, to Phillipsburg, MO with a population of 96. What a culture shock, but very enjoyable. Actually, we moved to a log cabin on Route 66. It was the best move that my parents ever made. I graduated from Strafford High School which was, at that time, nine miles east of Springfield. Today, the two cities share the same boundary line.

After learning I was too smart for college, I entered the Navy for a two-year period. Upon getting out of the Navy, I got a job at Royal McBee in Springfield. My Dad wanted me to go into business with him and signed me up for barber school in Kansas City. I quit my job in Springfield and headed to Kansas City, where I shared an apartment with two high school buddies. I worked part-time while waiting for barber school to open.

While waiting, I decided being a barber was not for me and started looking at other jobs. I saw an ad in the Kansas City Star that advertised the need for police officers. One of my buddies bet me $10 that I couldn't get on. Best bet I ever made. I used to read the police reports in the Springfield paper, and there were not many police calls each day. Turned out, I usually made more calls myself in an eight-hour shift than the entire police department in Springfield made all day.

I did go back to college while working on the police department and earned an associate's degree. Later, I obtained a bachelor's degree.

Since I retired from the department, my wife and I moved to Lake Pomme de Terre. Here I have the hardest job of all: a Muskie fishing guide on the lake, and I love every minute of it.

My K-9 Partner (Duke)

I was in the K-9 Unit for 20 years and had five different dogs while there. I considered all of them my partners. The dog's names were Bruce, Spook, Simba, Duke, and Champ. When my third dog went down, we looked around for a replacement and could not find one in the area. It was like someone was looking over us, because the Tulsa, Oklahoma Police Department called and said that one of their handlers had been promoted to sergeant and that they would rather let another police department have the dog than give the dog to the prison at McAlester, Oklahoma.

The decision was made for K-9 Officer Jim Martin and me to go to Tulsa to get the dog. We started off with just a muzzle to put on the dog for transportation back to Kansas City. We took my marked police car and decided to stop in Joplin to get something to drink. I checked the oil and found it to be three quarts low. The oil was checked before we left Kansas City; I guess the vehicle was not used to being driven at higher speeds for extended distances. We filled the oil back up, and the vehicle did not use another drop for the rest of the trip.

We made it to Tulsa, contacted their K-9 Unit, and met with the former handler. He showed us the dog, a big German shepherd named Duke. As a K-9 officer, I talked to a lot of people about dogs, and the main thing I noticed was that everyone had a dog that weighed 100 pounds. When you actually see their dog, it would be lucky to weigh 50 pounds soaking wet!

Well, Duke weighed 120 pounds and was a really bad son of a gun. He didn't like anyone. The handler put the muzzle on Duke for us and wrapped the lead leash around the back part of the rear window and shut the door. In a two-block drive Duke managed to get out of the muzzle and was trying to get to Jimmy. I swear

Jimmy's face is probably still imprinted on the dash of that car! We turned around and went back to the Tulsa K-9 Unit and had the former handler take Duke out of the car.

We then went to the Tulsa police garage where they installed a prisoner transfer cage in the back seat. We then had the former handler put Duke back in the car and we were off to Kansas City. Duke just laid there in the back seat after a while, and we could hear him almost all the way back, growling with a low quiet rumble in his throat. I later would learn that you don't mess around with Duke when he does that low rumble. It was apparent he was a mean dog.

Duke would take a 14-inch tire as his toy and flip it over his head, he was that strong. Gun fire would turn him on, but thunder and lightning made him want to crawl into the front seat and help me drive. I learned that during a storm I would have to tie him to the window to keep him in the back.

Upon arriving back in Kansas City, we pulled up to the K-9 unit and had to figure out a way to get Duke out of the car without getting bitten. We finally figured out a way and got him out of the car. We also put a sign on the front of the kennel for no one to agitate Duke.

I was the only one to do anything for him. For two nights, I went out to the kennel and sat and talked to him. When he put his body next to the kennel door, I would pet him only to be greeted with a show of teeth. I continued this method until he stopped growling and showing his teeth at me.

On the third day, after talking and petting him I decided it was time to get him out of the kennel and take him for a walk. It was a harrowing experience to go in there with that big dog, but it needed to be done. I took my lead, opened the kennel door and went in. To my surprise he came right over and I attached the lead. I opened the kennel door, and out we went. Duke started to pull me after him, but I guess it was just my training that made me jerk his neck with the choke chain to get him to heel and not lead. Duke turned around and looked at me kind of like, "do I take him now or not?"

I thought I had it made now, but putting him in a car was another matter. I did this by tying him to the rear passenger window and then getting into the driver's seat. Duke was going crazy growling at me. I would just tell him it was OK and talk to him a little longer. I would take him out of the car and just walk around for a few minutes, and then back in the car we would go. Each time, I would let the lead out a little further until he was right by me.

I then put him in the car on the driver's side and we went for a drive. I stopped every now and then to get out, walk around the car, and then get back in, to train him to this procedure. He finally accepted the way I was training him.

Without thinking, I reached into the back seat area from the driver's seat, to roll down the rear window so he could stick his head out and get some air. When I did this, I felt his mouth around my left elbow, but he did not put any pressure on my elbow with his mouth. I pretended it was nothing and rolled down the window, telling him it was OK. I then went about a block and rolled the window up and kept repeating this routine over and over until he paid no attention to me rolling the window up and down.

We started doing a little aggression with him while on lead. The guys who were wearing the big padded bite sleeve would really complain when Duke bit it. The dog really had tremendous pressure when he bit something. It was a good experience and I learned a lot training Duke, which helped make me a better K-9 officer.

Burglary Suspect

One arrest we made was that of a burglary suspect. Duke and I were dispatched to 18th and Woodland on a possible prowler on the inside. Upon gaining entry into the building with the aid of the owner, Duke and I proceeded to search the building. Once inside, Duke started with his low bear growl in the area of the loading dock. These docks were built up so flatbed trucks could just back down and be loaded from the sides. There was nothing in one of them, and Duke was standing over the end of another one looking down, I then notice a huge man down there and told him to come out several times. He refused, so I called Duke and had him jump down to the dock floor on the same level where the suspect was.

Duke immediately went to the suspect, a 275-pound man, grabbed him by the leg, and pulled him to me. The suspect kept kicking toward Duke, and I told him to lay still and I would take the dog off him. The suspect complied for awhile and then he kicked at Duke again, missing his head by an inch. Duke didn't miss with his second bite. I handcuffed the suspect and then called district officers to come in and take custody of the suspect.

We took the suspect to General Hospital for treatment of dog bites, before taking him to the jail for booking. At General Hospital, he refused treatment. We then took him to jail, and while booking him, one of the jailers was fingerprinting him when all of a sudden he jumped back and said, "What the hell is this?" Out of the nose of the suspect came this bubble which finally broke off and started floating in the air. It eventually fell to the floor and broke; I had never seen anything like that before nor since.

A few days later, I had to go to the preliminary hearing. A bunch of other prisoners were all handcuffed together, sitting on the back row. And then who comes in but my guy on crutches. On the stand, his lawyer asked me several times how many times my dog bit the suspect, and I kept answering twice. His lawyer then asked why he wasn't treated at General Hospital, and I told him that the suspect refused treatment. I could hear all of the other prisoners talking, saying what a dumb son-of-a-bitch that the suspect was for refusing treatment. Duke turned out to be an excellent partner for me, and I was really proud of the way he turned out after I trained him.

My K-9 Partner (Simba)

The second dog assigned to me as my partner was Simba. He was a great dog, weighing only about 75 pounds. He was everything you would want in a police K-9. I will never forget one of the calls that Simba and I experienced.

One early morning in April, 1975 at around 3 a.m., I was at the Pioneer Grill restaurant located at 12th & Baltimore having coffee with my sergeant, Richard Steffen. While inside, a bank holdup alarm went off at the bank at 10th and Baltimore.

We both volunteered for the call, along with the district officers. I told the sergeant that I would go down Baltimore, and he said he would go down Main and come up that way. When I got to the corner of 10th and Baltimore, I observed glass flying out of the window of the bank. A black male with a revolver then jumped out of the window and ran westbound up the alley toward the old Channel 9 building. I pulled into the alley and was pursuing him with my police car. The suspect ran about 200 feet and then turned around and started to raise the gun in my direction. I made up my mind if the gun came up another inch, I was going to scare the hell out of him with my left-handed shooting and then hit him with my car.

It is amazing how fast you can make this type of decision. He must have read my mind because he dropped the gun and took off running again. I could see he was tiring, and then I got out of the car and chased him on foot and caught him. He started to fight, so I hit him once and he started screaming, I didn't think I hit him that hard and I looked down. Simba was helping me by biting him on the ankle, calf, and leg until the suspect quit resisting and was placed under arrest. In the meantime, my sergeant had gotten involved with the second suspect, who ran eastbound on 10th Street, and then started to have a shootout with the police.

Upon talking to the guard at the bank, he told me that the one I had captured forced him into the bank lobby and made him show him the vault. The guard said the suspect then put his ear to the door and worked the combination, trying to gain access to the vault. The guard said, "The suspect watched too much TV." My suspect was arrested, but the other suspect had been shot by the police in a shoot-out and later died. The shoot-out took place on 10th Street between Main and Walnut.

Prowler on the Inside

On another occasion, I was dispatched to Elliot Arms in the 1500 block of Grand because of prowlers on the inside. Jimmy Martin responded to assist Simba and me with the building search. After searching for a while, Simba located the suspect hiding under some cardboard on the second floor. A few days later, I had to go to the preliminary hearing. Our case was the last one, and before hearing the case, the judge took a brief recess.

While sitting there waiting for the judge to return, the defendant said, "You guys don't have to stay, I am going to plead guilty anyway." We told him we had to stay anyway, but thanked him for the offer.

When Judge Hughes came back, I got up and testified about what had happened. The defendant then got up on the stand and pleaded not guilty. When Judge Hughes asked him why he was arrested, the defendant told him that Jimmy and I saw him walking down the street, threw him through the front window of the store and told him to hide from the dog. Judge Hughes evidently did not believe the defendant's story and bound him over for trial.

K-9 Demonstration

Officer Curtis Welch and I were assigned to give a K-9 demonstration at a school for little kids. While we were performing the demonstration, Curtis was using his dog, named Tip, and I was on the business end of the attack, using a bite sleeve on my arm. Curtis was doing the basic obedience stuff that Tip had been taught. Curtis moved away from Tip and gave the command to sit; Tip at this time proceeded to take a dump. Curtis, not being shook-up at all, shouted out very loud to Tip, "No, I said SIT," which got a big laugh from everyone!

Sergeant Dwight Rhodes retired from the KCPD in 2008, and is still active in the police reserves. In this photo, he is playing Taps at a police function. He is also very active in performing in orchestras. (Courtesy of the KCPD)

Chapter 29

Dwight L. Rhodes

Retired Sergeant, KCPD, 1978-2008

Disturbance: Party Armed With a Chainsaw

I think about the real "victims" in my shooting, and they are the spouses, children and other family members of the person who was killed. Over the years, I have heard indirectly from and about them, and, as far as I can tell, they are okay, but I don't want them to be re-victimized by having someone read a detailed account of the incident and point it out to them. This would intrude upon their lives, and it may be that one or more of them are still having difficulty with the situation. So, I won't refer to an address, date, or other identifying details. But if they themselves happen to be interested in police incidents, I think my thoughts and feelings will be of benefit to them and hopefully to others who are in similar circumstances.

At about 2 a.m. one night, the dispatcher put out a call: "Disturbance, party armed with a chainsaw." I was only a few blocks away when the call came out, but my backup was a long distance across town. As I got within a couple of blocks of the call's address, I turned off my lights and lowered my windows so I could hear if anything was happening. I approached the address of the call from around the corner, which is usually a good place to wait while not alerting people to my presence. I heard no signs of a disturbance or of a chainsaw.

A couple of empty lots were at the end of the block, so I stopped near the last house on the left side of the street. The empty lots were about four feet above street level, but over the embankment to my left I could see the back of the houses on the street where the call was located. I shut off the engine as I parked so I could hear better, and then I discovered that, because the corner lots were empty, I was actually within sight of the address of the call. A person was standing on the front porch holding something vertically that looked like a rifle or shotgun. A few seconds later, I was able to confirm that it was a shotgun because the person fired it. I notified the dispatcher that I had a shot fired at the scene of the call, but the suspect had not seen me yet and was just firing into the air. The dispatcher "held the air" as usual in such situations, and I started figuring out what to do.

It was apparent that if the suspect happened to look to his right and behind him in my direction he would see the top half of my vehicle with me inside. I didn't want to start the engine and draw his attention, so I quietly opened the door and got out, using the embankment as cover. A slight mist was falling. I saw him go inside the house, so I took that opportunity to get behind a large tree in the center of the vacant corner lot. This got me a little closer to the suspect's house, while maintaining a safe distance and good cover.

The suspect then came back out on the front porch, this time without the shotgun. I heard him yell as if to someone across the street; "Go ahead and call the police!" At this point, I figured that when my backup got there, I could probably take verbal command of the suspect and hopefully prevent him from going inside the house and creating a barricaded situation. But my backup was still several blocks away, and the suspect went back inside.

A few moments later, the suspect came back out onto the porch, this time with the shotgun again. I saw some headlights approaching at the crest of the hill to my right, and briefly wondered if that was my second officer. But quickly my attention was diverted by the suspect yelling at someone who was apparently approaching him from the street, which was below and to our left. I couldn't hear or see the other person, but the suspect said: "You can't take my house. I'm going to kill you." As he said this, he raised the shotgun as if to shoot, so I quickly took one step to my right from the corner of the house, pointed my handgun at the suspect, and announced "Police officer, drop the gun!"

Based upon a few previous experiences I have had with armed suspects, I expected him to partially turn and hesitate, and then put the weapon down. However, before that thought was even complete, he suddenly swung the shotgun around directly at me, and my finger immediately pulled the trigger twice, just as training had programmed me to do. I then quickly stepped back to my left alongside the corner of the house.

I didn't know if my shots had hit him, but I didn't hear anything for a few seconds, so I ventured a look around the corner onto the porch and saw the suspect lying on his back with the shotgun near his left arm. I said "Don't touch the shotgun." He said "I'm not touching it, man."

I could see a wound on his left wrist, and I could see that he was in no position to be able to immediately use the shotgun again, so I radioed to the dispatcher; "The suspect's been shot; I need a Code One ambulance." She asked "Who shot him?" and I said "I did." She then asked "Where is he shot?" I said "I can see a hole in his wrist." The suspect said "I've been shot in the stomach, too." I told him, "OK, I've got an ambulance on the way, just relax, you're going to be OK."

I then went up on the porch and moved the shotgun away from his reach, leaning it against the front of the porch. The suspect sat up briefly, and his shirt was raised up in the back where I could see a lump near his spine. A woman came up on the porch, saw us there, and she stepped over the suspect to go into the house saying "How is the baby?" I didn't know anything about a baby being around but, before I could say anything to her, she was already inside. Then a second, younger woman came up onto the porch, saw us, and stepped over the suspect, similarly expressing concern about a baby but disregarding the suspect.

Then my second officer came up to the porch, and we maintained the scene to preserve the evidence. Several other officers arrived, and I continued to reassure the suspect until the ambulance arrived. The paramedics quickly put him on a stretcher and took him to the hospital. The women who went inside the house had found the baby, a little girl, unharmed.

Other officers, commanders, and investigators arrived, and I told them what had happened. I turned my handgun over to investigators to be preserved as evidence. I don't remember checking the shotgun myself, but at some point someone discovered that it was empty of ammunition which, of course seemed a little surprising since I had seen him fire it, and he certainly had acted as though he believed it was loaded.

Even after being shot, when I told him not to touch the shotgun, he said he wasn't touching it, but he said nothing about it not being loaded. Of course, as I realized later, it is not very productive to speculate about the thoughts or behavior of another person. People are extremely complex and unpredictable. After I had provided all the necessary information at the scene, I was driven down to headquarters to give two statements, one to homicide detectives, and one to Internal Affairs. I was finished with the statements at about 6:30 a.m., in time to be reissued a replacement handgun and drive to my off-duty job at a bank.

Up until that time, I really had not been aware of any of my emotions, other than the normal level of anxiety and alertness that accompany any call where someone is known to be armed. Certainly, I was less anxious during this incident than I was on the first "party armed" or "shots fired" call that I had ever been on.

I do recall my feelings on that first call, which occurred on one of my first few nights of break-in. I had felt my heart start beating faster, a nervousness and anxiety came over me and I had (nonchalantly, I hoped) put my hand on the butt of my gun to reassure me it was there as I rode to the call with my break-in officer. I looked over at him, and he was just calmly driving as if to any other routine call. I think he probably smiled to himself a bit, enjoying my fruitless efforts to try to act as calm as he looked. When we got near the scene, we coordinated with our assisting car to check the area, found nothing unusual, not even a disturbance, and we cleared from the call with no incident occurring.

After a few such calls, and even when there are occasionally disturbances where people have been armed, you get accustomed to the fact that most people either get rid of the weapon before the police arrive, or they make no attempt to use it and you discover it during a search. So, when I say I had mild anxiety, this is the context in which I mean it. You try to suppress whatever anxiety you feel and concentrate on observing and responding objectively to the situation, hoping to maximize everyone's safety.

On the night of the shooting, the call was a little unusual because of the chainsaw mentioned by the dispatcher. The chainsaw was never a factor for me, but apparently the call originated from the suspect's wife, who saw him come home intoxicated with the chainsaw, so she locked him out. He attempted to cut through the front screen door with the chainsaw, but when he couldn't, he moved down to the garage door and started cutting it.

His wife took the opportunity to sneak out the front door with her young son and go across the street to her mother-in-law's house. From there, she called the police again to make sure we were on our way.

Of course, I was unaware of any of this as I approached the call, but I was cautious and alert for any sounds of a disturbance, especially the sound of a chainsaw. I heard no unusual sounds as I arrived, so I had no heightened emotions at that time, other than just being cautious and observant. The only time I would say that my anxiety increased to the point of fear was the split second when the shotgun was suddenly pointed at me. Before then, I had thought everything was going pretty routinely and was well under control. At the moment he turned on me, there was no time to think or feel — I just reacted by pulling the trigger and stepping back alongside the house. At that point, I feared that the shotgun would come poking around the corner to shoot me, and I was ready to return fire with my remaining ammunition; I had a six-shot revolver, so four rounds were left.

When nothing happened for a couple of seconds, I took the risk of looking around the corner and saw that the suspect was not in a position to use the shotgun. At that point, I felt relieved and back to "normal," so I focused on letting the dispatcher know what had happened and getting an ambulance for the suspect. Likewise, it felt pretty normal to give statements at headquarters, and there was no time to really feel emotional about the situation until after I had related as accurately as I could what had happened, and then went off-duty to drive to the bank.

At the bank, I started to think about how things had transpired, and I tried to figure out if I could have done something differently so that it wouldn't have been necessary to shoot the man. I knew that my actions were justified and I had handled the call the best I could. I just wondered if there were some tactical things I could have done differently that would have helped me handle future situations without shooting. Such thoughts occupied me for days and weeks afterward until I gradually came to some conclusions which I will summarize later.

While at the bank, I mentioned the shooting briefly to the girls who worked there, but I did not go into a lot of detail. They would later say that I had changed from that day forward by taking life a little more seriously than before. About 11 a.m., I received a call from my major, who informed me that the suspect had died, so according to normal procedure, I needed to report immediately to him and turn in my badge and gun. I was administratively suspended pending the outcome of the internal investigation. It actually seemed a little strange to me that the department suspends the officer only when someone dies instead of just doing it pending any shooting investigation.

The fact that he had died did not have a significantly greater impact on me than knowing that I had shot him and he was in the hospital, because I knew that his injuries were serious, and I doubted he would recover. I also knew that the shooting was completely justified, and I had long ago accepted the possibility that I might have to kill someone (or be killed myself) when I chose to be a police officer many years before.

When my major suspended me and took my badge and gun, he told me that there had been threats made against me by the suspect's family. This made the suspension process a little confusing again because if it is an administrative suspension, then why am I being disarmed while my life is being threatened? But, of course, the practical fact of the matter is that police officers have their own personal weapons in addition to their department firearms, so it is not like we are defenseless. And we have had people threaten us before, so we are prepared for that, as well.

I thought my suspension would last several days or a week, but I was back to work in just a couple of days. One of the investigators told me it was one of the simplest shooting cases he had ever seen. He said, "You said you fired two shots, and there were exactly two expended casings in your gun. One bullet went through the suspect's wrist, deflected off the stock of the shotgun and hit the ceiling of the porch. The other shot went through the suspect's bicep, into his chest and lodged in his spine. The trajectories of the bullets and the positions of his arms show that the shotgun was pointed directly at you. Everything is accounted for and consistent."

Predictably, a lawsuit was filed by an attorney on behalf of the deceased's family. Among the claims were the completely false ones that I had known the suspect from previous calls, that I knew he regularly threatened his neighborhood and police officers, and I went there with the intent to kill him. There was a statement from a neighbor across the street who said he was an eyewitness and that I shot the suspect in the back without warning. This is why, if I were a juror, I would never completely believe an "eyewitness" without corroborating evidence. I have seen too many cases where witnesses honestly believe they can identify someone or believe they saw certain things occur, when they are either completely or partially mistaken. I have no reason to believe that the witness in my case was lying or had any malicious intent, but I think the suspect turned so suddenly that the witness probably thought the shots came while he was still facing away from me.

I was interviewed in great detail by an attorney hired by the police department. He was satisfied that everything was justified, and after he relayed the necessary details to the attorney who had filed the suit, the attorney decided it was not worth pursuing and dropped the case. In addition to all the facts being consistent and leading to the conclusion that the shooting was a clear case of justifiable homicide, there was a recent court decision where the justices said that it was not an appropriate function of the court to second-guess a police officer who is faced with a sudden life-and-death decision.

As I mentioned earlier, knowing that my actions were justified did not prevent me from thinking long and hard about the circumstances and tactics involved. I finally concluded that there are as many different ways to handle a call as the number of officers who potentially could be sent to it. Every suspect is unpredictable and may react differently to different officers and their actions. We go into every situation with a limited knowledge of the realities that are present, and are limited by the training and experience we have at that moment.

We do the best we can to handle calls in a reasonable manner, and usually things turn out OK, even if we make mistakes. Sometimes, though, bad things happen; when they do, we have to realize that there are many factors involved, most of which are complex and unpredictable.

Some things can never be known, such as whether he unloaded the shotgun while he was inside the house, maybe thinking he would be able to tell the police it was unloaded if we caught him with it, or whether he had unknowingly fired the last round and believed it was still loaded. What was later determined from the autopsy was that he had both alcohol and marijuana in his system which made his behavior even more unpredictable. Even he probably didn't know what he was going to do next.

We can spend endless hours speculating, guessing and trying to draw out lessons for the future, but each situation will be unique and can be handled only as it occurs, knowing that even with the best of intentions, the world is a dangerous place. Each person present knows only part of the story, and that part is filtered through their senses and their mind as it interprets what is happening. All we can do is try to do the best we can with the knowledge and training we have at the time.

This photo of Detective David Parker was taken in the academy in 1971. He retired from the KCPD in 1997. He also retired from the Army Reserves as a lieutenant colonel. (Courtesy of the KCPD)

Chapter 30

David Parker

Retired Detective, KCPD, 1971-1997

I was twenty-three years old, serving in Vietnam as a first lieutenant in the Army Military Police Corps, when I saw an Army Times advertisement that the KCPD was hiring 300 officers. I had previously obtained my BA in criminology, and I was intent on pursuing a career in law enforcement. I also received my commission as an officer in the U.S. Army Reserve through the ROTC program at Indiana University of Pennsylvania.

Consequently, I wrote a letter to the personnel department, told them I was interested in applying for a job as a police officer and provided them with some of my background. My tour in 'Nam was scheduled to end in the fall of 1971, and that would end my two-year active duty obligation to the Army. I still would have a six-year active reserve obligation to fulfill, but more on that later.

The Army offered me an early out, and I took advantage of that opportunity. I was asked to take six U.S. military prisoners from LBJ (Long Binh Jail) to the post stockade at Fort Lewis, Wash. I was discharged from the active component of the Army in July 1971, after completing the prisoner transfer.

On my way back to Pennsylvania, I stopped in Portland, Ore., to take a prearranged test for the Multnomah County Sheriff's Department. I then headed home to Indiana, Pennsylvania, where I began submitting applications to other law enforcement agencies around the country. The KCPD subsequently had me come out for an interview and testing, and they were the first agency to offer me an opportunity to become a police officer. I jumped at that chance and began my 26-year career with the KCPD in September 1971.

My contract with the Army required a six-year active reserve assignment. I began looking around the Kansas City metropolitan area for an Army reserve unit to join; the only Military Police Unit in the area was the 493rd MP Detachment (CI). This was a Criminal Investigations Unit, with only one commissioned officer slot authorized, and that position was already filled.

I talked to the commander, Major Jack Maxwell, who turned out to be a Sergeant on the KCPD. He invited me to attend one of their drills, and I did. The members were associated with various law enforcement entities, many of them from the KCPD. Major Maxwell was able to work his magic and get me assigned to the 493rd MP Detachment (CID) in an "over-strength" capacity. I now was assigned as the executive officer of the unit. The unit members, affectionately I think, referred to me as 'Ensign' Parker. This assignment was the beginning of a wonderful and rewarding experience in the U.S. Army Reserve.

An early highlight of my initial assignment with the 493rd was annual training in 1973. The 493rd, along with all other USAR and National Guard CID units across the country, went to Fort Belvoir, VA, for consolidated CID command training. The high point of this two-week period in July was our unit's visit to the Hoover (FBI) Building in Washington, D.C.

A large number of members of the 493rd were also members of the KCPD. On June 27, 1973, the U.S. Senate confirmed Clarence Kelley's nomination to the post of FBI director, and he was sworn in on July 9th. Kelley was the first FBI director to be appointed through the nomination and confirmation process and only the second permanent FBI director. Kelley had been the chief of the KCPD before his appointment, and he was truly respected by both the sworn and non-sworn members of the department, as well as, the Kansas City community at large.

My career with the Army reserve did not end after six years. I continued in the program and eventually retired in 1996 when then-President Clinton decimated the military. My unit, the 102nd

ARCOM in St. Louis, was subsequently deactivated. I had been the provost marshal for the Command for several years before the deactivation, and my job simply went away.

During my 27-year career in the Reserves, the TO&E, (organizational structure) of the 493rd changed to authorize an executive officer and changed the authorized grade of the commander to a lieutenant colonel. I did manage to get back to the 493rd MP Detachment several times; once in the grade of major as executive officer and once in the grade of lieutenant colonel as the unit commander. I can't begin to say how much my association with the 493rd and its members meant to me. The organization, aside from being a professional one, was also a fraternal one.

Working the Gypsy Cases

While doing my time in the Army Reserves, I also enjoyed full-time duty with the KCPD. As with anybody who has served any time in law enforcement, there are a host of situations that would make for a good movie or book.

For instance, I was assigned to the Fraud Unit sometime around the mid-to-late-1970s. I started to specialize in the investigation of various confidence games. This was challenging because many of the "players" were travelers; they were in town one day and out the next. Early on I also worked on the Gypsy palm reader scam, and it was relatively easy to deal with. We never got prosecution, but we generally got restitution for the victims. This was because our sergeant, Ron Closterman, had a good relationship with the Gypsy King, Johnny Marks. All he had to do was call Johnny and tell him he had another complaint, and Johnny would negotiate with the victim and generally make restitution in exchange for no prosecution.

All this changed after Marks passed away in 1982. Before his death, John had confided in Sergeant Closterman that he was concerned that his wife, Julia, was going to kill him. It's my understanding that John admitted to Closterman that he had an affair with a redheaded beauty who was a non-Gypsy, and Julia found out about the affair.

After his death, the Homicide Unit did investigate the death.

The blood tests that were done on John Marks were inconclusive, and more extensive and expensive tests would be required to determine if Marks was possibly poisoned with a chemical that didn't show up in the first set of tests. A decision was made to close the case without pursuing additional tests.

Several years later, our problems with the local Gypsy palm reading scams began to grow. Mark's oldest son, Fred, assumed the position as the new king in the Kansas City area, and he was not into negotiating with their victims. Fred's wife, Nancy, and his brother, George, and his wife, Sandra, were the primary fortune tellers on the Missouri side of the state line, along with their mother, Julia.

Breaking the spell of the Marks' gypsy fortune-telling organization became a goal of mine after a series of victims, were identified with high dollar losses that were attributed primarily to Nancy and Julia Marks. I should add that my long-time friend and partner, Detective Bill Cosgrove, assisted greatly in this endeavor and our investigation was truly a team effort.

Let's start at the beginning, at least as far as Kansas City goes. In the mid-1980s the KCPD Fraud Unit began receiving egregious complaints relating to the Marks' fortune-telling operation. In the end, Cosgrove and I worked a number of the complaints for prosecution in 1984, three of which are detailed later. The events leading up to prosecution, however, had their own obstacles, not the least of which was an assistant prosecutor in the warrant desk of the Jackson County Prosecutor's office.

Two elderly Kansas City females, Lottie Randall and Ruth Avery, both had reported losing money to the Marks. Both women had serious ailments and issues that went with growing older. The Avery case came to the attention of the Fraud Unit in an unusual way. Ruth Avery's new husband had noticed that she was depleting her bank accounts, and he couldn't get her to tell him what was going on. He thought maybe someone was blackmailing her for something. The husband contacted Cosgrove, but he would only talk to Bill if he were talking on a pay phone.

Eventually, Bill was able to get the husband to bring Ruth to the Fraud Unit for an interview. After some intensive questioning, Cosgrove learned she had been the victim of a fortune-telling scam perpetrated by the Marks. Avery had diabetes and an elderly mother about whom she was concerned. I don't recall which of the three fortune tellers Avery met with first, but she was told she was "cursed," her diabetes was reportedly going to get much worse, and her mother was going to die in the near future. It was explained that only the Marks' "special powers" could exorcise the evil spirits that surrounded her.

During some of the visits Avery had with the fortune teller, she was told to take an egg home and rub it all over her body. She brought the egg back on a subsequent visit, where the egg was broken and when this was done she noticed what looked like a devil's head and blood in the egg. The fortune teller used this to show Avery that she was removing the "curse and the devil" from her body. Over a six-month period, Avery had paid the Marks more than $50,000 to remove the curse. Avery was promised she would get her money back once she was cured.

Similarly, Lottie Randall's sons, Jim and Chuck, brought their mother to the Fraud Unit in early June 1984, to make a report regarding the theft of more than $91,000 attributed to a fortune-telling scam. Randall told us she had been going to the fortune-tellers for about five years. She originally went to "Ruth" or "Sandy" (Sandra Marks) to have her fortune told. During that first reading, Randall was told she had a great deal of tragedy facing her in the future. It was emphatically suggested that she come back for more visits. Randall continued to visit the same fortune teller at the same Westport Road address for about six additional visits. Randall also gave Sandra $90 cash for some religious candles. After a half-dozen visits with Sandra, Randall was introduced to Sandra's mother. At the time, Sandra's mother was calling herself Marie; however, it was later confirmed this was actually Julia Marks. Randall told us she began going to 211 E. Linwood in Kansas City, where she continued to meet with Julia for consultations. During each of the meetings, with Julia she was asked to give several thousand dollars to Julia for the "church" to hold. She was told the money would be returned to her after her problems were resolved.

Randall continued to go to Julia for four more years, and she was always warned of the adversities she would encounter if she didn't continue with regular visits. These strong-armed tactics to get Randall to return and bring more money were reinforced with examples of what the fortune teller claimed to have already "cured" for her. Julia told Randall these problems included health issues for her husband, son and daughter-in-law. From the beginning of this confidence game and until the last visit, Randall withdrew money from her checking accounts and used her credit cards to give cash and merchandise to Julia Marks totaling $124,226.

Julia continually told Randall she was going to "hold" the money because this was the only way she could be healed and was the only way Julia could straighten out all of the Randall's' health problems. Julia repeatedly told Randall she would give all the money back, including the money used to purchase merchandise. Marks used tricks like the egg trick used on Avery; after the first egg was broken by Marks, the egg-white had turned to a gooey substance, and the yolk had turned to a solid matter with a picture of the devil embedded inside.

In another similar incident, an egg also was rubbed over her body and given to her to take home and place under her bed. When Randall returned for the next visit, Julia broke the egg, which contained what appeared to be dark hair; Julia explained that the foreign object was cancer that had been removed from her body.

Julia also purportedly burned $12,000 of Randall's money and $13,000 of Julia's money. The purported burning of money is not uncommon in Gypsy fortune-telling scams. The fortune teller already has a wrapped package of play money that is similar to the package that she would ultimately wrap containing the victim's money, and in this case, some of her own money. When the victim's attention was not on the wrapped money, there was a switch of packages and then the gypsy burns the prepackaged play money. This act was explained by the idea that money was the root of all evil and must be burned to help cleanse the soul.

The big losers in the Gypsy scams usually had some sort of health issue and/or serious relationship issue for which there appeared to be no solution. The fortune teller would tell the victim what they wanted to hear and make it believable for someone who wanted badly to believe. Perhaps, you had lung cancer and the medical community told you there was no cure, and that you only had eight months to live. Many people confronted with this type of news would get depressed and look elsewhere for cures. They might go to a fortune teller who told them what they wanted to hear, and this gave them some hope, especially if some of the other tricks the fortune teller pulled appeared to be legitimate to the depressed individual. Anybody can be conned; just look at the many influential and famous victims of Bernie Madoff. He was offering returns that were too good to be true.

Another particularly heartbreaking scam was investigated before the Avery and Randall cases were reported. This was a case involving a young Amish farmer by the name of David Warren from Jamesport, MO. David's father, Lawrence Warren, reported to the Fraud Unit that his credit card was unlawfully used to purchase a handgun at C&R Specialties in Kansas City for a customer identified as Fred Marks. Warren related that his son, David, had asked to borrow his credit card because he wanted to buy Christmas gifts for his children; he didn't have any money of his own to buy gifts for the kids. When the credit card bill came in, Mr. Warren questioned David about the C&R gun purchase. David got defensive and refused to talk about it. Consequently, Warren turned to the Fraud Unit.

When I got this case, I suspected immediately what was going on. Detective Cosgrove and I subsequently drove to Jamesport and interviewed Mr. and Mrs. Warren, the parents of David Warren. What we learned was truly a sad story. Their son and his wife had a farm in the Jamesport/Trenton area. David had medical problems and told the senior Warrens that he was in trouble and needed cash. He refused to tell them why, but his father gave him $3,000, anyway. He later asked for $10,000, saying he really needed it, but provided no reason, just that it was necessary and urgent. David's uncle eventually gave him $10,000 and then, later, $25,000 for what he said was an investment.

On May 1, 1982, David sold his farm just outside of Jamesport, along with all his livestock and farm implements. That Christmas of 1983, is when he borrowed his father's credit card to supposedly purchase gifts for his children. We took a police report on the fraudulent use of a credit device and presented the case to the Jackson County Prosecutor's Office. When Fred Marks learned of the pending charges, he immediately paid off the amount of the charge ($810) to avoid criminal prosecution.

When Lawrence Warren filed the police report on the credit card fraud, David told his parents he hated them and cut off all ties between himself and his parents. Lawrence and his wife were devastated. Not only had their son lost everything, but now the parents had lost their only child and grandchild.

Cosgrove and I tried, without success, to talk to David. We even stopped him one morning after leaving Nancy Marks' parlor on Main Street. He had not committed a traffic violation and, after being stopped, he became verbally abusive and simply drove off. We had no legal reason to go after him again. We could only hope that our attempt to talk to him would open the door of reason at some point in the future.

In spring 1984, we presented the Avery and Randall cases to the Jackson County Prosecutor's Office. After being presented for charges, we received a "yellow sheet" on the cases. A yellow sheet, as it was known then, was a declination to prosecute; it derived its name from the color of paper on which it was printed. I spoke to the assistant prosecutor, who made the decision, and his reason for tossing the case out was that the victims willingly gave the money to the suspects. He stated if they were that dumb to give that amount of money away, they deserved to be victims.

Officers are not supposed to get involved in their cases but after those comments, how could I not? I was irate, and everyone in the office knew it. I later talked to one of Lottie Randall's sons and told him the news. I suggested that if he and his mother were willing to talk to the news media, we might be able to give new life to these cases. He and his mother agreed to talk to a reporter. I also got Lawrence Warren's permission to involve the media in his situation. I talked to Cosgrove and told him what I was going to do, but I told no one else.

Sometime in early June 1984, I contacted KCTV Channel 5's (CBS) investigative reporter, Stan Cramer, and offered him a story that was sure to make headlines. Lottie Randall her sons, as well as Cosgrove and I, met with Cramer and his associate, Mike Sanders. When the Randall story was presented, Stan jumped at the opportunity to do an investigative series on the problem. He also was put on the trail of David Warren, again with Lawrence Warren's permission.

Over the ensuing weeks, a number of important and groundbreaking events took place. Lottie Randall and her sons went to visit Julia Marks. One of the sons was wearing a wire. Cramer and his TV crew were present to watch the meeting from a distance and monitor the conversation. Julia refused to talk about dollar amounts but agreed that none of the money given to her by Lottie Randall had been given back to her because "there was still work to be done." Four days later, Randall, her two sons, and Sanders went back to Julia's residence carrying a concealed video camera in a bag. They were told to come back in two hours, which they did. At that time, the Marks' family attorney, John Frankum, was there and he essentially said there was nothing to talk about and to take their concerns to the police or prosecutor.

The second impact that Cramer brought to the investigation was his visit with Lawrence and Doris Warren, parents of David Warren, who refused to acknowledge that their son had been victimized. Although David Warren denied involvement with the Gypsies and got physical with Cramer and Jim Pruitt, who had gone along to help, apparently their visit influenced David to think more about the situation, and he took their advice. During the midnight hour, he went to his minister's house and told him everything. The minister said that in 27 years of preaching, he had never heard such a story. The next morning, David called Cramer and said he wanted to talk to him.

Cramer and crew went back to Jamesport and set up a meeting with David, his wife Carol, and David's parents. Essentially, Cramer's perseverance got the family back together again, and this was all documented on film. David subsequently provided a statement concerning his involvement with the Marks. He first began his visits with Nancy who told him that he had so much darkness hanging over him that she would have to enlist the assistance of her mother, Julia. David told us one of the first things that made him and his wife believers was the fact that they made a comment to the fortune teller that Cathy–David's wife–couldn't have a baby. They explained that they had consulted two OB-GYN doctors who had both told them Cathy's tubes were twisted and she couldn't conceive. While at the Marks' parlor, both David and Cathy were told to urinate in bottles and bring the bottles back on the next visit. Not long after that, Cathy became pregnant. Around the time Cathy was scheduled to deliver their son, they were told by Julia and Nancy to bring $25,000 in cash. He was cautioned that if he didn't do it, terrible things would happen to his wife and child; the baby would be born blind, and Cathy would die in childbirth. In total, the Warrens gave Julia and Nancy in excess of $150,000 in cash and merchandise that was purchased on credit cards. Both David and Cathy were sworn to secrecy; if they broke that agreement, terrible things would happen. They also were told that the source of their curse was David's parents. He believed Julia and Nancy when they told them his parents were responsible for the death of his brother years ago.

Cosgrove and I continued putting new evidence together in the case files of all of these victims: Ruth Avery, Lottie Randall and David Warren. In the second week of July 1984, Cramer's "Breaking the Spell" hit the 6 p.m. news, for which Cramer later won a national award. It truly was this series that made possible the final outcome. As soon as it began airing, I was summoned to resubmit the cases for consideration. We were ready for the call, and Nancy and Julia Marks subsequently were charged with multiple-count indictments of felony stealing.

Although I never asked permission or even told anyone but my partner about my decision to involve Cramer in this investigation effort, the prosecutor's office surmised as much. Consequently, I was counseled not to do it again or I might face assignment walking a foot beat in the Missouri River Bottoms!

In 1985, Julia ultimately pled guilty and received a three-year sentence in the Missouri State Penitentiary. It's my understanding she died in jail. Nancy, on the other hand, was willing to take more of a risk. She went to trial, and the prosecutor was Marietta Parker (no relation to me). The state could not have gotten a better attorney for the task. Marietta was great. During the trial, I testified about Gypsy culture, and I also performed and later described how one of the egg tricks was done.

I came into the courtroom with a fresh egg. Marietta asked me to show the court and jury how the defendant would have made a devil's head show up inside an egg. I got out a large, red-checked handkerchief and palmed a plastic devil's head with dark hair inside the handkerchief. I was just putting the egg in the palm of my hand when defense counsel objected, saying a red handkerchief was not used. If you're going do it, do it like it's been alleged to have been done, he argued.

He offered me his white handkerchief, and I told him no. The attorney, of course, was trying to get me to fumble around and disclose the palmed devil's head in the red checked handkerchief. I recall, at the time, I was concerned about making the switch without being seen while all eyes in the courtroom were on me. I was able to rise to the occasion and accomplish the task without the trick being disclosed to the court.

I should also tell you that the previous evening I injected the egg with red food coloring using a hypodermic needle to make it look like blood was inside the egg, along with the devil's head.

While holding the white handkerchief containing a plastic devil's head concealed in my palm, I put the egg in the handkerchief, took my shoe off and smashed the egg with the heel while at the same time pushing the devil's head into the broken egg. I showed the results to the judge and then marched up and down the jury box with egg white and red food coloring dripping from my hands. The jury was impressed, but the defense was not interested in seeing the results.

After that demonstration was complete, I had to explain how I did it. I don't know how many cartons of eggs I wasted practicing making the food coloring injection, as well as practicing the actual maneuver to do the trick without being discovered; it certainly paid dividends. In the end, Nancy Marks was convicted. She received the maximum sentence of seven years in the state penitentiary. I don't have any recollection about what, if anything happened to Sandra Marks. I was told later by Marietta Parker that Julia and Nancy Marks were the first Gypsies in Missouri to be sentenced to prison for a confidence game.

At the end of Nancy's trial, Cosgrove purchased a bouquet of flowers and we gave them to Marietta for her commitment and her exemplary work on the cases. Marietta never forgot that, and years later, when she was first assistant to the U.S. Attorney, Western District of Missouri, she and a number of assistant U.S Attorneys and I were riding in the elevator when Marietta told everyone in the elevator that my partner and I were the only police officers who had ever brought her flowers for her work on a case.

For our efforts in the investigations, both Cosgrove and I were recognized at the 1984 Annual Kiwanis Law Enforcement Appreciation Banquet, and we each received a Certificate of Commendation from the KCPD.

If you are intrigued by the Gypsy culture and their life of crime, I would encourage you to read the novel King Con by Stephen Cannell. Although it is a novel with crimes ranging from murder to the most sophisticated confidence games, I would not put the events described in the book past any accomplished Gypsy.

Detective William Cosgrove retired from the KCPD in 1997. In this photo, he is working in the Fraud Unit, possibly around 1984. He was instrumental in working with David Parker and Stan Cramer solving the Marks Gypsy cases. (Courtesy of the KCPD)

Stan Cramer assisted Detectives David Parker and Bill Cosgrove in getting charges filed with the State Prosecutor's Office in the Marks Gypsy case. Cramer was a KCTV Channel 5's (CBS) investigative reporter that ran a series on television, "Breaking the Spell." He also won a national award for airing the series. This was in 1984–1985. (Courtesy of Stan Cramer)

The 493rd CID Unit, on a two-week annual training assignment to Washington, D.C., visited FBI Director and former KCPD chief Clarence Kelley in 1973.
Left-right: Robert Chapman, Donald Denning, Jack Maxwell, Albert Morton, Gary Howell, Robert Rennau, Edward Wolters, Paul Heathman, Clarence Robinson, Cecil O'Rear, William Price, Director Kelley, Delbert Knopp, Harry Hicks, George Mann, Mike McKinney, Miles Warren, Joe Liles, James Forbis, David Parker, Richard McLeod, and Jack Perry (Courtesy of FBI Director, Clarence Kelley)

This photo was taken around 1964 of Richard Schwieterman. (Courtesy of KCPD)

Chapter 31

Richard Schwieterman

Retired Latent Fingerprint Examiner, KCPD, 1964-1989

I joined the KCPD right out of the Air Force in November 1962. I was hired as a records clerk on the evening shift. They asked me when I was tested if I would like to be a police officer, but I said no, not at that time. But as I worked in close proximity with the fingerprint classifiers, I became fascinated with that science. So, I began studying on my own time, and I came in early to study with the ID Unit supervisor, Russell Griffing, who taught me how fingerprints were classified, filed, and recovered from files.

He also told me of some of the benefits of working in the ID unit, including higher pay, more vacation, and sick time. I think it was sometime in late 1963 or early 1964, that I was transferred into the ID Unit as a fingerprint technician 1 (classifier). At that time, we worked 22 days on and eight days off in a row. I got used to the 22 days on because I could look forward to the eight days off. It was shift work, but I volunteered for dog watch, and I worked that shift for about nine years.

At that time, the Latent Print Section consisted of Ray Bowman and Bill Green. The modern day lab was nonexistent as far as fingerprints were concerned. The officers in the field processed the crime scenes themselves, and this also was before the crime scene investigators existed in a separate unit. The two latent print men processed all homicide scenes and high-profile robberies. Paper items to be chemically processed were brought into the sixth floor of the police headquarters building where the latent print examiners processed the items themselves. I think it was in 1973, that Bowman decided to attend the academy and I made a strong plea to take his place as a latent print examiner and was accepted.

We mixed our own silver nitrate for processing, photographed the prints with our Polaroid CU-5 camera, marked everything, and put it in the property room. Looking back, I really don't know where we found the time to compare prints, write reports, and go to court, but we somehow managed to do it.

Ron Stein was brought over when we got that primitive searching machine called Miracode and was made operator of the machine. Then, when Bill Green left the unit around 1974, Ron became my partner.

Bill and I had a little different situation because we were under the law enforcement retirement system and were issued technicians' badges. Ron was too late for that, so he was under the civilian system with the standard civilian badge. My badge was the last technicians' badge to be deactivated when I retired in 1989.

Some of the major events that I worked on were the 1968 riots, the Hyatt Regency disaster, and the case of Robert Berdella, a serial killer who lured gay men to his house and performed experiments on them before killing each. He died in prison while serving his sentence.

There was a time when Ron and I trained all of the fingerprint people, one or two at a time, from surrounding cities in Missouri and Kansas. We also trained most of the crime scene personnel on the art of fingerprint examinations.

Crispy Critter Case

One of the strangest cases that Bill and I worked was that of a "crispy critter," a person who was set on fire. I believed this happened in Raytown. Just enough of one hand was left to get a couple of prints off each of two fingers. At the time, we didn't have any way to search them, so we just held onto the prints. We were hoping we could get a lead on who the person was.

A short time later, a woman in Raytown made a missing person's report on her son. He had never been fingerprinted, so we got permission from the distraught mother to lift latent prints from the young man's room. We processed some of his items at her home, brought the prints back to the office and were able to match the prints from the body with the prints from the items we had processed. So, in a way, we identified the body by coming in the back door, so to speak.

Identification of Homicide Suspect

One particular case I remember working was a homicide where no known suspect was identified. Latent prints were submitted from the crime scene, but there were no known suspects with which to compare the prints. I started searching, by hand, a section of our files for repeat suspects, and I was really fortunate to make a hit in a fairly short time in that file. I received the department's Meritorious Service Award, and I was also given two extra days off with pay for the homicide that had no known suspect. During my career, I have also received twenty-one letters of commendation from chiefs, prosecutors, and even an occasional defense attorney!

On another occasion, we solved a double homicide that occurred in 1974. A handbag found at the scene was brought to me for examination. Despite the difficult texture of the handbag, I lifted two latent prints. The homicide suspect was identified, subsequently convicted, and given a prison sentence of 50 years.

In 1977, I attended the Missouri Division of the International Association for Identification, along with other members of the KCPD. One of our department's former chiefs of police, Clarence Kelley, attended and gave a speech at the seminar.

Pictured, left to right, are Sergeant Alfred Fracassa, Sergeant Lloyd Hefner, Captain Bill Dycus, Major Ray Roberts, Richard Schwieterman, Sergeant John Cowdrey, Sergeant Lawrence Weishar and Officer Sherman Staffer. This was a photo taken around 1987 during a 25-year ring ceremony. (Courtesy of KCPD)

This photo was taken of Kathleen Hentges, who retired as a Forensic Specialist IV in the Fingerprint Identification Unit. She worked in that unit from 1989-2008 (Courtesy of Ann Mallot, KCPD Crime Lab)

Chapter 32

Kathleen M. Hentges

Retired Forensic Specialist IV, KCPD, 1980-2008

Fingerprints Have Always Been One of the Most Reliable Methods of Identification

In 1980, when I was promoted as the first woman latent print examiner for the KCPD, computers seemed to be light years away.

We examiners were just beginning to hear of a machine called AFIS (Automated Fingerprint Identification Systems). Somehow, you could enter latent or inked prints in this unknown computer system and receive a list of candidates for examiners to compare, based on pattern type, ridge detail, or minutia points. It was hard to fathom what this new and great technology could possibly do for an agency as large as Kansas City.

But before the department would purchase their first AFIS early in the 1990s, examiners relied on a system called Miracode. This was a microfilm-based way to search unknown latent prints lifted from crime scenes. And it worked. Search information was entered based on the information that detectives could provide on a suspect. Based on gender and race, the searching method time requirement could be cut in half by knowing any of this information.

Next, were the prints from the crime scene itself? Could you tell if it was a whorl, loop, or arch? Was it the right hand or the left hand? Once this information was known, you had the glorious challenge of searching roll after roll after roll of filmed fingerprints! I think you can catch my drift as to the true challenges of trying to identify these crime scene prints before increased technology came along. Detectives really had to use their investigating skills and work together to provide as much information as possible.

All of the latent cases were filed by location in the city. Many times, the same latent prints appeared on different cases, and the good Lord provided me with the ability to recall seeing the same print on another case. Examiners would then take all the cases in a certain area and perform a latent-to-latent search. Many cases were solved through this method. It was a thrill to be able to connect two or more cases together and let detectives know the same suspect was committing numerous crimes in the same area.

No crime was solved by just one individual. There had to be teamwork, beginning with the crime scene person or officer who processed the scene for fingerprints, and then submitting those prints to latent examiners to determine if there were usable prints for comparison purposes. Next, the detective had to conduct his or her investigation into who could have committed the crime.

We were fortunate to solve many crimes using the old Miracode machine and good old-fashioned detective work. As the years passed, new, improved methods for searching fingerprints were on the horizon. The KCPD was finally beginning to show interest in this new method of searching prints through a multi-million dollar AFIS computer. I was so honored to be part of the benchmarking team to search for the right AFIS for the department in the late 1980s.

During that era, there were only three systems available: NEC, Printrak and SAGEM Morpho. The Morpho system was chosen after numerous tests, which were based on the simplicity and accuracy of the system. One problem; how was the department going to convince the city that this was the greatest invention since sliced bread? Somehow, it happened, and the fun began in the early 1990s to prepare for half a million fingerprint cards to be sent to Tacoma, Washington for entry into the system. Not only did the system search latent prints, but also rolled inked impressions. Of course, everyone in the latent section and the ten-print sections had to endure extensive training to operate AFIS.

After training was completed, the hits started pouring in. The hit rate was incredible: for every 100 cases searched, we were identifying 22 to 25 cases. Homicides, rapes, and unsolved robberies now were being solved. Even though this AFIS was expensive, the hundreds and thousands of man-hours saved in detective work was worth it. The more cases we were able to identify meant that detectives could spend time on other cases that might not have produced evidence. It was nothing but a win-win situation.

Officers and crime scene personnel took extra steps to process scenes to obtain latent prints. The rewards were when we received a copy of an identification report with our names for processing the scene. Many officers, detectives, and crime scene personnel used to get a good laugh because I would always jump and shout when a crime would be solved through fingerprints.

There are so many cases that come to mind over my 28-year career in the Latent Section that stand out to me that were very rewarding. No one got more excited than I did to solve a crime. My job was to work for the citizens of Kansas City and to make their lives a safer place, to give closure to a family who wondered who took their loved one's life, to ease a little pain and grief with that closure. Those were the rewards.

And I was able to identify more than 8,000 individuals over my career. So many stand out, but there are four that are at the top of the list. Two cases were the result of hard detective work providing information that we used, and two were the results of AFIS searches. Have I talked about teamwork lately? It should be noted that not one case was the result of one individual doing all the work (how unlike TV crime shows). To solve a crime, everyone had to do their job, from the officer or detective who arrived at the scene to the person processing the scene, and then, of course, the latent section.

The Westport Rapist

Numerous rapes were occurring in the Westport area, south of downtown Kansas City. Women's lives were being violated in the 80s and early 90s. At this point, there was no way of searching for or identifying DNA evidence. Everyone relied on fingerprints, which still remain the most accurate form of identification. No two individuals have the same ridge arrangements.

Detectives were working overtime and spending numerous hours searching for clues and evidence to link someone to the crimes. One rape case was processed at the break-in point of entry, and a latent print was lifted from the inside window glass in the kitchen, and at least 100 comparisons had been checked against the latent print of value. No luck.

Then, one day the detectives received a tip about a possible suspect. A check of the name revealed a past criminal history with fingerprints on file. I was the lucky examiner who made the comparison and, Bingo! The Westport Rapist had now been identified. The main piece of evidence was the fingerprint, but unfortunately it was the only print left at one of the scenes, even though numerous rapes had occurred. The case went to trial, and, in the end, this suspect was convicted and sent to prison for life. Even though we could not connect this individual to the other rapes, DNA evidence was stored for future use.

In the past couple years, those cases were connected with DNA from each of the unsolved cases, but all along, everyone felt this same suspect had committed the other rapes, and now the DNA evidence proved it. The suspect already was serving his life sentence because of the identification of the latent print, but it was wonderful that these other victims could now also have closure, knowing the rapist had been behind bars and their cases were solved.

Jefferson City, MO, Prison

Another brutal rape occurred against an elderly lady and detectives were hot to find out who did it. The poor victim had returned home only to be brutally raped by someone hiding there. One of the sex crimes detectives informed me that crime scene personnel were hand-delivering lift cards processed from the scene to our unit. It was determined that the suspect had spent a lot of time in the home, snooping around each room and even raiding the refrigerator.

CSI personnel showed up and I evaluated the lift cards for any prints that were usable. There was one beautiful palm print lifted from the refrigerator door. First, we had to determine if the print belonged to the victim, but it didn't. The detective working the case came to the latent print section to inform me that he had received a tip over the hotline that the perpetrator could be a certain individual. This detective, in all the years of working sex crimes, had never received a tip that lead to the arrest of an individual on a rape case. But, he figured a lead was a lead, and we should compare this individual to the latent palm print.

After a computer check of the name, it was determined this possible suspect had previous arrests with fingerprint and palm prints on file. I retrieved the fingerprint card and began my comparison of the prints. I was shocked; the palm print matched the latent palm print. I ran around the room like a complete nut in excitement that this was, indeed, the suspect. Once verified by another examiner, I wrote the report. It was time to make my way to the second floor to find this detective so I could personally tell him the fantastic news. At first he didn't believe me, and then he ran and gave me a big hug because no tip had ever turned out to be positive for him.

The suspect, as it turned out, had arrived on a bus from the Jefferson City Correctional Center that very day and proceeded to break into the victim's home where he waited an estimated ten hours before brutally raping the victim when she returned home. In short, his new home was back in Jefferson City. These two cases were the result of dedicated team work by Sex Crimes Unit detectives, CSI personnel, and members of the Latent Print Section. AFIS was still not available, and when the department finally purchased the AFIS, palm prints could not be computer-searched, only fingerprints.

Early in 1990, the KCPD purchased an AFIS, and the hard work began of entering all the latent prints we could to help solve crimes. I could go on and on about the hundreds of cases that were eventually solved. The department ended up saving so much money in overtime hours that it really helped pay for the AFIS. So many crimes were being solved in a shorter period of time because of this new way of searching prints. The companies soon found ways to increase speed and upgrade their systems. The AFIS system was getting better and better, and results were coming back faster and faster. It was simply amazing.

Admiral Boulevard Convenience Store Murder

Teamwork is how crimes are solved. The following robbery-turned-homicide case shows how everyone worked together to identify a suspect in the murder of a convenience store clerk.

Two individuals walked into a store, one with a Styrofoam cup in his hand which he placed on the counter as he picked up some items. All of this was recorded on film from the store's cameras. The two proceeded to rob and cold-bloodedly shoot the clerk. The victim made no move to disrupt the robbery, so the suspects basically shot him for no reason. Detectives watched the film and noticed the cup on the counter.

CSI personnel examined the cup at the scene, but due to the curvature of the cup and its texture, they didn't want to take any chances of ruining the print by trying to lift it off the cup. They decided to hand-carry the cup in a sealed evidence bag to the lab to be photographed. The cup was logged into evidence, photographed by the lab's photo section, and then the photos were given to me to determine the value of the latent print.

If only all latent prints looked like this one! I stayed late and entered the print into the AFIS. It took less than six hours to identify the suspect and write the report. Everyone did their jobs in a professional manner and positive results were the rewards. Unfortunately, someone lost their life due to senseless violence and very little stolen money.

Rape of a Nun

The following case is one of the worst cases I ever worked and, to this day, it just breaks my heart. Everyone involved in police work has to be able to set aside the brutality and ignore their personal emotions and still provide the citizens with the best possible service they can give. Sometimes, however, there are cases that tug at your heart and you can't help but feel something deep inside. Police personnel are human, too.

This particular morning would forever change my thoughts about what human beings are capable of doing. In a normally quiet, very poor area of Kansas City, near the Missouri River, was a beautiful old church and rectory at Fifth and Campbell. In spite of outward appearances, it was a good neighborhood where the poor people attended Catholic Mass and were devoted to the church, and where five nuns lived and gave their lives for the needy. The five nuns lived adjacent to the church.

On this particular late night or early morning, someone broke into the living area where the elderly nuns resided. One nun was awakened by the intruder and was brutally beaten and repeatedly raped by this lowlife scumbag and worthless human being; please excuse my accurate description of him!

My supervisor received a call concerning this rape and called me into his office to tell me what had happened. The news hit very close to home with me because I was raised in the Catholic Church and could not fathom how someone could commit such a savage crime like this against a nun. The command staff wanted all available personnel to work this case. A special squad of detectives was formed as the crime scene evidence was hand-delivered to the latent section.

I was praying for just one fingerprint to enter into the AFIS for a search, and my prayers were answered. There were several partials, but only one that could actually be entered, and that's all I needed. The print was entered into the system as a priority one, the highest level of search capability. This means all other searches would be overridden by this search to receive a candidate list as fast as possible. After what seemed like forever, the AFIS finally showed up with the list of candidates. I had to calm myself down and take some deep breaths so that I could concentrate on doing the best job possible. My adrenaline started flowing and my body was tingling in hopes that a match would happen.

Then I saw the print. Quietly, I went to the fingerprint files to retrieve a fingerprint card to make a side-by-side comparison, not letting anyone know what was going on at this point. Could this really be that coldhearted dirt bag? I got up, sat down, got up, sat down several times in excitement. After completing my examination, I carried the inked fingerprint card and the latent print to my boss. He said to me, "You have got to be kidding?" My smile said it all. He then made the verification and I wrote the report.

As soon as the report was written and signed, the two of us went to the second floor where the special squad was being formed. They had not completed forming the squad when I looked at them and said, "We got him!" As long as I live, the looks on their faces will remain in my mind. Within an hour, we had this so-called human being in custody. I should just note that each case is handled with complete professionalism and importance, no matter who the victim was. For me, however, this victim was different, a holy person devoted to the people and her God. What really tugs at my heart is how frightened and scared these poor nuns were after this rape occurred. They no longer felt safe where they were, so they moved to another location in the city. And the poor people of that parish lost the heroes they looked to for salvation, help, and prayer. What kind of human being could commit such a crime?

The trial began and, after days of testimony, I was contacted by the prosecutor. He asked me to attend the closing arguments, something to which I had never been invited before. After the invitation, I just had to be there to see what really happens. I always respected the job of the prosecutor, but this really made me respect them for the hard work they do for the city. I sat in the very back of the courtroom, in a corner, not wanting to be noticed. The closing arguments referenced my testimony and the defense kept saying I said things that I had not. I kept thinking to myself, I did not say that! Sitting in the back gave me the opportunity to observe the people sitting in the other benches of the courtroom.

I had not met the victim or the other nuns, but they were there every day for the trial. But from simply observing, I knew just which one had been the victim. According to the defense attorney, every expert witness who testified had no idea what they were doing. When both sides were finished, the case was given to the jury.

As I left the courthouse, someone began yelling my name. I turned around, and it was the group of nuns wanting to thank me for the hard work we all had done. They hugged me. It was everything I could do to keep from crying in front of them. This case was very emotional, but I felt I had to maintain my professionalism. They had lost their home where they felt safe. Now, it was up to the jury to decide guilt or innocence. I turned away and began to cry, only after leaving the Sisters.

A few hours went by. I received a call that the jury had returned with a verdict and that I could come over to hear the results. Guilty on all counts, that's all I had to hear to know everyone did their job to their best ability. One of the local news stations contacted my supervisor to do an interview about how the AFIS worked and wanted to talk to me about this case and the results. Peggy Breit, from KMTV Channel 9 (ABC), and her film crew showed up to do the interview. I explained to her how we are really behind the scenes, just doing our job, testifying to our findings and it is the jury that decides guilt or innocence. Peggy turned and said something to me that I will never forget. She looked at me and said, "You are truly the silent witness."

Retirement

In April 2008, I retired to new adventures. I started out my career only using a simple magnifying glass and pointers, and ended up being able to search unknown prints in a computer system I could never have dreamed of. So many crimes were solved and so many more will be in the future.

Since I retired, the department has acquired the equipment to search palm prints, as well. I know I would have loved being able to search palm prints. Advancements in new techniques continue every day, and the speed of the new and improved systems is unbelievable. The time saved for departments and the speed and accuracy with which the crimes are solved is priceless, not only to the police, but to the victims, their families, and friends.

My Inspiration

My passion for police work came from my father, Robert "Bob" E. Brown, who retired from the KCPD as a major in 1980. He became Chief of the Independence, MO, Police Department in January 1980.

He was a policeman's policeman, if that makes sense. He never lost his roots as a street cop, even as he climbed to the rank of major. Everyone who worked for him loved to work for him.

He stood behind them as they tried to be the best they could for the citizens of Kansas City. Just months before he retired, he was chasing a robbery suspect down the street. Sometime later, some officers came by to tell me, "I can't believe your Dad was chasing that suspect." I asked them why, and they said because he was a major. I said, "My Dad is a cop, first and foremost. Just because he is a commander does not mean he doesn't still do police work."

My father was a World War II Army veteran who was a paratrooper with the 82nd Airborne that landed in Normandy on D-Day. He was fortunate to have survived; more than 60 percent of his group was killed. I found this out only two months before he passed away in May 1985.

My Dad is why I joined the police department. I started my career in August 1976, in the Identification Section, and retired from the same unit many years later. Not many civilians spend their entire careers in the same section. My family's roots can be traced back to a constable who came over on the Mayflower and, at the time I retired, someone in the Brown family had been in some sort of law enforcement position for over 280 years! So, I guess it really was in my blood.

My mother, Clara C. Brown, was also my hero. She endured being the wife of a police officer during the riots in Kansas City in 1968, not knowing if her husband would come home alive. Officers put their lives at risk every day for the citizens and the city. I have complete respect for each and every one of them and pray that, at the end of their shift, they return safely to their families.

This is a photo of Robert E. Brown, taken in 1980, when he was Chief of Police with the Independence Police Department in MO. He joined the KCPD in 1950, and retired in 1980, as a Major. He was the inspiration for Kathleen Hentges, his daughter, in deciding to join the KCPD. He passed away in 1985, of a heart attack, and was Hentges' personal hero. (Courtesy of Independence Police Department)

Stephen Wright is being promoted to Sergeant by Chief Norman Caron, 1978. (Courtesy of the KCPD)

Chapter 33

Stephen W. Wright

Retired Sergeant, KCPD, 1972-1996

I started getting interested in a career in law enforcement around age 15. I worked for a cousin who owned a Dairy Queen in Lee's Summit. Her husband was Ken Carnes, a Missouri State highway patrolman at that time. The Dairy Queen became a hangout for several of their highway patrol friends. It was an interesting group of men, with one thing in common; they all loved going to work. This was something new to me.

My Dad went to work in a coal mine at age 8, went to war, and then worked into his 60s in a back-breaking job. He certainly did not enjoy going to work; it was something he had to do. The fact that people looked forward to going to work was new to me. After being surrounded by this attitude all through my Dairy Queen days, I focused on a law enforcement career.

After graduating from high school, I started college at Central Missouri State University which had a law enforcement degree program. My college life could be summed up in one word, underfunded. After a junior year of near starvation in a $1 a day flophouse, I applied for a job in Higginsville, MO as a police officer. There were only two applicants for the job, me and a convicted felon. Because the uniforms fit and they felt the other applicant might not be able to carry a gun, I got the job. Things looked up. I married my wife, Susie, in December 1971, rented an 8x35 mobile home, and moved in with my new bride.

In 1972, I graduated with my Bachelor of Science degree. As it turns out, the degree was critical in securing a sworn position on the KCPD. At the time, the minimum height requirement was 5'8" and I was only 5'7" tall. My cousin, Kenny, said he knew a chiropractor who could stretch me a couple inches for long enough to get measured by the department's Personnel Unit. I decided not to go that route but, instead, try to get the job without running the risk of sustaining quadriplegia.

As it turned out, the department was willing to waive the height requirement because I had a college degree. That worked out well. The hiring process involved an interesting afternoon hooked up to a polygraph. I walked in with a few things that only I knew. When I walked out, there were two people that knew those things. After allowing a couple days for me to stew, I learned I was hired and would start the academy on July 5, 1972.

July 4, 1972 found me fired up to start my career, but it also found me with long hair. My wife, Susie, volunteered to cut it. We had dog-grooming clippers and a spacer that would give me about a one-inch buzz cut. She ran the clippers all over the front of my head; I was on the way to presentable. She moved to the back of my head and made a decisive move from my neck to the crown of my head. What she had not noticed was that the spacer had fallen off, so the clippers shaved a two-inch wide path up the back of my head. Imagine a reverse Mohawk. You can't fix that with dog clippers.

The best man at my parents' wedding was a barber. I called him at home, picked him up, and drove him to his shop. He did a good job of patching me up. I ended up with what military people call "high and tight," just really high.

My time at the academy was great. I made many friends that will last for the rest of my life. My first assignment was to the South Central Patrol Division. I worked relief throughout the division, which had me patrolling a variety of neighborhoods. It did not take long to figure out that I loved the job. I was on top of the world. I got to put bad guys in jail, help people at car crashes, get drunk drivers off the road, and got paid for doing it!

There were some ups and downs. Being a rookie, I had many opportunities to mess things up. I remember making a cutting call at a bar at 50th and Prospect Avenue. When I arrived there, I found an old guy at the bar, bleeding from a nasty cut to his arm. He pointed out the culprit, who still had the knife. After a brief struggle, the stabber was handcuffed and secured in the back of a paddy wagon. It was a slow night, so everybody showed up.

I got out my clipboard to get the information for the report. I asked the victim what had happened. As it turned out, it was some stupid argument. I asked the victim what he did next and he told me, "I shot him, twice." He made a V with his index and middle finger and pointed to the center of his forehead, an apparent guide to help me find the wounds on the guy I had just shoved into the back of a wagon. Did I mention it was a dark bar?

I ran out to the wagon, opened it up and there the gunshot wounds were, just as indicated. He went to General Hospital by ambulance. As it turns out, the bullets hit at a lucky angle, skimming the skull and exiting on top of his head. He was sent to jail with four Band-Aids and a good scare. Powers of observation grow with practice.

After a couple of years in patrol, I had a chance to expand on my experience as a member of the fledgling Crime Scene Investigation Unit. At that time, it was still a loose organization within patrol. After graduating from the CSI academy in 1975 (I'm the only one under 5'8" in the photo), I returned to the South Central Patrol Division where I occasionally rode relief in a sector car but became a CSI on most nights. What a time that was. The CSI Unit soon was formalized and made its own entity within the Investigations Bureau.

As the 1970s came to a close, I left the CSI Unit to take a position in the Planning Unit. I left there for Internal Affairs, and then was promoted to sergeant. I then was headed back to patrol. I got a call from an academy friend, a captain at the time, who wanted me to be his dog watch desk sergeant.

I'm not a night person, so I was flattered that he thought of me and politely declined. He thought I would jump on the transfer, and all he could say was that I was scheduled to begin in three days. Actually, it was a great experience. It was a fairly intricate job with a lot of things to learn.

But on Christmas Day 1979, the fire department was out on strike, and the police department had been pressed into quick action. Apparently, you can't inhale an entire building of smoke without repercussions. The bottom line was that I suffered smoke inhalation. I spent a couple of weeks in the hospital and six months in bed. For me, the late 1970s was mostly erased. I have vignettes, but most memories are gone.

When I returned to work, it was a struggle, and I soon accepted a position in the Audit Unit. Soon it was time to run a uniform by Konomos Dry Cleaning and head back to patrol after a brief taste of that assignment. In 1982, I learned of a position opening in the Regional Crime Lab. This was a unit within the department that also received grant money to serve the region. I got the job, and this is where I spent the remainder of my career.

I was supervisor of the Fingerprint Section and the Photography Section. I was also responsible for outside crime scenes. If a small city outside of Kansas City had a major crime, they would call me, and I would put together a crime scene investigation team and go gather the evidence. The downside was that I got a ton of calls in the middle of the night. To this day, years later, if we get a call at home in the middle of the night, I usually have my pants on before Susie has a chance to answer the phone.

Another of my responsibilities was coordinating a bi-annual CSI course during which we would train 16 people to become crime scene investigators. We also held seminars on blood spatter pattern interpretation, casting shoe prints, and crime scene photography. The blood spatter pattern interpretation was my favorite. I would go to the blood bank, withdraw about six pints, and take them to a facility where we had cubicles built and covered with cardboard. I would put on a motorcycle helmet with a blood-soaked sponge attached and someone would hit it with a baseball bat. It was messy.

The outside crime scene responsibilities were later expanded to assist with homicides inside Kansas City. This took me to a lot of murder scenes, but one stands out. Robert Berdella ran Bob's Bizarre Bazaar, selling oddities from around the world, such as human skulls, in the Westport flea market. After this story broke, the lab received a few skulls in the mail sent by people who had purchased them at Bob's Bizarre Bazaar. They turned out to be medical school skulls.

In his free time, Bob picked up men and took them back to his house, injected them with an animal tranquilizer, bound them up, and kept them as sex slaves until they died. That little secret went public when one of his captives freed himself, jumped from a second story window, and ran naked down the street screaming for help.

We found a skull in a closet with some mud caked on it, so we decided to poke around the back yard to see if we could find a grave.

Someone stuck a shovel in the ground, and out popped a skull. We ended up gridding off the back yard and removing a couple of feet of soil. Try that some time. What are the odds that the only find that we would make would be on the first shovel full of dirt?

Someone located stacks of Polaroid photos, along with notes regarding his victims. We found many references to the victims getting an EKG. Then we found photos of victims during their "EKGs." We found the device, 700-volt ballast that he would hook up to the victims. The photos and notes documented the captivity, torture, and assault of many young men. You could lay the photos out and see the physical decline of his victims before they succumbed to the effects of the torture Bob inflicted upon them.

I spent a month at Berdella's house. Because "Bad Bob" was kind enough to document his crimes with photos and written records, he pled guilty to avoid the death penalty. He was in jail for only a couple of years when he dropped dead of a heart attack, thus cheating his life-without-parole-sentence out of many years in a dingy prison cell.

I went to many murder scenes where the victims were badly decomposed. You would think that you'd get more accustomed to the smell the more you were exposed. Not the case. I eventually became extremely sensitized to the smell and became the resident puker.

Fortunately, I found a full-face, nuisance odor mask just in time to undress a badly decomposed victim. I pulled his boot off, and his foot came off in it. The odor was suppressed, but the visuals were too much and I filled my mask up to my eyes. I almost drowned in it. Co-workers started volunteering to perform some of my disgusting tasks, just because my retching was making them sick. To this day, my smell-meter is pegged on 10!

In fall 1996, I became eligible for retirement, after buying six months of service from my time in Higginsville. With a desire to get a full night's sleep on a regular basis, and to retain more of my meals, I set out to do just that.

The next year, my wife sold her business. In fact, we sold everything we owned and started our next adventure. We headed out in our motor coach to live as full-time RV'ers.

Wayne Staley was promoted to CWO2 at Fort Bragg, North Carolina. Jerry Borchers, his wife, Carol and daughter Beverly attended his promotion in 1980.
(Courtesy of Wayne Staley)

Chapter 34

R. Wayne Staley

Retired CWO3, U.S. Army CID, 1972-1993; Kansas City Regional Crime Laboratory, 1994-2010

June 1972, was quite the busy month for me. I graduated from Western Illinois University with a degree in history education, got married, and then received my draft notice. The strange thing about it was the fact I never did teach history, and the first marriage lasted only five years, although I did get a great son out of it.

This was when Vietnam was still going on, and with a draft lottery number of 3, I knew I was a sure thing. The other bad part was every third person reporting for the draft was being sent to the Marines, and I heard they didn't like draftees very much. When I did go for the draft, I managed to count ahead and shift over with the guy next to me so he went to the Marines and I got the Army.

The Army works in strange and mysterious ways. With all the battery of tests one is required to take when going in, my two worst scores were mechanics and electronics, with an almost perfect score in administrative areas. So, of course, the Army sent me to radio repair school and I got to play with electronics. I did actually graduate in the top 10 percent of my class, so I got sent on to advanced radio repair.

My first school was in Fort Benning, Georgia and from there I went to Fort Gordon, Georgia for the advanced class. The Army was trying something different with a go-at-your-own-pace school. With Vietnam waiting on the other side of the school, I was very slow about finishing. Indeed, I was the last one out. Finally, the orders for Vietnam came down, but these were canceled and I wound up getting sent to Fort McClellan, Alabama.

My first permanent duty assignment was with a Military Affiliate Radio Station (MARS) at Fort McClellan. My job was to use a shortwave radio to help GIs in Germany call home. Phone expenses from overseas at that time were cost-prohibitive. Instead, soldiers could go to their local MARS station in Germany, which would radio us, and we would place the collect call through the phone system with Alabama billing. But we had to listen to the call and have them say "over" when finished speaking so we could flip the off switch.

We definitely heard some interesting calls. I remember the wife who told her husband she was five months pregnant. After a couple minutes of figuring it out, he realized he hadn't been home for seven months. Oops! We had six people assigned to the station with only one radio, so I learned to play different card games.

From there, I was sent to Camp Humphrey, Korea. That was a learning experience in itself. Once again, I did not work as a radio repairman, which was probably a good thing, because I probably would have done more damage than good. My wife joined me in Korea, where we had to live on the local economy, which was interesting, to say the least.

After Korea, I went to Ft Riley, Kansas, home of the 1st Infantry, the "Big Red One." I got put into an administrative clerk position and decided that wasn't what I wanted to do. Actually, I wasn't sure what I did want, but I'd heard that CID agents got to wear civilian clothes, so I applied and got accepted. The CID was one of the best things that happened to me. I went to CID school at Fort McClellan and loved every minute of it. I was supposed to be assigned to Fort Campbell, Kentucky, but when I went in my unit to sign out, they told me my orders had been changed back to Fort Riley.

So, I did my probation there and learned from some great people. It was there that I met Jerry Borchers when his Reserve Unit came for their annual two weeks of active duty. It was a busy time for me, as I was going through a divorce and working a lot of hours. Jerry and I were teamed up and our first day was a day from hell. We normally worked 24-hour shifts and picked up one or two cases, but that day we had 16 investigations and six requests for assistance.

Among those was a cutting in which Jerry developed a palm print on a locker door to tie the suspect to the crime. Also, we investigated an officer's expensive sports car, damaged in a garage on base housing where we collected footwear prints that was later tied to local juveniles. Jerry and I really bonded that day, despite the fact he ate my peanut butter-and-jelly sandwiches and I wound up going hungry. The divorce process left me with very little money at that time, so I was living off peanut butter, jelly, and Tab sodas!

After Jerry's two-week active duty was up, he invited me to Kansas City. I decided to take him up on it, and I came to know his family, who all made me feel really welcome. His wife, Carol, was maybe a little leery of having a freshly divorced man in the house, but she and Jerry became my closest friends.

After the divorce was finalized, I requested a transfer and was assigned to Wurzburg, Germany, one of the greatest assignments I ever had. I was single again and looked forward to exploring Europe. In the time there, I worked hard and played hard. I would drive to Frankfurt to hop on a military flight going to someplace I wanted to see, like Greece or England. The one assignment I did not care for was the undercover narcotics position. That job often required a 120-hour work week, and the Army doesn't pay overtime. I also worked as evidence custodian and as a fraud investigator. I eventually applied for, and got, the rank of Warrant Officer.

From Germany, I was assigned to Fort Bragg, North Carolina as an investigator, which was great. Because of the 82nd Airborne and the Special Forces on the base, it was always busy and never boring.

Don't Sleep with a Bomb

The case I remember most dealt with a soldier who was planning to blow up his first sergeant with a homemade bomb in a canteen. It was well-made, but he had to wait until after dark to put it on the first sergeant's car. He lay down to rest and fell asleep with the bomb under his pillow. We found one ear on the ceiling and pieces of him outside, because all the windows blew outward from the concussion of the blast. We joked that it was an open-and-shut case.

Cross Country and Back

While at Fort Bragg, Jerry and his family came down to pin on my CWO2 bars. We had a great time. I talked my boss into supporting me for an assignment to the Protective Service Detail (PSD) in Falls Church, VA. I also requested the opportunity to attend German language school in Monterey, CA. Both requests were accepted, so I left Fort Bragg to head west to Kansas City to visit Jerry and his family. I was supposed to leave in plenty of time, but got sick for a day, so I wound up driving from Kansas City to Monterey in 33 hours straight. Quite a drive!

The German language class at the Defense Language Institute was an intensive eight-month course that gives you the equivalency of four years of college German. The class was great fun, but a lot of work. After leaving the school, I headed back to Kansas City to visit Jerry, and he arranged for me to meet a young woman who was separated and willing to try a blind date. We hit it off almost immediately. We dated long distance until she finally agreed to come to Falls Church where we got married. Gabriele turned out to be the soul mate I'd been looking for.

From Kansas City, I went on to Washington, D.C., and found an apartment in Falls Church, about two blocks from work, in a high-rise apartment building. It was great because I could actually see the fireworks at the Washington monument on the Fourth of July.

The protective service detail was a job I fell in love with. We provided protection for five VIPs, including Secretary of Defense, Caspar Weinberger; Assistant Secretary of Defense, William Howard Taft III; Chairman, Joint Chiefs of Staff, General John Vessey; Secretary of the Army John Marsh; and Chief of Staff of the Army, General John Wickham. During my three years in this assignment, I traveled all over the world and got to meet heads of state and royalty. We also attended hearings in Congress and learned a lot about the workings of the government.

A typical day in Washington would be to pick up the secretary of defense at his home at approximately 0600 hours. We would escort him to the Pentagon where we would get his schedule from his secretary. There was always an advance team to any location he was going to, as well as a chase car and an agent in the front right seat of his limousine. He could have meetings at the White House or a hearing at the Capital, but he could sometimes be in the office all day.

Usually, in the evening, he would start making the circuit of different political cocktail parties where you would always see him with a drink in hand, but you never saw him take a sip. After four or five cocktail parties, he would wind up at a formal dinner at approximately 2100 and finish around 2330. From there, we would drive him home and go back to the office to drop off the car and get home around 0030 hours. It would start all over the next day. One time, I did this for 41 days straight, including weekends. We often saw the Secret Service go through three shifts of people while we were still on the same one.

Sometimes Being Sick is Good

On one occasion, I was assigned to provide security for Mrs. Weinberger during a NATO-sponsored trip of spouses traveling by bus along the southern coast of Portugal. Mrs. Weinberger was from Maine and had a very reserved, New England manner. She was always very polite, but never really talked with the security agents. I knew that she would not want to stay with the bus the whole trip, so I followed in a car. We stopped for lunch and I had scallops and shrimp. After lunch, she indicated that she wished to return directly to the hotel, so she and two other ladies got in the car and we headed back.

It was about 70 miles and, halfway there, I realized that I was getting sick from the seafood. I was trying to decide whether it was better to get sick in the car and keep driving or to pull over. I finally decided to pull over and apologized to the ladies but told them I needed to be sick. I tried to keep the car in sight, but not make them watch me be sick. After I got rid of the food, I felt much better and got back in the car to drive the rest of the way.

The ladies were very solicitous, and Mrs. Weinberger volunteered to drive while I lay down in the back seat with my head on one of the other lady's lap. I didn't think my boss would appreciate seeing the car pull up to the hotel with Mrs. Weinberger driving and me sick in the back seat, so I thanked them and told them I was fine and did the driving. But after that, Mrs. Weinberger was always very friendly to me and would make a point to say hello and ask how I was doing. The other agents couldn't figure it out. I guess I humanized myself a little in her eyes.

Where are the Mountains?

On one trip to Honduras, we needed to fly to the southeast coast where the Special Forces were training Nicaraguan forces. The Honduran Air Force agreed to fly us up because it would have taken two days of back-country driving to get there. When we arrived at the airport, I saw a nice sleek jet and thought, how great. But when I headed to it, the pilot said no and pointed to a single prop plane for two people.

We took off and were flying through clouds so thick you couldn't see anything. I asked where the mountains were; he just pointed outside and said he was watching the altimeter, which would change numbers when he tapped it even slightly. After bouncing all over with turbulence, we finally made it through the mountains, in spite of a couple times when I looked out at a nearby peak looming higher than we were. After arriving at the coast, he turned and made it to a local airport and landed fairly hard. As we were taxiing up to the building, he ran out of gas. He said a storm was coming and he had to leave. On the way back, I called and got permission to rent a jet, which came out and picked us up and flew us back, well above the clouds.

Where is the Security Seat?

Whenever we traveled overseas, it was always a fight to ensure that the front right seat of the VIP's auto belonged to security. Everyone wanted to ride with the big guy. No matter how often it was stressed, invariably someone tried to scoot into the seat. We were in Japan with Secretary Weinberger and his military assistant, General Colin Powell, and the local embassy people were fighting us on their security. When the limousine arrived and we got the VIPS in the car, someone jumped into the front right seat, so I dragged him out and sat down. It was then I realized that this was Japan and the driver's seat was on the right side and I had pulled the driver out. I looked around and said, "It looks like everything is OK." I got out, let the driver back in, walked around the car and got in on the left side while trying to ignore Secretary Weinberger and General Powell laughing in the back seat.

During those three years, I spent a lot of hours in airplanes and airports around the world and was extremely disappointed that we weren't allowed to use the air miles we'd built up over the time. The job was definitely a lot of fun and I made CWO3 while on the job.

When my tour was about up, I decided to apply to the U.S. Army Crime Lab (USACIL) at Fort Gillem, Ga., in Atlanta. I loved photography, so I applied as a forensic photographer and got accepted. The training program was two years of intensive training. We handled evidence from all over the world and traveled to scenes across the country when requested by a local office. It was while we were assigned in Georgia that Gabriele and I decided to have another marriage ceremony in the Catholic Church and invited Jerry and Carol down to stand in as Best Man and Matron of Honor. They introduced us, supported us, and stood up for us.

From the Atlanta lab, I was assigned to the Frankfurt, Germany lab. I was supervisor of the photo section, handled the evidence room, and served as executive officer for several months between captains. I also served as acting lab director on one occasion. While in Germany, I wound up going to Saudi Arabia during Desert Storm. And again, after the war, I went for a second time. Living in a tent with blowing sand outside was not my favorite thing.

After three years in Germany, I decided to retire from the military and thought I had a job lined up with the U.S. Postal lab in Memphis. That didn't work out, so Gabriele and I decided to go to Colorado Springs and see what I could find. Of course, on the way, we had to stop and see Jerry and Carol Borchers in Kansas City. We stayed with them a while, and Gabriele wound up going back to work for the person she was working for when I met her.

Jerry then informed me that the Kansas City Police Crime Lab was hiring for a photography position, so I applied, got hired and went right to work. When Steve Wright retired, they civilianized his position and I replaced him. I took over running crime scene schools for our citizens and surrounding area law enforcement personnel. I expanded the course to three weeks and, with the help of the lab staff, made it one of the best CSI courses offered. During my time with the department, I ran 32 schools with 16 students per class from police agencies from all across Missouri and Kansas.

Diet Candy is Not Good for You

One scene we responded to was a rape in a local town on Christmas. It occurred at a daycare center that was closed for the day. A man traveling through the town had decided to stop, break in, and make himself at home. He had taken his clothes off and was washing them with the laundry machines, walking around in the nude.

A woman who worked at the daycare decided to stop by to borrow some milk, since the stores were closed. When she entered the building, the suspect grabbed her, raped her, and locked her in the bathroom. While he had been walking around, he had searched the desks for money or food and found a diet candy bar. He took a bite out of it, but apparently disliked the taste and threw it down. He washed the floor down where he had raped the woman, but we were still able to find one pubic hair. I also recovered the candy bar, and we cast the bite mark, which a forensic odontologist was able to match to the suspect. The pubic hair also was identified through DNA. This, together with the victim's evidence was enough to arrest him.

I worked at the RCL for 16 years before retiring a second time. During that time, with the help of so many good people, I took the photo section into the digital age and, subsequently, on to forensic video. I left it in good hands and feel that the time spent with the Army CID and the Kansas City Police Crime Lab was well worth the long and often strenuous hours.

This is a photo of Missouri State Highway Patrolman Michael Leavene that was taken in the academy in 1972. (Courtesy of Michael Leavene)

Chapter 35

David M. (Mike) Leavene

Retired Sergeant, Missouri State Highway Patrol, 1972-1999;
Retired CWO2, U.S. Army CID Reserves, 1987-1997

How I Started My Law Enforcement Career

I have been a commissioned peace officer with three states, Missouri, Arizona and Texas, and an accredited special agent with the U.S. Army Criminal Investigation Command. After more than 40 years in law enforcement, I know hundreds of stories, some sad, some funny, and some downright scary. I will share a few with you here.

In 1948, I was born in Moberly, MO. My father, Howard Leavene, sold cars most of his life, but later retired as a guard with the medium-security prison south of town. It was during his years as a salesman for the local Dodge dealer that I got to know several state troopers who brought their patrol cars in for repairs. Men like Roy Robinson, Leo Prenger, Roy Beal, and Lloyd Swartz had no idea how much I was influenced by them. But I knew then, when I grew up, I wanted to be a Missouri State highway patrolman. I was lucky because I got to live that wish and more.

Like many other police officers, I began my law enforcement career by joining in the U.S. military, enlisting in November 1968. I graduated from the U.S. Army Military Police School in Fort Gordon, GA. in 1969, and was then assigned as a MP for 13 months in the Republic of Korea, Second Infantry Division. The remainder of my three-year enlistment was served with the 63rd Military Police Detachment at the Military Ocean Terminal in Bayonne, New Jersey as a patrol supervisor. Serving those three years as an MP proved to me I had made the right choice in my career path as a law enforcement officer. I liked the Army and got to know and respect some true professional military law enforcement personnel. I came close to re-enlisting; but due to draw-downs at the end of the Vietnam War, cancellation of re-enlistment bonuses and a new baby girl, my wife, Linda, and I decided to leave the active military. I would pursue my career in civilian law enforcement. After completing active duty in December 1971, I applied with the Missouri State Highway Patrol, was accepted, and began six months of recruit training on July 1, 1972.

The first 10 years of my career on the patrol, I was stationed in Troop B which served 16 counties in Northeast Missouri. My first assignment was Zone 1 in Macon County, and my field training officer (FTO) was Trooper Larry Murdock. A good FTO has a profound effect in molding a new officer, and I had one of the best. I would later be transferred to Zone 3 in Canton and assigned as the only trooper in Knox County. The Canton zone covered four Northeast counties and had five officers assigned to it. This is a rural community with no federal highways and a population of around 5,000.

At that time in the early 1970s, it was not uncommon for officers to be assigned to cover large rural areas and, at times, especially at night, be the only law enforcement officer on duty. The law enforcement knowledge and experiences I gained there would prove invaluable during my career.

In 1977, I enlisted in the U.S. Army Reserves and for the first six years, I was a drill sergeant with the 85th Division Armor Training in Quincy, Illinois. I would later serve four years in troop command headquarters over military police units of the Missouri National Guard, during which time I transferred from Troop "B" to Troop "A" in Kansas City during 1982. In 1987, I switched back to the Army Reserves and was accredited as a special agent in the U.S.

Army Criminal Investigation Command and graduated from the U.S. Army Reserve Component CID Special Agent School in Fort. McClellan, Alabama. As an Army Reserve accredited special agent with the U.S. Army's Criminal Investigation Command, I advanced to the rank of Chief Warrant Officer Two before retiring in 1997, as special agent in charge of the 493rd Military Police Detachment (CID). With international and domestic assignments, I obtained experiences in a wide range of investigations, from crimes against persons to fraud.

Strange Lights South of Memphis

While stationed as a trooper in the Northeast in the 1970s and early 1980s, there were times when we were dispatched on calls to investigate very strange occurrences. During this time there were a lot of UFO sightings by the public.

There was a reported UFO encounter I remember quite well. It occurred late one fall evening, south of Memphis, MO. Troop B sent me and Trooper Lee Tipton (assigned to Memphis) to investigate a report of strange lights. I traveled north out of Edina and he came south from Memphis. The weather was cool and fairly clear that fall night. When we came into the area where the lights were last reported, we took up stationary positions and started watching the surrounding area for anything unusual. It wasn't long before I observed a bright light moving along the top of a tree line between my position and Trooper Tipton's. We started converging on the area where I had seen the strange light and soon discovered the light was not actually above the trees, but was shining up through the trees. We worked our way closer to the area through winding gravel and dirt roads and soon I was in a position where the light was coming towards me along a fence row. I turned off my car and lights, and then waited to see what the source of this illumination was. I didn't have long to wait. Out into the open came a pick-up truck equipped with a very bright spotlight which was the source of the strange light that had been reported by the public. As soon as I saw what the source of the light was I had a pretty good idea of what was taking place, due to the time of the year and the spotlight shining into the trees. Raccoon season was still a few weeks off and, at that time, the fur industry was very good. Good 'coon hides were going for $25 to $50, depending on the quality.

As the truck came near my position, I turned on my lights and activated the emergency lights to pull the vehicle over as it came onto the dusty road. The chase was on! It wasn't long before I saw a large bag being thrown out the window on the passenger side and I radioed Trooper Tipton its location so he could retrieve it. The culprits soon realized they were not going to get away in a pick-up truck from the big Chrysler Newport with a 440 hemi-magnum police interceptor engine, and within a couple miles they came to a stop. We then called the local "Possum Sheriff" (State Conservation Agent) who was glad to assist in summoning these culprits into the local magistrate for hunting 'coon's out-of-season. Don't get me wrong about the term "Possum Sheriff." It is nothing more than a little friendly jab at officers for whom we all had the greatest respect, no different than when others called us, "State Bulls." The game agents probably have one of the most dangerous jobs in law enforcement when you realize that practically all of their law enforcement contacts are armed when they approach them or when those potential violators are watching them through a scope at a distance. At that time, most of the state conservation agents held a reserve deputy commission in the county where they worked so they could assist law enforcement in the rural regions.

As it turned out, the two culprits in the pick-up were well-to-do local farmers. The local magistrate had no mercy on hunting wildlife out-of-season, and they both ended up losing their guns that night and their hunting privileges for a long time, on top of a pretty stiff fine.

Transient Criminals

After retiring from the Missouri State Highway Patrol in July 1999, Linda and I moved to Phoenix. I went to work for the state of Arizona Registrar of Contractors (ROC) in November as a criminal and civil investigator. Statewide, at that time, there were close to 30 investigators, many were former or retired law enforcement officers within Arizona or from across the country.

As a criminal justice agency, investigators enforced Title 10,

Chapter 32, of the Arizona Revised Statutes; routinely filing criminal charges with local jurisdictions for violations of Arizona's contracting laws. Investigators also filed felony charges for theft and fraudulent schemes when these offenses were uncovered while conducting unlicensed contracting investigations. ROC investigators did not have Arizona peace officer status, so their activities were limited to the investigation of violations of state contracting laws and related offenses.

During my early years at the ROC, I was actively involved in investigation of the fraudulent activities of transient criminals. I gathered intelligence information and coordinated contacts with other law enforcement agencies nationally, which resulted in the arrests of several suspects wanted by the federal government and other agencies outside Arizona.

This was not my first experience with transient criminals. During my early years on the highway patrol in Northeast Missouri, we had several contacts with them conducting barn painting, lightning rod sales, and termite inspection scams.

From December 1999, to January 2000, the ROC investigated approximately 35 cases involving asphalt-paving fraud. The financial loss on these cases was approximately $150,000, not including the cost of repairs or replacement because of poor workmanship. One suspect cashed more than $60,000 in checks at a check-cashing store in Mesa. This was for just one crew. We suspected that as many as six different crews were working in the Phoenix area.

Many of these crimes go unreported. Victims are either embarrassed to report the scam or in the case of some of the commercial businesses, the victims are afraid to initiate an investigation for fear of losing their job. Sometimes, the cases are reported to the police and victims are told that it is a civil matter between them and the contractor. This was caused primarily by a lack of understanding on the part of law enforcement officers about the nature of the crimes being committed.

Most cases occurred in winter. The transient criminal organization consists of thousands of individuals nationwide who have been known to interact with each other, and whose migratory livelihood revolves around scamming the public by performing shoddy home repairs. They often target the elderly in established neighborhoods, retirement communities, and mobile home parks to commit home improvement frauds.

In addition to poor workmanship, the scammers also specialize in the use of poor quality materials. Typically, members of these groups will dilute their paint with water, while roof coatings and asphalt coatings will be mixed with diesel oil or gasoline and other cheap fillers.

By all appearances, these transient criminals may look like legitimate contractors. They may present identification; however, it is usually a fraudulent or stolen driver's license. Business cards and contracts use fictitious names and do not have an address on them; they usually list 800 numbers or cell phone numbers that are connected to an answering machine or answering service. They will claim to be licensed and bonded and give a false license number, if asked for one.

The trucks and equipment that the transient criminals use usually are clean and appear to be rather new. Occasionally, the trucks will have the company name painted on the door or magnetic signs on the side with the company name, or no markings at all except for a department of transportation number. The trucks pull flatbed trailers with paving equipment. The rollers, pavers, and Bobcats are usually rented. The trucks and trailers are owned by the transient criminals, but the registration usually checks to a female.

In the case of asphalt scams, the standard method of operation involves approaching a business or residence and claiming that they have just completed another job down the road and have leftover asphalt or materials that they will sell for a bargain price ($2 a square foot or less). Victims usually believe the asphalt will only cost a few hundred dollars and are totally surprised when they are handed a bill for several thousand dollars. If the victim is reluctant to pay, the suspects may try to intimidate the victim by threats of a lawsuit or appear to get angry. These ploys usually result in the victim agreeing to pay an amount that is lower than first listed on the contract.

When the asphalt is applied, they do not coat the area before paving, and the asphalt that is applied is usually a low grade patch asphalt, costing approximately $25 to $30 a ton, that is spread thin (1/2-inch layer) and which will crumble and crack in a short time. (A quality asphalt driveway is about 2-1/2 inches of highway-grade asphalt, compacted to 2 inches on a properly prepared sub grade.) Suspects also cover a much larger area than the victim wanted or ordered, so the bad guys can inflate the bill. They also charge for more square footage than was actually applied. Suspects usually are not at a job site for more than one or two hours. If the victim informs the suspects that they have contacted the police or the ROC office, the suspects will leave before law enforcement can arrive on the scene.

Because of the nature of the crimes committed by these groups and the vulnerability of their primary victims, they were operating with little or no threat of criminal prosecution.

Transient criminal activity is monitored by networking with such organizations as the National Association of Bunco Investigators (NABI) and the National Association of Construction Investigators (NACI). The sharing of information with other law enforcement agencies has resulted in several felons, wanted in other states for fraud, being located and arrested in Arizona.

Although transient criminal activity remains a major issue, it is being addressed through better training and communication among law enforcement agencies. The majority of the credit for attacking this transient criminal activity should go to the members of NABI, a great organization of professionals from all over the United States and Canada who continually work together on cases around the country involving transient criminals.

Case of Disbarred Attorney

I was hired as a detective by the Maricopa County Attorney's Office Investigations Division on April 12, 2004, and obtained my Arizona Peace Officer Certification on July 8, 2004. Detectives primarily were assigned to locating individuals, witnesses and/or victims, serving subpoenas, conducting interview, and performing other follow-up investigations on crimes submitted by other law enforcement agencies for prosecution. Occasionally, the unit would be assigned a case where our detectives would be the primary case agents. They actually would open the investigation and follow it through to the end.

In February 2005, I was assigned a case that tested my knowledge and skills as an investigator. This was a fraud case that later would be described as a career investigation because of its magnitude and complex nature.

During the investigation and trial of Gary Karpin, I was placed on special assignment to the Special Crimes Unit and tasked as the primary case agent. This proactive investigation was initiated by the Maricopa County Attorney's Office and resulted in the suspect, Karpin, being charged by a grand jury with 25 felony counts of fraudulent schemes and theft.

I was assigned to work with Maricopa County Deputy Attorney Annie Laurie Van Wie to investigate a complaint of fraudulent schemes made by the Arizona State Bar. The complaint was against a disbarred attorney known as Gary Jay Karpin, who was from Vermont. This case would span three years, and it would involve more than 300 victims and numerous witnesses before Karpin would come to trial.

For almost a full year, this case was my primary duty. Initially, I was given two boxes of material sent to the Maricopa County Attorney's Office from the Arizona State Bar concerning complaints and a civil law suit that had been filed against Karpin by the Arizona State Bar. I immediately set out to research this man and the complaints filed against him, and it did not take long to see a clear pattern of deception and manipulation by a man who would later be described as a predator.

Consumers began filing complaints against Karpin in 1996, for the unauthorized practice of law. Forty-three complaints were filed between December 1996, and September 2005. A total of 16 complaints were filed with us between 1999 and 2005, including six complaints filed with the attorney generals by the Arizona State Bar. No investigations were ever initiated by the attorney general's office.

Karpin continually ignored warnings to cease his unauthorized practice of law in Arizona. He had been operating his business in Maricopa County since at least 1996, under several different names: Divorce with Dignity, Divorce Associates, and Relationships with Dignity, G.J. Karpin and Associates, and A Dignified Divorce. The Arizona State Bar brought civil litigation against him for practicing law without being a member of the bar, but this did not stop Karpin from continuing his practice in defiance of the state bar and Arizona Supreme Court.

My investigation, from interviews with victims and witnesses, revealed Karpin was operating a fraud scheme in the operation of his divorce mediation business, known as "Divorce Associates," aka "Divorce with Dignity." He claimed or implied to all of his clients that he was a licensed attorney, when, in fact, he was a disbarred attorney from Vermont and not licensed to practice law in Arizona. I would later learn he was being sought by the state of Maine, which also wanted to serve him with disbarment papers. Karpin was warned on numerous times to cease his activities of practicing law.

One of my first tasks was to obtain a certified copy of the disbarment proceedings from the Vermont Supreme Court. Karpin was charged by the Vermont Professional Conduct Board with four counts of misconduct in November 1992, and disbarred from the practice of law by the Supreme Court of the State of Vermont in March 1993. The reasons listed included: lack of diligence, lack of competence, lack of candor, failure to maintain the public trust, false statements, fraud, misrepresentation, and submission of false statements in connection with the disciplinary process. With disbarment like this, he would never be licensed to practice law in any state.

My investigation revealed that Karpin moved to Arizona within four months of being disbarred and got a job selling cars at a local dealership. It wasn't long before he left that field and set up a business where he would practice law under the guise of divorce mediation. He advertised as a divorce mediator and emphasized to his clients he was a former prosecuting attorney. He even framed a badge from his former employer and hung it on a wall in his office.

Karpin worked for the Orleans County Attorney's Office in Vermont from November 1987, through September 1988, before being fired and going into private practice. When I contacted his former boss, the main thing he could remember about Karpin was that he gave him two boxes and two hours to "get his ass out of his office." The fact Karpin was being investigated and would later be arrested came as no surprise to him.

Karpin told many of his clients that he was an attorney and did not disclose that he had been disbarred and was not licensed to practice law in Arizona. He advertised his services in several Maricopa County newspapers and magazines, with advertisements still running after his arrest in July 2005. The advertisements had various claims about services provided, but all were deceptive in implying Karpin was an attorney by mentioning his past employment as a prosecutor, Jurist Doctorate degrees, and listing him as a Maricopa County Justice Court mediator, a non-existent title. The more than 300 victims who believed he was a licensed attorney agreed they would not have hired him if they had known, at the time; he was not licensed to practice law.

Karpin exploited vulnerable couples financially through his divorce mediation business. It was pretty easy for him because the first thing he would have a couple do was fill out a form that gave full disclosure of their finances. He knew exactly how much they had or, in some cases; if they had a relative or someone else to turn to for financial help. Financial losses to known victims exceeded $1.19 million. Karpin also established personal and physical relationships with several of his female clients during the divorce mediation process to further his financial exploitation of those victims. Many of his female victims described him as "creepy." We were not allowed to enter this evidence at trial later, due to a ruling by the court.

Many victims interviewed gave similar accounts. Karpin would tell them that he had filed papers with various courts, but they later would learn that the documents were never filed. He also prepared documents for some clients to file, only to find out later that the document was not properly prepared. Karpin misrepresented facts and continually tried to obtain more money from his clients than what was previously quoted, telling victims he would not file paperwork until he was paid even more money. A lot of victims had child custody issues mishandled by Karpin.

None of the victims were aware that Karpin was filing their divorce papers as "pro per" in the courts. The term means that the victims actually were representing themselves as their own attorney, when they believed Karpin was their attorney. Their lack of knowledge of legal terms such as this and the fact that Karpin was having the courts mail any notifications to his business office prevented his clients from being notified that some documents were not properly prepared. Legal document preparers are licensed in Arizona, and Karpin had no such license. Even the person he was using to prepare the documents for him was unlicensed. She also believed he was an attorney and cooperated fully with the investigation. She provided a lot of evidence and would later testify against him.

Karpin routinely threatened people with lawsuits when he discovered they had complained to the Arizona State Bar or state's attorney general's office, and he threatened others into not making complaints.

Some victims reported that Karpin told them he was a doctor of psychology and child psychologist. He even used the term "Dr. Gary" on his answering machine. Karpin was involved in filing Chapter 7 bankruptcies for clients, as well as drawing up contracts, divorces and representing himself as an attorney for child custody cases. He also sent documents out of state that listed him as the "attorney for the respondent."

Victims reported that Karpin maxed out their credit cards and told them he would use those funds toward their account. He didn't' provide proper receipts and charged clients for visits they did not make to his office. Several licensed attorneys in Maricopa County had to assist clients with divorce and custody problems created by Karpin's fraudulent practice, and they also filed complaints against him with the Arizona State Bar.

On July 7, 2005, Karpin was charged in a 16-count felony indictment for fraud schemes and theft by a Maricopa County grand jury, and an arrest warrant was issued. Listed on the warrant were two counts of fraudulent schemes and artifices and 14 counts of theft. Bond was set at $250,000, cash only. These charges would later be amended before his trial in 2008.

On July 11, 2005, he was arrested by me and other detectives from the Maricopa County Attorney's Office. Because of observations made in his office during his arrest, I obtained a search warrant and secured a large quantity of documentation to support our case against him. More than 20,000 documents and items were logged and labeled into evidence. The documentation on this case filled more than 15 five-inch binders.

In December 2005, his bond was reduced to $75,000, which only required a 10 percent posting. Karpin's relatives posted his bond, although he remained under court supervision (ankle monitoring) until his trial.

I seized nearly $225,000, cash from Karpin's attorney's account under a racketeering (RICO) lien when I learned he had transferred the money from an account back East to post his original bond. We also placed a lien on Karpin's home, which had equity estimated at more than $700,000 at the time of his arrest. Karpin's scheme allowed him to live well, purchasing the house, Corvette, truck, motorcycles, horses, and take expensive vacations. Karpin had prepaid for his Divorce with Dignity office space, at approximately $2,000 per month, through December 2005.

We believed there may have been more victims of this fraud, but many may have moved out of state or were not aware of the fact that they were a victim of this criminal activity.

On August 11, 2008, the trial began in Maricopa County Superior Court and lasted for more than eight weeks. Forty-nine victims and witnesses testified for the prosecution, and several hundred documents were presented as evidence. After a three-month trial, Karpin was convicted on all but one count and sentenced to serve a minimum of twelve years in the Arizona Department of Corrections. His cash and assets later were ordered forfeited, and restitution was ordered for the victims.

My Current Law Enforcement Academy Assignment

On August 1, 2010, with a background as a law enforcement officer, soldier and instructor in Missouri and Arizona, I began a new career as a full-time instructor at the Southwest Junior College Middle Rio Grande Law Enforcement Academy. Since then, I have worked with Basic Peace Officer classes, training a total of 60 cadets. It is not uncommon when we start an academy class that we lose almost a third of the recruits before the class is finished. The first class that I assisted in training, according to academy coordinator Lloyd Dragoo, had the highest average on the state licensing exam in the 34-year history of the academy.

On April 29, 2011, I passed the Texas Peace Officer licensing exam, administered by the Texas Commission on Law Enforcement Officer Standards and Education and was commissioned as a Reserve Deputy Sheriff with the Uvalde County Sheriff's Office on May 13, 2011. I have also received my certification as an instructor from the Texas Commission on Law Enforcement Officer Standards and Education.

I hear regularly from some of my former cadets who now are in active law enforcement, and I am proud of their accomplishments. The men and women in law enforcement are special. It takes special people to do this job. As I tell each class at the beginning of the academy, they have one thing when they start this career that no one can take from them, and that is their integrity. Protect it and wear it proudly.

This is a photo of Michael Leavene on the left and
Kevin Eckhoff on the right being promoted to WO1 at
Ft. McClellan, Alabama in 1988. Both were members of the
493rd CID Unit in Belton, MO. (Courtesy of Leavene and Eckhoff)

This photo is of Reserve Deputy Sheriff, Michael Leavene with the Uvalde County Sheriff's Department Uvalde, Texas, 2011. (Courtesy of Michael Leavene)

The above photo is of David Eads, a trooper with the Missouri State Highway Patrol. This photo was taken in the 1980s. (Courtesy of David Eads)

Chapter 36

David Eads

Retired Sergeant, Missouri State Highway Patrol, 1978-2005

I was born in 1953, in Trenton, MO. My grandfather started a fuel delivery business in 1933, and my father took it over and expanded it after World War II. In 1971, after my high school graduation, I enlisted in the U.S. Marine Corps and, when discharged, returned home to take over the family business. I had no intentions of ever being in law enforcement because I had everything I thought I needed at home and in Trenton. But in the summer of 1977, one of the local state troopers came into one of our stations and wanted his big patrol car washed. I admired the two big red lights with the big chrome siren on top of his car and his neat, professional uniform. As I was cleaning the interior, I listened to the police codes on the radio. The line was being laid out, and I just didn't know it yet.

Within a few weeks, I was asked if I would like to go on a ride some evening. I did, and now the hook was set; this was something I had to try. During the next several months, I went through the hiring process and started my recruit training in August 1978, at the MSHP Headquarters in Jefferson City.

Six months later, I thought I owned the world. During my 28 years in the police department, I was promoted to corporal and, eventually, to sergeant, a zone commander in Cameron, MO. I was a firearms instructor for 14 years, a sniper for 20 years, and I was on the Patrol's pistol team and served as a troop armorer. I was blessed supervising numerous talented troopers, and I had a very good career. There was not one day that I did not want to go to work because of being burned out, which is a common issue in law enforcement.

As a state trooper, our primary job was traffic enforcement; but being in rural areas, most sheriffs' departments were a four- or five-man department. The local police departments were also small. We often were called to assist in all areas of law enforcement. That was the nice thing about being a trooper: domestic violence calls, property theft or damage was handled by the other departments. We got the icing-on-the-cake calls: pursuits, raids, manhunts, and assisting the other departments on more serious crimes. Of course, we worked a lot of wrecks, especially in northern Missouri during the winter months.

I have a great family that has always supported me in my career despite all the moving around we did. I have been married to my wife, Charla, for 36 years now, and we have two daughters and one son, who is a new police officer, working in Lenexa, Kansas.

My First Car Stop, Sort Of

We had a huge snowstorm when I was first breaking in as a "newbie." Some of the snow drifts were 6 feet high, taller than the light bar on our 1978 Mercury patrol car. Corporal Mike Hooker was going to be my FTO (Field Training Officer) for the next three months. Interstate 35, being a north-to-south road, was mostly open; however, U.S. 136 was now one lane, thanks to a snow blower brought in by the state highway department. They had only one in the entire state, and, thank goodness, it was located where we were.

Mike would drive over to Albany and get to my house, and then all we could do was drive 5 miles west to a gas station, drink coffee, and then back to Albany and drink more coffee. The roads had blown shut again, but we kept busting drifts, drinking coffee at one place, and driving to the other to use the bathroom.

During the first five days of the FTO program I just rode along and watched how things were supposed to be done – the right way. I learned how to drink a lot of coffee while riding with Mike. Eventually, most of the snow melted and I could now show Mike what I had learned in the last six months at the academy.

Mike decided it was time for me to issue my first ticket while working stationary radar. We were west of Bethany in the White Oak Bottoms, and he told me to back onto the old road and we would catch someone coming over the hill to us. We backed onto the frozen, snow-packed, side road and in a matter of minutes here came a poor sucker driving too fast.

Mike had informed me that as they got close I should just activate the red lights and they would stop. Here came the pickup, getting closer, getting closer, and on went the red lights. The plan worked, the pickup slowed down and stopped on the shoulder about 200 yards away. I had the big 1978 Mercury, about as big as an aircraft carrier, in drive and started to pull out onto the road. Unfortunately, we were stuck, wheels spinning and red lights on.

After Mike waved for the farmer to go on, I found out you do not get stuck with your FTO present. I was able to push the car free, and we pulled up about 5 feet where we knew we were okay and decided to try Plan B. The next sucker to fall into our devious trap would be stopped by me activating my lights and then walking onto the road.

About 10 minutes after my first chewing out, here came the second violation of the day. I turned on my red lights and as I got out, the stupid high wind caught my brand new hat and away it went, eastbound. I paid a lot of money for that hat and only a gun battle would keep me from chasing it. It slid faster than I could run on the hard-packed, deep snow. The only reason I got it back was it hung itself up on a fence about 100 yards away. I guess Mike motioned for that driver to go on, too because, when I finally retrieved my hat, he pulled the car down the road to where I was and picked me up. We drank a lot of coffee the rest of that day.

Don't Move

Trooper Jimmie Linnegar was shot and killed when he stopped a van in south Missouri in April 1985; we had a training seminar on it a few weeks later.

One night, I checked a box-style van with no windows on Highway I-35, and it rapidly took the off ramp at the Highway 69 spur at Bethany. I stopped it under I-35, a good place to do something without any witnesses seeing anything. I observed two people in the van on the car stop, and I had the driver get out. As he got out, I saw, through the van's rearview mirror, the passenger jump out and run to the back of the van trying to flank me. I thought I was in the same scenario Trooper Linnegar was in when he was killed.

I grabbed the driver, an old man, by his hair and swung him in front of me to use for cover. I placed my .357 revolver next to his ear and pointed at the person that was coming around the back of the van. His stupid son came running around the corner of the van and darn near got shot. He threw his hands up and screamed, "Oh, my God!" I replied, "No, it's the devil, don't move." His hands were so high I thought he could touch the moon. It turned out there was no problem; he just wanted to see his Dad get a ticket.

FFA Car Stop

Corporal Hank Bruns, Trooper Dan Hough, and I were out working I-35 one nice summer day when Iowa called and said a station wagon was going southbound on I-35 with three girls in the back holding up a sign that read "Help, we are being kidnapped." Iowa had two cars running south to overtake it, but were unsuccessful.

H2 scales, near the state line, called me and advised the station wagon had just gone past them, still headed southbound, and there was a sign in the rear window. We met the car near the 100-mile marker and it just did not look right. It had been a slow day and I thought what the heck, we'll practice a felony car stop, anyway. I pulled in directly behind the car, Hough pulled over one car length onto the grass to use my car for cover, and Bruns stopped on the inside shoulder. We all three got out with our Remington Model 870 shotguns, and, as the driver got out and looked up from his billfold, there was a very loud Oh-My-God scream.

I had the well-dressed driver walk backwards to me, even though I knew something was wrong here, some type of joke being played. I explained to the extremely nervous and shaking driver why we approached him this way, and he stated he was just a teacher taking these three students to Kansas City for the Future Farmers of America (FFA) National meeting.

I informed him that there were signs in the car, and he asked the girls for the signs. He returned saying there were no signs there. This time I got more demanding and, on his second approach to the girls, he hollered and cursed for them to give him the signs, which they did. He really gave them a chewing-out. I still laugh today at that one and can still see his expression looking up from his billfold at the three of us. Those poor girls must have had a long trip back home, and I am confident the next year's trip had more ground rules explained.

Neon Light

In the early 1980s, it seemed like a lot of the truckers were buying gimmicks to try to defeat our radar units as we had a "push" to slow the truckers down and a lot of enforcement activity was focused on them. We saw a lot of ingenuity in the devices they came up with, which, of course, didn't work. A lot of them had aluminum foil tied to their valve stems or anywhere on their tire rims, thinking this would mess up our radar beam and they would not get caught.

West of New Hampton one night, I stopped a tractor-trailer unit well over the limit. As I had the driver in my car issuing him a ticket, he started bragging about his homemade radar detector. I issued him his citation, and he wanted me to come back up to his truck to show me his new device. It was a neon light bulb, 18 inches long and wrapped with an electrical wire. Both ends of the wire were soldered to the end of the light bulb. The wire was neatly wrapped around the bulb, with about a two-inch space in the middle where you could still see the glass. If our radar beam hit it while it lay on the truck dash, it was supposed to light up. He said he bought it in California and it had worked all the way to Missouri but, apparently, we had some new type of radar. "Oh, well, back to the drawing board for that guy."

What's Them Lights?

I got called up to the scales at Eagleville one summer night to check on a driver who was acting like he was on drugs. When I arrived, the inspectors said something was wrong with the guy and they did not want to release him. I met the truck driver and the first thing out of his mouth was "I don't use drugs and I don't drink. I'm a Christian, but something's wrong."

He said he had been driving down the road and these lights kept blinking everywhere in front of him. He had been seeing them for several miles and felt maybe he was having a reaction to what he had eaten for supper. He kept looking outside the building like the UFOs were getting close again and rattled on about the lights. All of a sudden, he hollered "There, don't you see them?" and went outside. I didn't see anything unusual, because he was pointing everywhere. Eventually I figured out this guy was a new truck driver from Oregon. This was his first trip to the Midwest, and he was seeing lightning bugs. I grabbed one, ripped off the light and put it on my finger as we did as kids, and he was really embarrassed.

Fatal Wreck

Throughout my 28 years with the patrol, I worked a lot of fatality accidents and saw some rather impressive ones. You got used to these, but giving the death message to the family was always the hard part. One that stands out in my memory was a "height and distance" double fatality. After reconstructing it, it was determined the car was traveling 101 mph as it went around a curve. Unfortunately, it missed the curve and struck an embankment, ejecting an 18- and a 20-year-old. Both kids went airborne more than 35 feet high, clearing some trees and finally landed 160 feet out into a soybean field; that's over half a football field.

The car also cleared the 35-foot trees and came straight down like a yard dart hitting the ground nose first, staying put. It looked like someone had deliberately put it there that way. Needless to say, there were no survivors.

The Tracks

One day we had a big snowstorm come through and I was the late car. It was snowing enough that the highway department gave up trying to plow it. The truck stops were full and no traffic was moving. I decided to make a long trip up I-35 to the state line to make sure no one was stranded. It was a boring trip; I was it, no headlights or taillights anywhere to be found.

On the return trip, I decided to play around and drove from the right shoulder clear over to the left shoulder feeling the road edges, just being stupid. At Eagleville, I dropped off the inside shoulder and was almost sucked into the median; time to stop and just head back to Bethany. There were no other tracks on I-35, as I was still the only car out. Once getting back to Bethany, Troop H radio called and said there was an accident at the 106 mile marker in

Eagleville. It took quite a while to return back up there and, upon my approach, there in the median was a van on its side. The driver was walking around picking up very expensive camera lenses and photography gear.

I picked the driver up and went up to the crossover to be able to come back to the starting point where the van had left the road. The driver said he had been southbound and was following some tracks that he pointed out to me. He said, "All of a sudden I ran off the road into the median here!" He had been following my tracks. It's all I could do to keep from laughing, so I informed him it may have been a drunk who should have been paying more attention. There was no way I could issue him a citation.

Iraq Mission

I retired from the MSHP on December 30, 2005, and had been considering going to Iraq as a private contractor to teach the Iraqi police how to shoot. The salary was very good: I could make in one year there what I made as a zone sergeant in five years. My son was doing his first tour in Baghdad with the 101st Airborne Unit. I had met some of his friends he'd brought home and developed a high respect for these young soldiers.

On October 31, 2005, Kelley called from Iraq, their third day there, and said his best friend who had stayed with us and three others had all been killed by an I.E.D. At that point, my attitude changed. I didn't care about the money; it was a personal thing now. I was now determined to go with the idea that if I can train the police to catch just one terrorist and save just one innocent American or Iraqi life, then I would have succeeded. This really shook me up, knowing my capabilities and just sitting around doing nothing; what a waste.

I retired at my first chance and was in Iraq by January 23, 2006. My family supported my decision, which helped. While there, each night I wrote what had occurred that day, usually some unbelievably stupid stuff you cannot comprehend unless you were there.

I have 56 pages of stories, far too many to include here. Basically, my job was a range officer; I made sure things were going as outlined in our Glock and AK47 training programs. We were not on a military base but located outside of Mosul at the "Alamo," so named because it had been overrun three times before my arrival.

We did not have the luxuries of a military base, a nice chow hall, movie theater, gym, etc. Our daily meals were chicken twice a day, peas and carrots, and some type of potato or a tomato and zucchini dish. We got mortared weekly and at the range, the local sniper would periodically shoot at us. We had 500 students attending a ten-week course, in two groups of 250.

In June, it appeared from reports that we were starting to make a difference. Killing Iraqi police officers was a high priority for the terrorists. Often, some students would not return, and we learned they had been killed over the weekend. A typical scenario had someone knocking on your door, asking if you are so-and-so, and if you were, they simply killed you at your house. No student wanted his picture taken, as we often did, because they all were afraid we might put it on the Internet to mark their death.

Even the instructors had nicknames — Hollywood, Superman, etc. — and fellow officers did not know what their real names were. Oftentimes, we had terrorists right in the class, and, after week two or three, the MPs would arrive to arrest them. A background check was a simple phone call; the Iraqi General would call his friend and ask if he knew Mohammad, and he was hired. That was it.

I was pretty naïve when I arrived in the country and felt sorry for the Iraqis after seeing what they did not have. As the year passed, my attitude changed. Their way of life had been this way for 2,000 years and more, and the ones now have only understood Saddam's leadership. We had night fire with the classes the last two nights. I felt so sorry for these students. They, in no way, can make a decision because, in the past, if they did and it was wrong, it cost them their lives. I could see they were desperate to learn, so much eagerness in their eyes. Everyone said it was like teaching fifth-or sixth-graders, and now I fully agree.

They had only one chance in their lives to shoot a night fire course and each student received only 25 rounds, absolutely no "light-on, light-off" technique, just very basic turn on a flashlight and point to shoot. Flashlights are called torches and the worst flashlight you see at Wal-Mart is far better than what they have there. I can really see now when they are attacked why they often run - lack of proper training and equipment. I felt like all we were doing was getting them ready to be killed.

Car stops in a Third World country are completely different than in the United States. Each car has four officers in it; pickups have six officers. Pickups also are equipped with our version of the M60 machine gun, mounted in the bed. It is mandatory that at least two cars perform a car stop, usually more, so, at the very least, they have eight officers on one car stop. Two perform rear security watching for suicide bombers, four are outside the 360-degree perimeter watching for ambushes, two are the arrest team, and two are the front team.

Police here are the bad guys. The day I flew in, the recruits were leaving to go home. We were short six students because on their way home they were ambushed. Two were killed and four injured by small-arms fire, a normal event. One family had four sons in one class; two were killed and everyone says the others will be killed also.

Corruption is rampant. The pay master pays the officers, and then the officers pay him to get paid. Applications are free to apply for the police force, but the person accepting it charges anywhere from $500 to $1,500 to file it. Our major in Iraq was a shepherd before applying to be an Iraqi officer. After paying another $2,500, he graduated and became a major. An Iraqi uniform will sell for $2,500 to the Taliban, so if a student says he has lost one; it usually means he has sold it because he only makes $300 per month.

A colonel makes $500 and a general earns $700 a month. Before the war, an Iraqi colonel made $41 per month. Doctors, lawyers, and engineers are commonly seen going through the police academy, because they make almost nothing. No one has money to pay them.

Kosovo

I came home from Iraq for three months and ended up in Kosovo with the United Nations in a special operations group consisting of a Witness Protection Unit, High-Risk 1 Prisoner Movements, and a Close Protection Unit. Unfortunately, I had to sign an agreement not to talk about our mission there. Fifty-seven different countries involved, and it was a completely screwed-up operation, as far as I am concerned. I spent a year there, and then came home.

After taking almost two years off, I am employed again at the federal courthouse in Kansas City, where my good friend, Jerry Borchers, asked me to contribute to his book.

David Eads took a one year assignment to Iraq in 2006, to train the Iraqi Soldiers in firearms training. Eads is standing by his SUV holding a Bushmaster M-4 assault rifle. (Courtesy of David Eads)

David Eads is pictured with an Iraqi receiving gifts for children from the USA. The above photo was taken in Iraq in 2006. (Courtesy of David Eads)

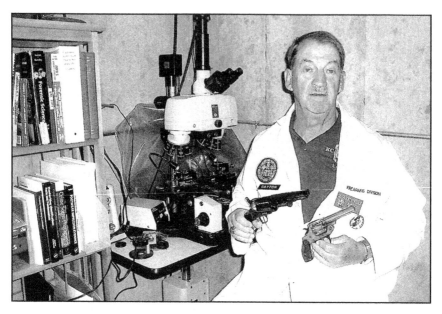

This is a recent photo of John Cayton. He is sitting at his Forensic Ballistic Comparison Microscope located at his Access Forensic Laboratory, located at 11851 N.E., A highway in Cameron, MO. During the past 43 years, John has spent thousands of hours making ballistic comparisons. He has analyzed everything from the bullets recovered in the Jesse James casket, matching bullets from a homicide at the U.S. Army Range in Korea, to "making" knife cuts on human tissue. John is still actively working several homicide cases at his lab. You can reach him at 816-632-4867 or cell 816-617-3372. His e-mail address is forensiclab@msn.com. (Courtesy of John Cayton)

Chapter 37

John C. Cayton

**Retired Kansas City Regional Crime Laboratory, 1967-1999;
Retired CWO4, U.S. Army (CID), 1970-2000**

Tatoo Case

The North Kansas City, MO, Police Department answered a call on a burglary of a gas station. The burglar had broken the front window and a lot of cigarettes and other things were missing. A large pool of blood was found outside the broken window during a crime scene search and was submitted to the KCPD Lab for examination. The case was assigned to me to work up the blood to be analyzed. I looked through the large clot of blood and found a hunk of skin, which I cleaned off. There was a piece of skin with some blue lines on it. About the same time, a man showed up at a local hospital with a large cut on his left upper arm which he said was made when he was attacked by a machete.

I went to the NKCPD to check his wound and saw that the man had a cast on his left arm and there was a tattoo of an eagle appearing over the top of the cast. I removed the cast and compared the photograph of the piece of skin that I had examined at the Lab with damage to some missing eagles feathers on the suspect's left upper arm. The examination revealed a perfect match which was able to solve the burglary.

41-Year-Old Cold Homicide Case

It was February 1961, when a cab driver by the name of John Orner was robbed and shot to death in Columbia, South Carolina. The cab driver was a retired disabled Army soldier. His cab was found a day later with blood in it. Two days later, John Orner was found near a creek 20 miles away, where the victim had been dumped over a cliff.

The autopsy revealed he had been shot in the back of the head and a damaged .32-caliber lead bullet was recovered from the victim and sent to the SLED Lab.

Three weeks later, an 18-year-old soldier by the name of Edward Frieburger, from Ft. Jackson, was hitchhiking and was picked up by a Tennessee Highway Trooper. The trooper was taking the person to town to get a bus ticket, but when he padded him down, a loaded .32-caliber revolver was found in his pocket. He arrested him and contacted the Army, who responded and took custody of Frieburger.

It was learned through the investigation that Frieburger had been committing burglaries at local offices and was pawning office equipment. He used the pawn money to buy a .32-caliber Harrington & Richardson revolver and a box of ammo the day before the victim and cab came up missing. This made Frieburger a prime suspect in the robbery and shooting death of the victim.

The examiner at the SLED Lab could not match the bullet that was recovered from the victim with a test bullet that had been fired with the revolver that had been recovered from Frieburger, due to being damaged. Frieburger spent a year at the prison in Ft. Leavenworth for the burglaries and the homicide case went cold.

In early 2002, I received a call from a retired CID Agent, Carl Craig. He had worked on the case in 1961, and asked if I would look at the revolver and bullet. I agreed to conduct an examination. I cleaned up the bloody bullet fragments, saving the tissue for possible DNA. I test fired the revolver. The examination resulted in a positive identification of the spent bullet fragment that was recovered from the victim's body matching the test-fired bullet from the .32-caliber revolver that was recovered from Frieburger. I informed the Richland County Sheriffs office of the match.

The cold homicide case was solved and Edward Frieburger was again arrested at Ft. Wayne, Indiana, at the age of 58. He was later tried for the robbery and killing of John Orner and found guilty of First Degree Murder in a jury trial, after only two and a half hours of deliberation. He was given a life sentence.

Police Officer Rick Friesen was a reserve officer with the KCPD from 1982–1985. The above photo was taken of Rick Friesen and his wife Glenda in 2012. (Friesen family photo)

Chapter 38

Rick Friesen

**Reserve Police Officer, KCPD, 1982-1985;
Executive Pastor, Abundant Life Baptist Church,
Lee's Summit, MO, 2000-Present**

What is a Reserve Police Officer?

I was a reserve police officer for Kansas City from 1982 to 1985. I now am an executive pastor at Abundant Life Baptist Church in Lee's Summit, MO, and a police chaplain for the Lee's Summit Police Department.

Maybe you're asking at this point, what is a reserve officer? At the time I was a reserve officer, we were commissioned officers. Like regular police officers, reserve officers graduate from the police academy; but instead of working full time, they volunteer to work part-time. The state requires us to complete the academy and serve a minimum of 24 hours a month with our respective departments.

As a volunteer commissioned officer, the reserve officer, just like the full-time officer, falls under the jurisdiction of the state and city, and must comply with all laws and regulations from both entities, as well as all the general orders of the KCPD. This service of 24 hours a month or more usually includes working the streets in a district car, filling in for a regular officer who is sick or on vacation, or just being an extra patrol car during periods of high activity.

There were times when the entire complement of full-time officers from Metro, East, Center, South or North Patrol Divisions would have a picnic or in-service training and we were asked to man the whole division during that time. On other occasions, we were asked to help in specialized divisions within the police department, usually based on a particular skill we possessed in our regular civilian job. The bottom line is we were assigned where the department needed us.

The Reserve Unit was under the command of a full-time captain. During my three years with Kansas City, I worked for Captain John Bartlett and Captain Robert Pattison. Both men were great to work with and appreciated the dedication and the seriousness of our job. In addition, we had our own cadre of sergeants and captains. Our sergeant reported to our captain and he reported to the full-time captain.

At the time I was "employed," there were approximately 150 reserve officers serving on KCPD. I worked with some great reserve officers, including: Mike Sharp, who is now the Jackson County, MO, sheriff; Hugh Mills, who is now the Jackson County Undersheriff; Craig Sarver, who eventually went full-time with Kansas City and served in various capacities within the department; Dave Bernard, who went full-time with the department and became a homicide sergeant; Capt. Bill Schaeffer, Sergeant Mike Caponetto, Jim Ogren, and Tom Caponetto, just to name a few.

Why would anyone want to be a reserve officer? After all, you don't get paid, it's strictly a volunteer position, and there are a lot of hours, in addition to those of your regular job. There's the potential of being seriously injured or sued, which, in turn, could jeopardize your full-time career. The reasons are as varied as the men and women's personalities who sign up to be reserve officers.

My reasoning may have been a little different than most. At the time, I was trying to decide if I wanted a full-time career in law enforcement, with the ministry, or in some completely different career. At this point you may be thinking, wow, police work and the ministry are worlds apart. But they're much more closely aligned than you may think.

My Struggles with God's Calling

At age 18, I felt strongly that God was calling me to a full-time vocational ministry. Just three years before, I'd accepted Jesus Christ as my personal Savior, and it was a good thing because there is no telling where my life would have turned without God. I came from a dysfunctional home. My mom and stepfather that I lived with maybe went to church twice the whole time I was growing up. Needless to say, we were not a religious family.

My mom and stepfather were alcoholics. My stepfather would get drunk, beat my mom, and beat us kids. There were constant verbal assaults on our character. I remember having to get on the floor and eat out of the dog dish for having what my stepfather perceived as poor table manners.

One day I walked in on the unthinkable. I opened a bedroom door, where I saw my stepfather molesting one of my four sisters. Even with both my sister and me telling what happened, it was all swept under the carpet. I was a bitter young man as a result of this incident. I had such hatred for my stepfather there were times I actually thought about killing him, but I was too chicken to try.

I remained bitter and angry until the day I met Christ at age 16. A youth pastor shared the gospel with me and told me that God loved me so much he sent his Son, Jesus Christ, to die on the cross for me. All I had to do, according to the Bible, was admit I was a sinner and invite Christ into my heart. Romans 10:9-10, tells us "That if you confess with your mouth to the Lord Jesus and believe in your heart that God has raised Him from the dead, you will be saved. For with the heart one believes unto righteousness, and with the mouth confession is made unto salvation."

I bowed my head and said, "Lord, you know that I am a sinner. You know the bitterness in my heart. Please come into my heart and save me." Jesus did just that. Almost immediately, a weight was lifted from my shoulders and God took away the hatred and bitterness I had for my stepfather. I still can't explain it today; I just know it was no longer there.

Eventually, my stepfather died of emphysema and liver issues from his drinking. I was with him the last week he was on this earth. Some of my family members couldn't understand why I would be there with him during his dying days. They would ask, "How can you do it after all that he has done to our family?" I would answer them, "I don't know. All I know is that God has changed me, and I actually have compassion for the man."

Answering the call to ministry took a little longer than my salvation. I say God was calling me because one thing I have learned over the years is that you don't choose the ministry, the ministry chooses you through God's calling. Most people would not choose the ministry on their own. I ran as far away from God's call as I could for many years. Because of the dysfunction in our home, I convinced myself for many years that God had it all wrong. I was not the right material. I thought I was not "holy" enough to be one of God's ministers. It was years later I discovered God calls people from all types of backgrounds.

My first step in running from God's call was signing up to be a reserve officer with the KCPD, and, yet, as I look back on my experiences I can see how God was preparing me to be a minister, even though I was fighting it. I experienced many things while I was an officer for Kansas City that prepared me for the ministry, from the calls I went on to the officers I met. I learned a lot about treating people with dignity and respect, even in some of the toughest situations. I learned that officers, while tough on the outside, are also human and need someone they can talk to. Because many knew that I was serious about my faith, I sometimes served in the role of chaplain, as well as police officer.

During the first year-and-a-half of being a reserve police officer, I was not married and was out of work. Because I was out of work, I took on many off-duty jobs with various businesses, such as, banks, shopping malls, diners, and bingo halls. These businesses wanted commissioned officers to run their security. Because of working so many off-duty jobs, I was on duty almost 24/7. I would work off-duty jobs early morning until late afternoon, and then go into the station almost every evening and work a district in a patrol car.

The full-time officers loved that I came in every evening, because it allowed some officers time off or gave them an extra car to answer calls. I remember many calls and various situations working off-duty and in a district car, but two really stand out in my mind.

Rick Friesen

Investigate the Cutting

I eventually married, and my wife and I had just moved into the Deerhorn Village Apartments. I was working the South Zone on the dog watch shift when the dispatcher called my radio, 522. I responded "522, Ervin Junior High School." The dispatcher then called 524. Radio 524 gave its location, and the dispatcher proceeded to give us the call, "522, along with 524, investigate the cutting at 10604 East 98th Terrace."

I thought for a moment, "Where is 10604 East 98th Terrace?" Apparently, the caller did not give an apartment number. I started to get my street guide out when it hit me: that was the address we just moved in to. My heart started racing, knowing my new bride was at home sleeping. I never got to a call so fast in my life, and I'm sure I broke every department traffic-related regulation along the way, hurrying to check on her. I was the first officer to arrive and went bursting into our apartment with my gun drawn. I did not wait for backup. I looked all through the living room, the kitchen and bathrooms, and then made my way to our back bedroom, where my wife Glenda was sound asleep. There was nothing out of the ordinary in our apartment.

I was so focused on checking our apartment that I did not hear the calls from 524 looking for me. The apartment had a double-door security system, and 524 could not get in. 524 saw my patrol car, but could not see me, so he put out an "assist the officer" call. I did hear that and quickly called the assist off. Because it was a slow night, many officers showed up, anyway. I went to the first security door to let the officers into the building, which housed four apartments, two upstairs and two downstairs.

After letting the officers in the first door, I let them all in our apartment. I believe there were five or six officers in our apartment talking very loudly and Glenda still did not wake up. Just as we were going to check out the other apartments, we heard a loud commotion in the apartment upstairs and ran to investigate. It was a domestic disturbance that led to the wife stabbing her husband. We called an ambulance, took statements, and placed the wife under arrest. We now had officers, paramedics, all the neighbors, a police wagon on the scene and my wife never did wake up!

I told her about the incident the next morning, and she didn't believe me. It wasn't until the neighbors told her that it was true that she believed the story. To this day, a tornado could come through our house, and my wife would not wake up. Fortunately, I'm a light sleeper.

Officer Assault Call

The other call that really sticks out in my mind involved an officer assaulting another officer. I will leave the names out of this story to protect their family members. Only the old-timers will be familiar with this story, anyway.

I got the call as a secondary officer to assist the primary officer, who was dispatched to the scene first. When I arrived on the scene, I thought it was a little odd that so many officers, along with the primary officer, were standing out in the front yard instead of being in the house where the victim was and where the assault took place.

I could tell they were all there waiting for me to arrive on the scene. The officers knew I was a reserve officer and, as I approached the house, one of the officers said, "Hey, why don't you take this report? It's all yours." I thought about saying no and I wish I would have gone with my gut feeling. But instead, I thought, "No big deal, it's still early enough in the shift and I'll have the report done in between calls by shift's end."

Apparently all the officers standing outside the house, I learned later, knew who the victim was, knew who the suspect was, and knew why the suspect assaulted the victim, but they did not share that information with me. One downside, as well as a blessing, to being a reserve officer is you don't know all the scuttlebutt going on in the department, nor do you get to know most of the non-patrol officers like the full-time officers do.

I took statements at the scene from those in the house and tried to take a statement from the victim, who was going in and out of consciousness. I followed the ambulance with the victim to the hospital, where I thought I would finish my report. It was at the hospital I got the full picture of what was going on.

When the ambulance arrived at the emergency room doors, I

saw what appeared to be all the brass on the police department, including Cruiser One (the radio call sign for the Chief), huddled inside the emergency room doors. I thought, "What in the world have I gotten myself into?" The victim was rolled into a room, with brass in tow. I was intercepted by a captain, who told me what the officers on the scene had not told me: the victim was a Kansas City detective.

After the brass came out of the room where the victim was, the captain filled me in on the rest of the story. The victim was a detective, and the suspect was a sergeant on a Special Weapons and Tactics (SWAT) team. The detective was having an affair with the sergeant's wife. After the sergeant discovered the affair, he went to the detective's house and knocked on the door. As the detective opened the door, the sergeant burst in and beat the detective with what I recall to be brass knuckles. The sergeant then left the scene.

I never received so much coaching on how to write a report as I did that night. And I don't mean coaching as in covering up; I mean coaching as in good report-writing. The command staff handled everything in a professional and forthright manner. It took me the rest of the night to write the report, with no calls in between. If my memory serves me correctly, the SWAT team members went out that night to go to the sergeant's house to arrest one of their own.

Halfway through writing the report, it dawned on me I was going to have to go to court and testify as the reporting officer. No wonder the officers on the scene did not want to take the report. It's uncomfortable for an officer to testify when another officer is on trial. The disposition of the trial is a matter of public record.

This incident really caused me to start thinking: would I really want to do this job as a full-time career? Don't get me wrong, many officers are trying to do the right thing every day and have strong family relationships, but this incident left me watching other officers closely. What I noticed in a lot of the older officers were great guys who developed cynical, sour dispositions over the years. I thought if I was a full-time officer, would I become the same?

My answer came one day when I was walking down the street at 12th and Locust on my way to court. A gentleman walked past me. There was nothing unusual about him. His dress was professional and looked as if he had business downtown. He was just an ordinary citizen going about his business. As he walked past me, I thought to myself (and not out loud), "Asshole." As soon as I thought it and said it in my mind, God spoke to my heart and said, "What's the matter with you? You don't even know that person. Who are you to say that about somebody I created? As far as you know, this person has not done, nor ever will do, anything wrong."

I knew at this point I probably could not make a career out of law enforcement. The type of cynicism I had toward the young man who walked past me was not a part of whom I really was or wanted to be. My thought then was, "If I'm doing this after three years, what would it be like after 10 years?"

So, my wife and I built a house outside the city limits, and I accepted a full-time position at the old Bendix plant, which became Allied Signal, then Honeywell. Because you have to live inside the city limits as a Kansas City police officer, I left KCPD and became a reserve officer with the cities of Raymore, and then Belton.

I ended up being at Allied Signal for 15 years. In that time, I received a master's degree in human resource development, worked in security, taught total quality management classes, and ended my career there in labor relations.

But even though I had great jobs at Allied Signal, I still was miserable. I was still not doing what God wanted me to do. Even though I was making great money with great benefits, I looked in the want ads every single week. It drove Glenda crazy.

Eleven years ago, I went on a mission trip where I finally surrendered to God's call. On that trip, I got on my knees and said, "God, if you will still allow me to be your full-time servant, I'm yours lock, stock, and barrel. God, I'm tired of running from your call, and I'm tired of being disobedient. If you will allow me to serve you, I promise I will serve you 120 percent for the rest of my life!"

About four months after that promise, a full-time ministry position became available at Abundant Life Baptist Church in Lee's Summit. I am still there today and have not looked at a want ad for 11 years.

While I did not make law enforcement a career, I still have a special place in my heart for police officers. They have one of the toughest jobs on the face of the earth. Everything I learned as a police officer has served me well in ministry. My answer to the question, "How do you start out thinking about law enforcement and ending up in the ministry?" is that there are many similarities. You're in the people business in both.

You deal with people at their worst and at their best. Both are stressful jobs. Both require long hours. Although there are many similarities, there are two striking differences. First, most people do not go up to an officer and start confessing crimes. However, it is amazing what people will confess to a pastor. Second, officers take the initial call, write the report and testify in court, and then they are usually finished with the case and rarely see or hear from the victims or suspects again. As pastors, we minister to the "suspects" and "victims" usually long after the incidents have taken place.

This is a photo of J. Michael Brady, AIA, LEED AP, in his office in Sacramento, CA, in 2003. He is a cousin of Jerry Borchers. He was a reserve police officer for two years with the San Luis Obispo, CA, Police Department in the late 1970s. He is now living in West Sacramento, CA and is the principal architect at CSHQ, a Design Collaboration. (Courtesy of J. Michael Brady)

Chapter 39

J. Michael Brady

AIA, LEED AP, Principal

Architects are trained problem solvers; this was my motivation for wanting to be involved with police work. I did some ride-a-longs in the late 70s in San Luis Obispo, CA, and then they initiated a Reserve Police Officers' program. I applied, was accepted, and completed the required training. I was teamed with full-time officers when on duty. This was a volunteer program. I worked 8 to 12 p.m. or 12 to 4 a.m. duty shifts to keep a low profile in the community. I did this for two years and came to realize a couple of things:

First, my position as a part-time officer did not allow for in-depth follow-through and problem-solving situations on cases that full-time police officers have in their day-to-day police work. Tactics and logistics, along with being mentally prepared to expect the unexpected, are the skills that were required.

Second, the risk factor became something I had to deal with. The experience of encountering suspicious situations and responding to unknown conditions in a part-time volunteer role made me experience a level of risk that I didn't think I was prepared for, based on the mental shift required to feel confident in my ability to be prepared for the conditions that confront an officer.

Police work requires a full-time career focus and continued training to perform at your best in the line of duty. I stopped the program and returned to my career as an architect. But the experience was enlightening and helped me to be more observant and aware as a citizen.

In the early 1990s, I returned to a ride-a-long program, this time in Kansas City, MO, where my cousin, Detective Jerry Borchers, was a crime scene investigator. He invited me to ride along with him on one of his shifts. Now, this was more like what I was looking to experience. This police work was investigative and involved the problem-solving that I was originally interested in pursuing. The perspective of an observer was great at this time for me.

One ride-a-long remains clearly in my mind. It was a summer evening, I reported to the station at 11 p.m. to ride. Jerry was following up on some existing cases at the station when the call came for a possible fatal auto accident. This was on a rural stretch of Highway 40 where we found the body of a male victim in the roadway, apparently run over by a van that had stopped and reported hitting something in the road. Upon arrival, the scene was secured and both lanes shut down.

The crime scene was about 150 feet long, as articles of clothing, shoes and body parts and waste were evident along this stretch of road. The process of working the scene began. Items found were marked and logged, and we set up a camera. The method of photography used was unique in that a single negative plate was used to capture the scene through a series of sequential exposures. We moved in about 20-foot segments using multiple light flashes on both sides of the road to light the roadway sequentially. This particular type of photography is called "painting by light." I was on one side of the road and Jerry on the other and the end result was a one time-lapsed photograph that captured the entire crime scene. This method of photography allowed the scene to be photographed without waiting until daylight or keeping the road shut down.

I noticed that the male's body had a tattoo on his upper right arm that read "Victor" in a scrolled ribbon background. I thought this could be his name.

As the evidence was being collected, the body was removed and transported to the morgue for processing. As we were putting away the photo equipment, there was a lot of yelling coming from down the road, as a pickup truck had entered the blocked-off crime scene area and was headed our way. Fortunately, he was stopped before entering the critical crime scene area. Evidently, the officer that was posted at that end of the road closure was distracted allowing a pickup truck to barrel on through.

The van that was involved in running over the victim was towed for further examination. We left the site and went to the morgue to finish working the accident case. There we had a controlled setting to examine the body and recover any evidence for further investigation. Upon entering the examination room, the body was already on the table. Jerry and another technician proceeded to remove the clothing and examine the body. There were several stab wounds in the victim's chest and his skull had been caved-in near the back of his head. An autopsy later revealed he had received stab wounds that were fatal but the blow to the head was from being run over by the van.

When the van was examined, hair and tissue fragments were recovered from the under-carriage of the vehicle. (This corroborated the theory that the van probably caused the crushing blow to the victim's head.) The detectives believed that the victim had probably been dumped in the roadway after being fatally stabbed in the chest, and then the van drove over him in the roadway.

I was able to observe Jerry and the other technician conduct a full-scale examination of the body and also obtain his elimination fingerprints. These fingerprints were hand-carried to the Fingerprint Identification Unit to identify the victim. His full name was later discovered. As it turned out, his first name was Victor, so my initial tattoo clue was correct. To this day, I don't recall if a suspect was ever identified. But I can say that this was a night on the ride-along program that I will never forget.

Retired USCG-CGIS Special Agent Donnie Bowerman, (Senior Chief Investigator, E-8), standing in his driveway in front of his beloved "Silver Twinkie," aka Airstream! This photo was taken in late 2008 or 2009, before heading to an annual 55th Wing (STRATCOM) Birthday Celebration at Offutt AFB in Omaha, NE. (Photo courtesy of Donnie Bowerman)

Chapter 40

Donald A. (Donnie) Bowerman

U.S. Navy, U.S. Army and U.S. Coast Guard Reserves, 1969-2002;
Civilian Law Enforcement, *et al*, 1974-2002 and 2005-2006

My law enforcement career spanned from 1974 to 2002, with a short stint during retirement from 2005-2006, It included service in Missouri at the Central Missouri State University Campus Police, the Independence Police Department, followed by the Kansas City Missouri Police Department, followed by the Jackson County Sheriff's Department (from which I retired in 1996), followed, finally in Texas, by the US Drug Enforcement Administration, Dallas Field Division, from which I resigned in October 2002. During this never "routine," occasionally exciting, and, sometimes, "very ugly" career, I was able to work in a challenging variety of capacities: district officer, planning and research project officer, traffic officer (radar car, motorcycle, Special Events Squad), accident investigation specialist, academy instructor, member of the Missouri state governor's protection detail, CSI detective, road deputy, D.A.R.E instructor, and an intelligence analyst for the DEA.

In 2005 and 2006, while laboring under the various physical and mental stresses of retirement (!), the Pottawattamie County Attorney, in Council Bluffs, IA, made me an offer I couldn't refuse and I became his Chief Investigator. During that period of time, my entire focus was on the one-man enforcement of the recently enacted

Iowa state law barring registered sex offenders from living within 2,000 feet of a school, licensed day care, or other child care facility. I won't even begin to touch that "hot potato" now, but, suffice to say, not a single county attorney nor county sheriff throughout the state agreed with the law, but, of course, the state legislature never asked for their opinions first before they wrote it!

My military career began in November 1969, and also ended in October 2002, when I applied the brakes to my law enforcement career. During my Navy years, I served as a Quartermaster (navigation duties) on ships supporting the Vietnam War from the Tonkin Gulf, two destroyers and an aircraft carrier. When I came home and later "shipped" over to the Army, I served in the 159th Military Police Battalion, the "parent" organization for the 493rd CID, which has been mentioned many times in this book and which also, means I worked with or around most of the fellows who were assigned to it. Then, for twenty years, while serving in the United States Coast Guard Reserves, I was a special agent in the Coast Guard Investigative Service. I retired with the rank of Senior Chief Investigator (E-8). Reserves, in the context of the CGIS, definitely do not mean the typical once-a-month, weekend warrior with a two-week summer camp. I was on call 24/7, and worked many major cases and/or events that took me away from my police job for much longer periods of time. (Don't tell my former employers, but, for me, military ADTs and TDYs were more like vacations from the common drudgeries of police work!)

Just another Day at the Park

Contrary to the popular image of police work as portrayed for decades on television and the silver screen, those of us who have worn the badge at one time or another know that the job generally consists of ubiquitous mountains of paperwork, anything but "routine" patrol activities, and endless hours of investigative duties that lead to countless dead ends. Then, there are those proverbial, albeit few, moments of sheer chaos and terror, and fewer still the moments of very profound internal satisfaction. The latter will manifest it in various forms and situations and will often go completely unrecognized by anyone beyond the immediate participants. However, when it occurs, those previously boring hours and days and weeks and, perhaps, even months seem to fade into distant regions of the mind and the event at hand makes it all seem worthwhile. It can even happen when one is engaged in working that oftentimes, financially-mandated, off-duty job. One early evening, that's just where I found myself and this book's author, Jerry Borchers, my longtime friend, police department co-worker, and off-duty partner at baseball games of the Kansas City Royals at Kaufman Stadium. Funny thing is, we both know this event happened, and we remember a lot about what happened, but the passage of time and the absence of that aforementioned external recognition have left each of us scratching our heads trying to remember exactly when it happened. We've settled on sometime near the end of the 1970s. Jerry and I had long partnered together and "patrolled" the stadium's upper deck level, affectionately referred to the "nose bleed" seats. Most of the time, we ate copious hot dogs and peanuts, watched the game, and let our police-uniformed presence serve as the deterrent it was meant to be and, thankfully, usually was.

It was just another nice evening ballgame until a woman in our vicinity started screaming. For the first two seconds, I simply tried to get oriented to who was doing what, where. As I looked to my right and above where we were standing, I saw a considerable crowd of people begin to stand and look in the direction of the same screaming that I was trying to focus on. But I was also instinctively moving in the direction of the "event," with Jerry hot on my heels. I began parting the crowd, yelling "Police, get out of the way," trying to not-so-gently move those whose focus was on the screaming woman and not on me rushing up behind them. Jerry and I had to jump a few rows to get to the woman, but upon arriving by her side, she quickly pointed to her son, a young lad of eight or nine years of age and told us that he was choking. Without a moment's hesitation, I grabbed the boy, hefted him out of his seat and into my arms where I applied the Heimlich Maneuver and, after just a couple of upper thrusts to his mid-section; out popped the offending chunk of wiener. Spontaneous applause quickly erupted, and I received my first "warm fuzzy" of the day. Knowing that the ballpark's on-site medical personnel should also check the boy's condition, I requested that Jerry radio them and meet us on the outside concourse level. We led the mother and boy there where we met with and turned the boy over to the EMTs for a check-up. The mother hugged Jerry and me; my second "warm fuzzy," thanked me profusely, and we soon parted ways. Jerry and I returned to our "routine" off-duty job.

Neither of us can remember the name of the boy or his mother, let alone the date, as I mentioned. There was no external recognition beyond the hugs and the applause we received. Truth be told, that was the best reward of all. Maybe I saved a life and maybe I just beat someone else to the scene that would have done the same thing. But it was my turn that day and I was glad to be of help. First and foremost, police work is paperwork, followed by the never "routine" patrol-type activities, but once in a while, if you are in the right place at the right time, it can all come full circle and you will find joy and satisfaction in knowing why you put that badge on day after day after day.

And maybe, just maybe, a once-young lad of eight or nine is now a police officer himself. That's a really nice thought...and another warm fuzzy for this retired "fuzz."

Some Thoughts on Other Chapters, in No Particular Order

As I helped Jerry with this book, I was able to get a sneak peek at what others wrote. Sometimes I laughed, I reflected a lot, and, a couple of times, I got a little misty-eyed. I would like to add a few brief thoughts of my own to some of the stories you've read.

Ruby!!!

Few people have impacted my life more than Ruby McIntyre. I loved the "soul food" she cooked, the atmosphere in which it was served, and the personal friendship we shared for nearly thirty years. Like Bal Rast, I had to "clean my plate" of more food than I thought I could ever eat. I know all about the robbery that initially claimed the lives of two of the bad guys; she related that story to me countless times. A couple years later, a nearby traffic accident caused one of the disabled cars to plow into and take out the entire front of her restaurant. A few years after that, the liquor store, located adjacent to her café, burned to the ground, taking half her building with it. But through it all, I never observed a more resilient and determined individual than her. Ruby lovingly called me her "white son," and I very proudly called her "my Black Mama." I always will.

Coates House Fire

My first permanent district was in Sector 110, Car 114. Smack in the middle of it was the Coates House. I made several calls-for-service to that location. Each time, I was met by the sights, sounds, and smells of a once majestic hotel. Now, she groaned from decades of neglect and abuse, and she reeked of cheap wine and urine. On one occasion, late in 1977, I recall passing by open rooms, into which I could look, where I often saw a gas stove with all the burners aflame. It was the only source of heat for so many of the transients that now occupied the floors. A short time later, this former grand dame of Kansas City hotels was literally a burned out, three-walled shell. My district meant it was my job to help stand watch over the efforts of CSIs like Dennis Gargotto from the warmth of my patrol car as he and the other CSIs labored in that frigid January winter air of 1978. And, I, too couldn't help but occasionally cast my eyes to that top floor and the scorched remains of the man who was draped over the former window sill.

Hyatt Skywalk Collapse

For no less than two years, I'd been trying to obtain a date with a nice young lady from church. When she finally gave in to my romantic intentions, with incessant pressure, I found myself standing at her front door on Friday evening, July 17, 1981. When she opened the door, her family was gathered around the television, watching the newsflash on the collapse of the skywalks. I told her that I'd take a rain check, but I had to go. I don't know what she or I missed, but I never cashed that rain check. That night, just as for Leon Cook and others, my personal plans came to an abrupt end; and, like so many others, I did not leave the scene until late the next day. No one who remained there will ever forget the sight before our eyes as the last skywalk was raised…never.

Chapter 41

Police Career's Impact on Family

Brenda Savage (Nee Borchers)
My Life as a Policeman's Daughter

I am the oldest daughter of my parents. I was born in 1961, at Williams Air Force Base in Chandler, Arizona. I have two sisters, Bonnie and Beverly. I have been married to Daniel Savage since 1978, and I have seven children and fifteen grandchildren. I presently live in Sequim, Washington, where my husband is the pastor of the Cornerstone Baptist Church.

It was always a comfort to know my Dad was a policeman. I felt safe and proud to be his daughter. Some of my fondest memories were sitting around the table, watching my Dad shine his shoes and clean his gun. I can vividly remember the smell of the shoe polish and the smell of the gun cleaning oil. I remember the care taken to get them just right. I always hoped Dad would never have to use his gun. We had many happy conversations about police work around the kitchen table.

It was also a blessing to have a policeman for a father, on one occasion, especially. I was 16 years old and just starting to drive. I was driving my car down the street and dropped a pencil on the floor of the car. I accidentally ran up over a curb as I was reaching for the pencil. I ran into the front yard of a residence down the street and struck a small tree, putting a large dent in the middle of the front bumper. I drove home because there were no persons or other cars involved. I didn't realize that it was wrong to leave the scene, and I didn't know that I would be in trouble. Soon, Dad and Mom came home. I was so upset, and Dad told me I had done wrong for leaving the scene. Before we had a chance to go back to the scene, the police showed up at our house to investigate the accident. I was so glad that Dad knew the police officers and took care of the situation.

Another thing I remember was that Dad helped my sisters and me to not be naïve about things like marijuana. Dad had brought something home that had the smell of pot on it so we would know what to avoid. I was glad that Dad educated us about that. I remember when Dad worked at the Youth Unit and how it made him sad to see the conditions some children lived in.

One Christmas, Dad really had no desire to exchange gifts as we normally did. He suggested that we collect toys from the neighborhood to take to foster homes where children did not have the luxury of having toys. That really stuck in my mind and made me grateful for what we had, compared to those poor, and disadvantaged families we helped that Christmas.

I also remember how much fun the annual police picnics were. It was great to be around so many policemen at once, knowing that these were the men and women that were protecting our city. I didn't really live in daily fear for my Dad's safety, but on the other hand, it was quite a relief at the end of the day when I saw him walk through our door, safe and sound.

Bonnie Blangiforti (Nee Borchers)
My Life as a Policeman's Daughter

I was born in California when my Dad was in Bangkok, Thailand, in the Air Force. When he left for the overseas assignment, Mom was six months pregnant with me. He was gone so long that I was already nine months old before he got to come home. Can you imagine? He didn't get to see me, hold me, play with me, or bond with me during those precious first months. He must have felt such a loss and a longing during that time away from the family.

Back at home, while he was away, Mom would tell me stories about my father while showing me his picture. She obviously expressed so much emotion during these times, because I picked up on how much I should love this "man in the picture." Mom told me when I first saw him, on his return from Thailand; I recognized him right away and reached out my little, chubby baby arms and cried out with joy. My mom told me he cried like a baby when he got to finally see his little creation and hold me close.

I was so blessed with a stable childhood. Plenty of affection and acceptance was always balanced with appropriate expectations and discipline. Balance is definitely an asset that both my parents possess. "Heart and logic" had equal value. It's easy to respond well to strictness when a child feels safe.

Most kids typically start lying around 6 years of age. Usually, with good parenting, they could evolve out of that bad habit around 9 or 10. My timing was a bit quicker. In fact, the first lie I remember telling might have been one of my last childhood lies. Having a detective for a father, who then investigates your story, finds the lie and sentences you to a week-long grounding, can smash a child's expectations of gaining any benefit from lying. And if we only achieve punishment and no relief from our lies, because our parents are too smart, then why choose that strategy?

The details of that one, vivid moment are still so clear in my mind. I had arrived home without my new shimmery purple coat, and my Dad asked where it had gone. "Oh Daddy, it was horrible! A dog attacked me and tore off my coat. I barely got away!" My 6-year-old reasoning had decided that my Dad couldn't fault me for what a dog had done, so I thought this would be the end of it. Oh, no. I hadn't counted on how angry he would be at the owner of such a dog. He left in a huff and came back with the real story.

He found the house and the dog I had described, knocked loudly at the door and paced the porch until the owner of the dog was available for my father's questioning. "Why, Sir, our dog has been in his fence all day. See? Look, the gate has a lock on it." They walked together along the tall, wooden fence and spotted my tattered purple coat in the back of the yard. That's about the time that the shade of red on my Dad's face shifted from "angry red" to "embarrassed red."

I was always able to count on hugs and approval from my parents, so the disappointed look in my Dad's eyes when he arrived home was heartbreaking for me. "Bonnie Lynn!" he roared, "tell me what really happened." Between sobs, I told him how I just wanted to play tug-of-war with the dog, so I poked one part of my coat through a gap in the wooden fence. But the dog was too strong, and he pulled the coat out of my hands.

Well, I'm glad you told the truth," he said, "but I'll have to ground you for lying. That way you'll learn that it is the wrong choice for you to lie to us again."

He held me to my punishment until he saw how genuinely sorry I was to have displeased my mother and him. He told me he trusted me and knew I would choose better next time.

One other thing I remember from those years was hearing the door open, knowing Daddy was home. I'd run to the door and reach up for a hug. My future perceptions of the world were impacted by the simple act of that daily hug: a strong, tall, handsome man in uniform, lending security and affection to his little girl. It must have been the safety and the joy I felt at his return each day, linked with the image of the police uniform that gave me such respect for people who choose his job. And as I got older and learned of the dangers and sacrifices he endured, my admiration only deepened.

Now, whenever it just so happens that I see the same type of uniform cautiously approaching my driver's window to write me a speeding ticket, I feel empathy for the man in the uniform. I see him as a Daddy who reaches down each day and hugs his child, a husband who works hard to support his family, and a servant who is willing to risk his safety to keep us safe. Yeah, and then I try to talk the officer out of the ticket, like we all do!

Beverly Eldridge (Nee Borchers)
My Life as a Policeman's Daughter

As a young girl, I would beg my Daddy to put his police handcuffs on me so I could try to escape from them. After much pleading, he would finally give in and shout in his deepest voice, "You are under arrest, little girl!" I'd feel the cold metal of the handcuffs close around my wrists and hear the ratchet sound of them clicking shut behind my back.

I didn't waste any time manipulating my skinny little arms and legs to bring the handcuffs in front of me. I'd squeeze my hands completely out of those handcuffs and mockingly wave them in front of him. No matter how many times he watched this performance, he would always laugh and act surprised. The time came when I was too big to escape the cuffs. I was truly stuck. This time my father acted scared and told me he lost his key. He had me squirreling. He told me that his handcuff key must be at work and that he was going to have to call the police to have them respond to unlock the handcuffs. This really scared me, and I did not want the police to come and have to take the handcuffs off. But then he reached in his pocket to produce the key and made everything all right again.

One day, when I was a bit older, I snuck into my parents' room to play with Dad's police gear. I was comfortable with a gun in the house and was instilled with the knowledge and fear to never play with guns, and I didn't. However, I felt Dad's other gear was fair game. I remember lifting his very heavy bullet-proof vest over my head and onto my shoulders. Feeling the weight and testing the thickness of it, I prayed that if he ever had to take a bullet, his vest would save him. I put on his blue police shirt, pinned on his police badge and swept my long red hair up under his police hat to keep it firmly on my head. Viewing my reflection in the mirror, I imagined what it would be like to get called to a dangerous scene. I wrapped my hands around his baton, thankful he had it for protection.

As you may know, policeman wages are not very high. Dad always worked a couple of security jobs on the side to provide extras for the family. Mom also worked full-time and still coordinated the cooking, cleaning, shopping, and all of the other activities that came with our busy household. With the heavy workload on my parents' shoulders, we still managed to take family camping trips, canoe trips, or magical short trips to a fishing hole where we would laugh and enjoy each other's company. We even had fun doing yard work together. When the neighborhood kids would see my father raking leaves with us, they would bring their rakes over to join us. Sometimes, they would even knock on the door and ask, "Can Jerry come out to play?"

My fondest memories took place in our little 1970s décor kitchen. Sitting in black bucket swivel chairs, dinner was lovingly placed on the glass table by our mom. We could see our terrier, Todd, underneath the glass, waiting for scraps to be "accidentally" dropped. We always anticipated the new police story Dad had to tell during dinner, but we never knew what to expect. His stories were interesting, funny, and shocking, but sometimes left us wondering if he was making them up.

Some of the memorable stories occurred when he worked as an evidence technician and dealt with dead bodies. Needless to say, Mother wasn't happy with him sharing those during dinner. His children, however, enjoyed the stories and encouraged him. I guess Dad saw a lot of tragedy on his job and I think he dealt with it by searching for the humor in things and sharing that humor with the ones he loved.

I felt safe having a policeman for a father. As I got older, I realized the risks police face. After learning of Dad's re-occurring dreams of being stabbed to death on that rainy night in the Benson

Lumber yard, I know someone powerful had given him warnings so we wouldn't lose him that day.

As we got older, Dad would encourage my sisters and me to join the reserves or the police force. I would laugh and tell him he was nuts. If there was a dangerous situation, I'd want to run from it, not toward it. I think he secretly wished one of us would follow in his career footsteps. But being a police officer takes a special courage that not everyone possesses. I am so proud my father is one of them. When I see police officers on the streets, I nod my head to them and inwardly thank them for keeping us safe so we can enjoy those magical moments with our loved ones around dinner tables and at fishing holes.

Carol Borchers
My Life as a Policeman's Wife

(Courtesy of Olin Mills Studios)

"Honey, I'm home!" Jerry would exclaim as he came through the front door. His voice was always a glad sound to our ears. The girls ran up to their Dad, full of hugs and kisses. He'd give a quick kiss to me as I started dinner in the kitchen. Then, he would say "I'm going to lie down for 20 minutes. Wake me up for dinner."

This was Jerry's usual routine when working a part-time job after putting in a full day at his regular police job. I learned to have a clean uniform ready, with missing buttons sewn in place, and dinner ready in time for him to eat. Maybe even have a lunch packed or a thermos of coffee ready for him to grab as he flew out the door.

This was in addition to working my full-time job at Bendix Corporation, and keeping three girls dressed, fed, and car-pooled. Laundry got done, but not before a Mount Everest-like pile of dirty clothes built up in front of the washing machine each weekend.

Housekeeping was our Saturday job. Afterwards would come the dreaded "white glove inspection" by me before the girls could go out to play with their waiting friends.

Sometimes, between my work shifts and Jerry's, we only had a chance to wave to each other while driving past on the road. That's why time together was so special. We'd plan ahead for those one or two weekend days a month we could get together as a family. When the weather was nice, we'd usually go camping or fishing. If time was short, we'd just go to the park with a picnic basket, blanket, and a ball. As soon as the station wagon engine shut off in the parking lot, the car doors flew open and the race was on to see which of us could get to the swings first. (I liked to swing, too.)

During winter months, we'd take in local events like the American Royal Rodeo or a Christmas play. At Christmas time, after a few grumbles, Jerry would drive us through the crowded Country Club Plaza streets in Kansas City to view all the magnificent holiday lights and decorated shops. This was all the more appreciated by the girls and me as we knew he would rather stay home, away from the crowds that he had to deal with all the time on the job.

American Royal events were fun because Jerry often worked part-time there, and he provided security for the rodeo cowboys and show-horse performers in the building where they were housed. It was especially fun when Jerry would bring the children and me to meet the rodeo clowns. They were real heroes. They exhibited bravery and courage in rescuing cowboys whose hands or feet got tangled in the rope on a wildly bucking Brahma bull.

Between the planned times together, we would find and snatch moments to play a game, watch a TV show, or play with neighborhood children. I always worried there weren't enough good times tucked into the day-to-day rush. But, fortunately, the good times seem to be what the girls remember.

Having little time together can be hard on a marriage. We would sometimes find ourselves growing apart in our separate worlds. It took a conscious effort to plan some time just for us. One anniversary, Jerry surprised me with a trip to an unknown destination. I thought it would be to a nice hotel in town, but then we drove past town toward the airport. I had no idea where we were going. When we arrived at the airport, Jerry showed me the departure schedule board and had me guess which flight was ours. It turned out to be a trip to Chicago. We stayed at the Weston Hotel, where he wined and dined me. Exciting surprises like that go a long way toward keeping a marriage strong. It really didn't matter where we went; it was the idea that counted.

Sometimes being a policeman's wife meant sitting and listening while he vented his frustration, disappointment, and/or anger at something that wasn't going well on the job. Maybe there was friction between Jerry and someone he worked with. Maybe it was working hard on a case, gathering witness statements, evidence, and writing it up to present to the prosecutor's office before the deadline, only to have it yellow sheeted (rejected) and the suspect let go. Of course, I also listened as he told the funny things that happened on the job.

When Jerry first became a Los Angeles policeman, I naturally worried about his safety. I'd pray every night that he would come home safely to his three daughters and me and that he would act wisely in each situation he might find himself in. After a while, I figured God was tired of hearing the same prayer every night, so I trusted that the prayers already said were enough and, instead, offered thanks.

Jerry would sometimes share details about the cases he was working. One case really touched my heart. A woman reported her young, but legal-aged daughter missing. Usually, a missing person's report of an adult is not worked for 72-hours because, most often, the "missing" person returns and wonders what all the fuss is about. Besides, it was a three-day weekend and young people go to the lake with friends. But the mother's fears seemed well grounded. I empathized with her. I couldn't imagine how it would be to have one of our daughters missing.

I was glad Jerry took the case and immediately started the investigation. I prayed for the safe return of the young woman, even though I knew, if foul play had befallen her, any prayers would probably be too late. So, I also prayed a contingent prayer that the daughter would be found and the scoundrels brought to justice so the mother could at least have closure. That was, of course, the case of Karen Keeton.

I suppose most policemen's wives are familiar with prayer. Because I have mentioned it a few times already, I thought I'd also mention that I don't think my prayers are any better than anyone else's. I believe it's not about the pray-er; it's about the goodness of the One prayed-to.

I knew about the recurring nightmares Jerry had of being stabbed to death at the lumber yard while answering a prowler call. One night, I was awakened by his dream-screams (you know, the ones you try to scream, but they never really vocalize fully). He was sitting straight up in bed, his skin in a cold sweat. We worried about the dreams just then, in our minds and hearts, but life's current has a way of sweeping us along a path filled with daily activities and responsibilities. So, the next day broke and the dream was pushed back and forgotten, almost.

Chapter 42

The Real Prowler Call

One night in April 1972, I reported to work on the dog watch. My shift started at 11 p.m. and ended at 7 a.m. A couple of officers had called in sick. Instead of being on my regular assignment, I was assigned to the area around Benson Lumber Company, located at 18th and College. I became quite nervous. It was raining, just as it had been in those five nightmares I'd had, and I was on the same shift.

The night was really slow because of the rain. At one point, I remember looking at my watch, as I had during the dreams. It was 1 a.m. Lo, and behold, I got a prowler call. Another car was dispatched with me to an address on 19th Street, near College. The hair starting raising on my arms.

I arrived quickly. The other car was coming from another district; I got there first. A middle-aged woman told me the same story as the one in my dreams: a man had been looking in her window and had run away. He had not attempted to break in or threaten her. She had last seen him running north on College towards 18th Street. I believed, at this time, that the dreams were a warning: if I chased after the man into the Benson lumber yard, I would be stabbed to death.

My back-up arrived and wanted to know what was going on. I told him I was going to "HBO" the call. This means that the officer has handled the call, without any further action being required. I explained to the officer that it was only a prowler and no crime was committed. I asked the officer to meet me at the parking lot down the street. Once we arrived at the parking lot, I told him about my disturbing dreams. He agreed that I'd made the right decision by not pursuing the prowler. Death did not claim me that night. What might have happened, I will never know. Would I have been stabbed to death if I had chased the prowler into the Benson lumber yard? Who knows? I might have caught the prowler. But now, at age 74, I am retired, still alive, and finally free from those disturbing dreams.

About the Author

Gerald R. Borchers was born in Kansas City, Mo., and at the age of nine, became an avid storyteller with the neighborhood children. His storytelling continued throughout his life when his family finally encouraged him to share his stories with others by writing a book. Jerry is married, with three daughters, and had an extensive law enforcement career that included the Los Angeles Police Department, the U.S. Army Criminal Investigation Division, together with twenty-five years on the Kansas City, Missouri, Police Department. Now in retirement, Jerry enjoys fishing, traveling, and "spinning a yarn" or two for those who still listen to and enjoy hearing him tell them.

Made in the USA
Monee, IL
02 March 2020